OUTLANDER KITCHEN
To the New World and Back Again

OUTLANDER KITCHEN

To the New World and Back Again

The Second Official Outlander Companion Cookbook

Theresa Carle-Sanders

Delacorte Press
New York

Copyright © 2020 by Theresa Carle-Sanders
Foreword copyright © 2020 by Diana Gabaldon

Published in the United States by Delacorte Press,
an imprint of Random House, a division of Penguin Random House LLC, New York.

DELACORTE PRESS and the HOUSE colophon are registered trademarks of Penguin Random House LLC.

"The Diet and Cookery of Eighteenth-Century Highlanders" originally appeared in
The Outlandish Companion (Volume 2), 2015.

Some of the recipes contained in this work were originally published on the author's blog,
Outlander Kitchen, outlanderkitchen.com.

This work contains excerpts from the following novels by Diana Gabaldon, published by Delacorte Press, an imprint of Random House, a division of Penguin Random House LLC: *Drums of Autumn*, copyright © 1996 by Diana Gabaldon; *Lord John and the Private Matter*, copyright © 2003 by Diana Gabaldon; *Lord John and the Succubus*, copyright © 2003 by Diana Gabaldon; *Lord John and the Brotherhood of the Blade*, copyright © 2007 by Diana Gabaldon; *Lord John and the Haunted Solder*, copyright © 2007 by Diana Gabaldon; *An Echo in the Bone*, copyright © 2009 by Diana Gabaldon; *The Scottish Prisoner*, copyright © 2011 by Diana Gabaldon; *Lord John and the Plague of Zombies*, copyright © 2011 by Diana Gabaldon; *A Leaf on the Wind of All Hallows*, copyright © 2012 by Diana Gabaldon; *The Custom of the Army*, copyright © 2012 by Diana Gabaldon; *Written in My Own Heart's Blood*, copyright © 2014 by Diana Gabaldon; *Virgins* copyright © 2017 by Diana Gabaldon; "A Fugitive Green" from *Seven Stones to Stand or Fall*, copyright © 2017 by Diana Gabaldon; *Besieged* copyright © 2017 by Diana Gabaldon. Reprinted by permission of Delacorte Press, an imprint of Random House, a division of Penguin Random House LLC.

Photographs on pages x, 13, 16, 19, 69, 92, 103, 126, 140, 145, 152, 168, 172, 182, 183, 186, 212, 214, 235, 250, 263, 280 are by Theresa Carle-Sanders, copyright © 2020 by Theresa Carle-Sanders

All other photographs are by Rebecca Wellman, copyright © 2020 by Rebecca Wellman Photography

Hardback ISBN 978-1-9848-5515-2
Ebook ISBN 978-1-9848-5516-9

Printed in China on acid-free paper

randomhousebooks.com

2 4 6 8 9 7 5 3

First Edition

Book design by Virginia Norey

To Rita, my mom.
Your old-world lessons and resilience gave me the grounding
to find my way in this very modern world.
I'm grateful every day.

CONTENTS

Foreword by Diana Gabaldon   *xi*
Introduction   *xiii*

FOREWORD

What makes a vibrant, thriving culture? The language you speak, the stories you tell, the songs you sing, and the food you eat. And when people are forced to leave their place of origin, they often take these precious things with them.

If you hang around in Scottish academic circles these days (and who doesn't . . . ?), you hear a lot about the Scottish Diaspora. This refers to the Scots (both Highland and Lowland) who—over a period of some three centuries—emigrated from Scotland and settled in other parts of the world. Some went willingly to find new opportunity and adventure, some were transported as prisoners, and some left because their homeland could no longer support them.

Regardless of reason, though, these Scots settled in places from Argentina and Brazil to Canada, Chile, the United States (and, prior to that, the American colonies), Australia, New Zealand, Ireland, and Poland. And they arrived in all these places with the treasures brought from their homeland: songs, stories, and food.

Now, songs and stories are easily portable, and while they naturally change a little with time and custom, they're mostly recognizable, no matter where you encounter them. Food, though . . .

What comes to mind when you think of Scotland and food? Well, oatmeal. Whisky! Or, if you've been to Glasgow recently, maybe deep-fried Mars Bars. . . . Scots may have strong traditions, but they're nothing if not innovative, let's put it that way.

So, arriving in new places that might be lacking in the foods they were used to, they promptly adapted their tastes and recipes to the foods that they found in their new settlements. Nor were the Scots the only ones to do this: French and German and Irish immigrants did the same thing.

Scottish food goes much further than oatmeal and Mars Bars, and Theresa's interpretations take in a variety of foods developed in the New World as well as in

Scotland, using the traditions of the original settlers (and the indigenous people) as inspiration for a wonderful array of new and delightful dishes, in addition to classic takes on original ones.

I met Theresa some years ago, when she wrote to ask whether I'd allow her to quote bits from my books as an accompaniment to recipes inspired by the mentions of food in the *Outlander* story—these to be used in her blog, where she would demonstrate the preparation and cooking of the dishes she had created.

I thought that was very cool and said of course—and here we are, *two* wonderful cookbooks later!

One of the hallmarks of Theresa's wonderful cookbooks is the dexterous way in which she handles traditional recipes—sometimes straightforwardly, but more often with a spirit of humor and joyous adventure. And, may I add, with the skill of a professional chef who knows what makes food taste good.

Bon appétit! [Ith gu leòir!]
—Diana Gabaldon

INTRODUCTION
To the New World and Back Again

I was deep into my first-stage love affair with *Outlander* when My Englishman, Howard, and I moved to Pender Island from Vancouver in 2003. I had read each of Diana Gabaldon's books, up to *The Fiery Cross* (the last book available at the time), at least twice before we pulled into the driveway of our little house in the woods, searching for a new way of life beyond the stressed, overworked existence we knew in the city.

And although we had no dreams of living off the land—we're on a third of an acre—looking back, I can't imagine the first years of our semirural life without the influence of Jamie and Claire. I took advantage of our first backyard and planted a small herb garden and a larger one of vegetables, then spent the next few seasons learning why most of the veggies I planted did not thrive in our decent-looking soil. (The answer is cedar trees. They're big, greedy feeders with clumping roots.) I hung our laundry on the line and chopped wood. I walked every day in the woods and along the shores of this small island, and embraced a slower rhythm of life, long forgotten to me in my big-city life with my big-corporate job.

Not that it wasn't hectic at times. We moved here within a month of first viewing the property, and without much of a plan about how we were going to make a living. We were very sure that the exponentially rising cost of living in Vancouver wasn't going to work for us in the long term though, so with a sense of adventure, and semispontaneous, life-changing inspiration, we took our savings and cast our home-hunting net far enough to include the Southern Gulf Islands between Vancouver and Victoria on Canada's west coast. We quickly narrowed the choices down to Pender, because, unlike some of its neighbors who were still using dial-up, high-speed Internet was available—an essential in the twenty-first century, even when you're trying to simplify.

I used that connection with the outside world, combined with an old-world skill taught to me by my mom, to start an online business selling yoga accessories that I sewed on a little table under our bedroom window. (Just one of the essential life tasks Mom made sure to teach us all. I still have the felt elephant eyeglass case my eldest brother, Trev, sewed before I was born, and my other older brother, Ron, executes the neatest line of hand stitching you've ever seen.)

My most popular item was a silk brocade eye mask lightly filled with flaxseeds and lavender. It took off after a couple of mentions on "alternative lifestyle" forums, especially in Great Britain. For almost two years, I collected the orders from my computer in the morning before sitting down at the machine to sew, on average, a dozen eye masks per day. From there I'd head to the island's post office and ship them off to their new owners across the Atlantic.

Meanwhile, Howard was working at whatever he could lay his hands to as well. We were earning a living, but it was tight. When my dad died unexpectedly and rather quickly in 2007, I found myself reevaluating everything in my grief. As a result (thank goodness for an understanding husband), I fulfilled a lifelong dream by returning to culinary school the next year. And the year after that, a random thought during a walk in the woods with the dog had me pondering what the rolls stuffed with minced pigeon and truffles from *Voyager* might taste like.

Diana was supportive of the idea from the beginning. She posted my first recipe for Rolls with Pigeon and Truffles on her website, and when that was a hit, posted my next one, Brianna's Bridies from *Drums of Autumn*, a couple of months later. I published my first blog post for OutlanderKitchen.com in October 2010, and eventually, years of work, hundreds of blog posts, dozens of recipes, and a couple of seasons of *Outlander* on TV, culminated with the publication of *Outlander Kitchen: The Official Outlander Companion Cookbook* (henceforth known as OK1) in 2016.

Two years later, on another long walk in the woods, I was thinking about one of my favorite characters (Outlander is never far from my mind), Lord John, and why I enjoy his stories so much. This description of him from Diana in her introduction to "A Plague of Zombies" in *Seven Stones to Stand or Fall* sums up his circumstances well:

The thing about Lord John's situation and career—unmarried, no fixed establishment, discreet political connections, fairly high-ranking officer—is that he can easily take part in far-flung adventures rather than being bound to a pedestrian daily life. To be honest, once I started doing "bulges" (that is, shorter pieces of fiction) involving him, I just looked at which year it was and then consulted one of my historical timeline references to see what kinds of interesting events happened in that year. That's how he happened to find himself in Quebec for the battle there.

Lord John is the original International Man of Mystery. His lack of attachment combined with substantial independent income and well-developed sense of adventure mean his life is never boring. He wines and dines in London, fights in Germany, governs in Jamaica, and, in his spare time, runs the occasional rescue mission to help those in need. He is always a gentleman, lives for good food, and never fails to make me laugh.

It was that walk with Lord John that rekindled my second-stage love affair with Outlander. I started my new reread that night, with, of course, the entire Lord John series. I then dove back into *An Echo in the Bone* and *Written in My Own Heart's Blood* from the main series and finished with Diana's *Seven Stones to Stand or Fall*, a collection of Outlander novellas published in 2017.

Outlander Kitchen: To the New World and Back Again features recipes from my reread. It follows Jamie, Claire, and friends on their revolutionary adventures, voyage to Scotland and back again, and eventual resettlement at Fraser's Ridge. Others are on the move as well: Roger, Brianna, Jem, and Amanda, after finally settling into Lallybroch in the twentieth century, are separated and forced to return to the past to save their lives. Lord John, not to be left behind, makes more journeys to the New World and back again than anyone else in the Outlander universe. Add in stories like the prequel about Jamie and Ian Murray as young mercenaries in France, "Virgins," and the story of how Hal Grey met and married Minnie Rennie, "A Fugitive Green" (both from *Seven Stones to Stand or Fall*), and this fictional cookbook author has a lot of culinary inspiration with which to work.

I often get asked how I choose the recipes that I feature on the blog and in the cookbooks. It all starts with my journals filled with Outlander food. Soon after Diana gave me permission to pursue *Outlander Kitchen* in 2010, I began recording EVERY mention of food I came across in all of her stories, large and small.

Sometimes the mention of food is very specific within the text, such as Ragout of Beef with Oysters (page 82) from *Lord John and the Brotherhood of the Blade* and Cranachan with Brian and Jenny (page 249) from *Written in My Own Heart's Blood*. Other times, it is more vague, as with the mention of a thick soup in an excerpt from *Lord*

John and the Haunted Soldier, which gives me a chance to use my culinary creativity and turn it into a delicious Leek and Potato Soup (page 49). I also regularly draw inspiration from Diana's characters; when everyone's favorite pig appeared from the burned ashes of the big house in *An Echo in the Bone,* I created The White Sow's Crispy Pork Belly and Apple Slaw (page 125).

What was, at the beginning, a straightforward choice from my handwritten lists for the week's recipe on OutlanderKitchen.com (Mrs. FitzGibbons's Overnight Parritch from OK1 was the first recipe posted on the blog) grew into a more involved and complicated set of tasks as I assembled the first, and now this sequel (hereafter, OK2), cookbook.

From my handwritten journals, I began OK1 and OK2 by entering the long, unedited list of foods (more than 600 entries for OK2) from the source books into a spreadsheet. From there I am able to sort the information any way I want, delete what I don't, and work until the chosen remains resemble the rough draft of a cookbook's table of contents.

When I have multiple excerpts to choose from, for an oft-served dish like bannocks or biscuits, for example, I review my choices over and over, juggling them around in my head with my twenty years of reading Diana's stories, including the last ten years of food-specific interactions. The excerpt that wins in the end generally is emotionally charged, whether it be poignant, funny, or, as with many of Diana's scenes, both—one that puts the reader right back in touch with the characters, like the one introducing Almond Biscuits (page 260), featuring Germain at his mischievous best.

As I discuss in the essay "The Diet and Cookery of Eighteenth-Century Highlanders" (page 311), which I originally wrote for Diana's *The Outlandish Companion Volume 2,* the plentiful corn and pork in the new lands of America meant a change in diet for those coming from old-world Europe. Puddings made from wheat were changed to incorporate corn, and pork became the mainstay protein for all economic classes. Squash, beans, and greens added much-needed variety and nutrition to their diets.

Eventually, much of the North Carolina and surrounding colonies' diets were based on pork and corn, with the average person consuming five pounds of pork for every pound of beef. This "hog and hominy" diet, as it came to be called, stretched across all levels of society, with the wealthiest consuming the choicest cuts of the animal and leaving their workers and slaves with what remained. All parts of the animal were consumed or repurposed, and the diet was supplemented with a bevy of collard greens or cabbage.

We are going through a food revolution similar in its scope here in the twenty-first century. In the four years since OK1 was published, our food has continued to transform at a blinding rate. Alternative diets such as gluten-free and low-carb that were once just whispers on a few lips have become permanent fixtures. Veganism is on a steep rise and has attained mainstream status. At the same time, ironically, convenience foods are more popular than ever, from chips and cookies in the snack aisle to whole precooked dinners from the deli. They continue to contribute to rising obesity rates, diet-related illness, and gaps in nutrition across the globe.

From a historical/fictional cookbook author's perspective, our new food world could be viewed as fraught with culinary hurdles and potholes. Fortunately, in the pages of the past, we find old-world replacements for many of the foods causing dietary distress in the twenty-first century. Oats, long an *Outlander Kitchen* staple, combine with rice flour (used mostly to powder wigs in the eighteenth century) to make a delicious and versatile gluten-free Press-In Crust (page 17) for pies and tarts. Mushroom Catsup (page 307) is a hundreds-year-old condiment that makes a delicious, umami-filled vegan substitute for Worcestershire sauce, and Chicken and Cornmeal Stew (page 113) comes together faster than delivery can get a pizza to your front door.

To help cooks navigate this new food landscape, at the top of every OK2 recipe you will find letters that identify each as gluten-free, dairy-free, vegetarian, vegan, or easily adaptable. Recipe adaptions are listed at the bottom of the recipe in Notes. See the Dietary Legend on page 7 to learn more.

Cooking new-world/old-world sometimes requires you to venture out past your favorite supermarket. My recipes don't call for an excessive number of hard-to-find ingredients, but specialty stores, farmers' markets, and online vendors are where you will find those items that are new to you. If you can't find the king oyster mushrooms used in Mocktopus with Tomatoes and Olives (page 70) where you usually shop, check an Asian market if you have one in your area. Similarly, health food stores are an excellent source for the nutritional yeast used in Vegan Sausage Rolls (page 75), as well as for nuts, alternative flours, and grains. They often offer these items in bulk, so that you can buy as much, or as little, as you need to get started.

Outlander Kitchen: To the New World and Back Again contains more than 100 recipes, 90 of them brand-new, the rest chosen from fan favorites on OutlanderKitchen.com. In the continued spirit of OK1, the recipes to follow are a mixture of authentic old-world *receipts*, new-world adaptions, and humorously delicious character-inspired dishes, all created to satisfy your hunger and insatiable craving for everything Outlander.

Welcome back to my Outlander Kitchen.

—*Theresa Carle-Sanders*

OUTLANDER KITCHEN
To the New World and Back Again

PANTRY NOTES

Beer, wine, and spirits

- Beer: The barley and wheat commonly used to make beer is not gluten-free, so look for a specifically gluten-free beer if that's a concern. Nor is all beer vegan. Some breweries use products like isinglass (collagen from the air bladders of fish), egg whites, and gelatin in the filtering and clarification process.

- Wine: Reaction to gluten from wine, sherry, or port is very rare. Unless you or one of your guests has reacted to a specific wine in the past, it shouldn't be a big worry. However, for the same reasons as above, not all wine is vegan. The same animal products used to clarify some beer are also used by some wine producers.

- Spirits: All spirits and liqueurs are gluten-free, as the distillation removes all traces of gluten. Similarly, almost all distilled spirits are vegan except for cream-based liqueurs and products that mention honey on the label, such as some rums and whiskies.

Cream I use whipping cream (30 to 35% fat) and heavy cream (36% and up) interchangeably. For extra richness, use double cream (up to 48%). Light cream, also known as single and table cream depending on your location, contains 18 to 20% fat. The higher the fat content of the cream, the more heat and acid it can withstand before curdling.

Dairy-free Those who follow a dairy-free diet eat no milk, cheese, yogurt, or other dairy products, or any products with hidden lactose or milk proteins, like many margarines and some packaged chicken stocks. When cooking for those following a dairy-free diet, always check the packages you buy to ensure the manufacturer guarantees the product to be dairy-free.

Egg substitutes for baking For each egg, stir 1 tablespoon ground flaxseeds (flax meal) or 1½ tablespoons chia seeds into 3 tablespoons hot water. Mix well and proceed with the recipe. This mixture provides moisture and body to recipes that use eggs as a binder, such as Corn Bread and Salt Pork Stuffing (page 203).

Fats

- Butter: Always OK's first choice for fat. At home, with family-size recipes, I use salted and unsalted butter interchangeably. The difference is negligible when cooking for smaller numbers.

- Refined coconut oil: An excellent dairy-free and vegan replacement for butter in pastry and frying. While unrefined coconut oil can have a distinctive flavor, refined has a subtle, neutral taste.

- Vegan margarine: Another dairy-free and vegan option to replace butter in baking.

- Lard: The best lard for baking is rendered leaf lard, which comes from the hard fat surrounding the pig's kidneys. It has a neutral flavor and keeps your pastry light. The pastry for the Game Pie (page 144) is flakiest when made with half lard and half butter.

- Extra-virgin olive oil: I keep extra-virgin olive oil in the pantry for dressings and pan-frying.

- Vegetable oil: I use sunflower, grapeseed, or avocado oil for dressings and pan-frying, and peanut oil to deep-fry.

Flours

- All-purpose: I use Canadian all-purpose flour, with a protein content of about 13%. OK2's recipes were tested by bakers all over North America, using different regional flours, all with successful results.

- Brown rice: This is OK2's primary go-to gluten-free flour. Although you can also use white rice flour, I prefer the brown's nutty taste in the Press-In Crust (page 17) and Fish Fried in Batter with Tartar Sauce (page 171). Store brown rice flour in an airtight container in the fridge or freezer to maximize its shelf life.

- Oat: Grind rolled oats in a food processor or coffee grinder until they are the desired texture. Pulse three to five times for a coarse meal, or six to ten times for a finer texture, closer to that of flour.

- Gluten-free: Most commercially blended gluten-free all-purpose flours are made to substitute cup for cup with all-purpose wheat flour, and are the easiest way to create gluten-free versions of the bread and baking recipes in OK2.

Gluten-free People's approach to their own gluten sensitivities and allergies varies from body to body. If avoiding gluten is an absolute priority, always check the packages you buy to ensure the manufacturer guarantees the product to be gluten-free.

Plant-based milk A number of OK2 recipes can be made dairy-free with the simple substitution of plant-based milk for whole dairy milk. Choose from commercially prepared milks such as almond, rice, or soy, or make your own. Vegan Cream (page 20) is an excellent stand-in for light, whipping, or heavy cream in sweet or savory recipes.

Spices To toast whole spices, heat a cast-iron pan over low heat and add the spices. Toast, shaking the pan occasionally, until they begin to release their aroma and brown just slightly, 2 to 6 minutes. Do not allow to burn.

Sugar

- Sugar beet: Sugar made from sugar beets is always vegan but may contain genetically modified ingredients.

- Sugarcane: Bone char from cattle is used in the sugarcane refining process, meaning the resulting granulated sugar is not vegan. This also applies to brown sugar and confectioners' sugar. If there is any question, contact the manufacturer.

- Raw, turbinado, demerara, natural, organic: These are all labels for sugarcane sugar that has been boiled down until it crystallizes, without any further refining. All of these sugars are vegan.

Vegan Someone following a vegan diet has eliminated all foods sourced from animals, including dairy products, eggs, and honey. Their diet consists of only plants (such as vegetables, fruits, grains, and nuts) and foods made from plants. There are a number of nonvegan ingredients hiding in our everyday packaged foods. Check the packaging and research online to ensure what you're buying is truly vegan.

Vegetarian There are as many different versions of vegetarian diets as there are vegetarians. If you're cooking for a vegetarian for the first time, check with them first before finalizing your menu.

Yeast I use instant yeast (also known as fast-rising, rapid-rise, quick-rise, or bread machine yeast) exclusively. It is easier to use, as it does not require proofing in water like active-dry yeast, and I find its results more consistent.

Conversion Tables

Although not exact equivalents, here are a number of practical conversions, rounded for convenience, that are commonly used in international kitchens.

Temperature

250°F = 120°C = Gas Mark ½
275°F = 135°C = Gas Mark 1
300°F = 150°C = Gas Mark 2
325°F = 165°C = Gas Mark 3
350°F = 175°C = Gas Mark 4
375°F = 190°C = Gas Mark 5
400°F = 200°C = Gas Mark 6
425°F = 220°C = Gas Mark 7
450°F = 230°C = Gas Mark 8
475°F = 250°C = Gas Mark 9
500°F = 260°C = Gas Mark 10

Length

⅛ inch = 0.25 centimeter (cm)
¼ inch = 0.5 cm
½ inch = 1.25 cm
1 inch = 2.5 cm
6 inches = 15 cm
12 inches (1 foot) = 30 cm

Volume

½ teaspoon = ¹⁄₁₂ fluid ounce (fl oz) = 3 milliliters (ml)
1 teaspoon = ⅙ fl oz = 5 ml
1 tablespoon = ⅓ fl oz = 15 ml
¼ cup = 2 fl oz = 60 ml
⅓ cup = 2⅔ fl oz = 80 ml
⅔ cup = 5⅓ fl oz = 160 ml
¾ cup = 6 fl oz = 180 ml
1 cup = 8 fl oz = 240 ml
1 pint = 2 cups = 16 fl oz = 500 ml
1 quart = 4 cups = 32 fl oz = 1 liter
1 gallon = 4 quarts = 3.75 liters

Weight

½ ounce = 15 grams
1 ounce = 30 grams
2 ounces = 55 grams
4 ounces = ¼ pound = 115 grams
8 ounces = ½ pound = 225 grams
12 ounces = ¾ pound = 340 grams
16 ounces = 1 pound = 450 grams

Dietary Legend

GF—Gluten-free

DF—Dairy-free

V—Vegetarian

VGN—Vegan

(a)—Adaptable

For example, the recipe for Simon Fraser's Grits with Honey (page 39) is GF | DF(a) | V | VGN(a). That means it is gluten-free and vegetarian as written. Because the recipe contains milk, it is neither dairy-free nor vegan as written, but it can be adapted by following the Notes at the bottom of the recipe:

- *To make this recipe dairy-free, substitute extra-virgin olive oil or refined coconut oil for the butter, and plant-based milk or thinned Vegan Cream (page 20) for the whole milk.*

- *To make this recipe vegan, make the above substitutions and replace the honey with maple syrup or your favorite sweetener.*

Chapter 1

Basic Recipes

Preserved Lemons

GF | DF | V | VGN

Lemons preserved in salt are a North African and South Asian condiment used to enhance dishes with their slightly tart and intensely lemony flavor. Traditionally used whole in Moroccan tagines and as a home cure for stomach ailments in Ayurvedic cuisine, recipes for lemon pickle, as it is also known, first appeared in English and American cookbooks in the latter half of the eighteenth century.

Use them in Asparagus and Gruyère Quiche (page 185), Scones with Preserved Lemon (page 237), and Hot Rum Punch with Preserved Lemon (page 288).

Makes 1 quart (1 liter)

Ingredients

8 to 10 medium blemish-free lemons, preferably organic, plus additional for juice

Coarse or kosher salt

Method

Wash a 1-quart (1-liter) mason jar and its lid in hot, soapy water. Rinse thoroughly and set on a rack to air-dry. As always, before you start any recipe, wash your hands in hot, soapy water and shake them dry.

Scrub the lemons under warm water with a brush to remove any dirt and impurities. Slice off both ends of each lemon. Standing them upright and starting at one end, cut the lemons in half lengthwise, stopping about ½ inch before you reach the bottom. Repeat the cut at a 90-degree angle to the first so you have cut each lemon into quarters—but not all the way through; they should still be attached at the bottom.

Add 2 tablespoons salt to the bottom of the sterilized jar in an even layer. Pack salt into the lemons, liberally sprinkling it between the quarters. Arrange the salted lemons in the jar, squeezing and pushing down firmly to release their juices. Fill the jar about ¾ inch from the top. The lemons should be completely submerged in their own juice. If necessary, juice an extra lemon or two and add it to the jar. Sprinkle 2 more tablespoons salt over the top and close the jar with the lid.

Let the jar sit at room temperature for 2 to 3 days. Each day, turn it upside down and shake it to redistribute the salt and liquids. Refrigerate the jar on the third day, and turn it upside down every other day or so. The lemons are ready when the rinds have softened, 3 to 4 weeks.

To use, rinse the lemons thoroughly in cool water to remove the excess salt. Discard the seeds and proceed as instructed in the recipe.

Store in the refrigerator for up to 6 months.

Notes

- *Use spices such as cinnamon sticks, bay leaves, coriander seeds, cloves, peppercorns, dried chiles, and cardamom pods for additional flavor.*

- *Use as a substitute in most recipes calling for lemon zest, such as Young Ian's Sage and Garlic Sausage, Nettle Rolls, and Apple Fritters from OK1, or to introduce a spike of lemon to other recipes in this book, including Mocktopus with Tomatoes and Olives (page 70), Herb-Roasted Salmon (page 169), and Mayonnaise (page 18).*

Quick Vegetable Stock

GF | DF | V | VGN

A flavorful broth made from pantry basics in under 30 minutes that adds depth and umami to all your soups and sauces. Save time while making whole, homemade food that everyone can enjoy.

Makes about 1 quart (1 liter)

Ingredients

1 large onion, chopped

2 medium carrots, chopped

2 celery stalks, chopped

1 medium tomato, chopped

½ lemon, cut into 2 pieces

½ ounce (15 grams) dried wild mushrooms, such as chanterelle, porcini, or morel (see Notes)

2 fresh thyme sprigs

12 peppercorns

Method

In a large saucepan, combine the onion, carrots, celery, tomato, lemon, dried mushrooms, thyme, and peppercorns with 5 cups cold water. Bring to a boil over high heat, then reduce to medium-low and partially cover. Simmer briskly for 15 minutes.

Strain into a heatproof container and cool.

Store, covered, for up to 5 days in the refrigerator, or freeze for up to 1 month.

Notes

- *Mushrooms are full of umami. If you don't have dried, consider adding mushroom stalks, like those from button and shiitake mushrooms. Freeze any mushroom trimmings you collect and add them to stock for a punch of deep flavor.*

- *Add a rinsed whole preserved lemon to create a flavorful poaching broth for fish and seafood.*

- *Find recipes for chicken and beef stocks in OK1.*

Vegan Short Crust Pastry

DF | V | VGN

A multipurpose, melt-in-your-mouth vegan crust for sweet or savory fillings. While pastry made with coconut oil requires gentler handling than that made with butter or lard, this crust is still substantial enough to hold up outside of the pan, as with Vegan Sausage Rolls (page 75).

Makes one 12-inch crust or two 9-inch crusts

Ingredients

3 cups all-purpose flour, plus additional for dusting

2 teaspoons sugar

1 teaspoon kosher salt

1 cup refined coconut oil, chilled (see Notes), in small chunks

½ cup ice water

1 teaspoon lemon juice

Method

BY HAND: In a large bowl, stir together the flour, sugar, and salt. Add the coconut oil and work it in with your fingertips until the coconut oil is reduced to pea-size lumps and the flour looks like wet sand. Make a well in the center of the bowl, whisk together the ice water (see Notes) and lemon juice, and pour into the well. Use your fingertips to bring the dough together into a shaggy ball.

IN A FOOD PROCESSOR: Alternatively, combine the flour, sugar, and salt in the bowl of a food processor. Pulse three times to combine. Scatter the coconut oil into the flour. Pulse four or five times, until you have mostly pea-size lumps. Whisk together the ice water and lemon juice. Add to the bowl and pulse eight to ten more times.

Pour the dough and any loose flour from the bowl onto the counter and knead it quickly and lightly into a smooth ball. Divide the dough in half and form it into two 1-inch-thick disks. Wrap tightly in plastic and refrigerate for at least 30 minutes and up to 2 days, or freeze for up to 1 month.

To roll out the dough, lightly dust the counter with flour. Use even pressure to roll the dough out from the center in all four compass directions. Turn and loosen the dough occasionally as you continue to roll the pastry into a circle or square shape that is an even ⅛ inch thick, unless otherwise directed in the recipe.

Roll the pastry lightly onto the rolling pin and transfer to a tart pan or pie plate, or cut it into shapes and use as directed.

Notes

- *Coconut oil is solid at room temperature. Although it shouldn't be kept chilled, putting it in the freezer for 10 minutes before you begin makes for easier handling and better final results.*

- *Unrefined coconut oil has a strong coconut flavor, while refined is much more neutral tasting.*

- *If it's very humid, hold back a couple of tablespoons of water when you first mix the dough. Add more, a teaspoon at a time, if needed.*

- *If you prefer, substitute the same amount of butter or lard for the coconut oil. The recipe for Short Crust Pastry in OK1 also includes an egg yolk for additional sturdiness without sacrificing a tender crumb.*

Simple Syrup

GF | DF | V | VGN

A 1:1 sugar-to-water syrup used to sweeten cocktails and cordials such as the Gin and Orange Flower Cocktail (page 272).

Makes about 1½ cups

Ingredients

1 cup sugar

Method

In a medium saucepan over medium heat, combine the sugar with 1 cup water. Heat gently until the sugar has dissolved, then increase the heat to high and bring it to a boil. Maintain a low boil for 1 minute, remove from the heat, and cool.

Store covered in the fridge for up to 2 weeks.

Notes

- *Not all sugar is vegan. See Sugar in Pantry Notes (page 5) for more information.*
- *To infuse the basic syrup with flavors, such as the chai syrup used in Whisky and Coconut Milk (page 277), submerge the flavorings immediately after you remove the syrup from the heat, and remove them once the syrup has cooled completely.*

Press-In Crust

GF | DF | V | VGN

A quick and easy crust that is pressed into the pan without the fuss and bother of a rolling pin. This crust is great for quiches, pies, and tarts, but will not hold up outside the pan.

Makes one 9-inch piecrust

Ingredients

2 tablespoons vegetable oil or melted butter, plus additional for the pan

1 cup oat flour (see Notes)

½ cup brown rice flour or gluten-free all-purpose flour

½ teaspoon kosher salt

¼ cup ice water

Method

Move the rack to the middle rung and heat the oven to 350°F. Brush a 9-inch pie plate lightly with oil.

In a medium bowl, stir together the oat flour, brown rice flour, and salt. Drizzle in the oil and ice water. Mix well with your hands, ensuring the dough is evenly moistened and in smallish clumps. Pat it into the prepared pie plate, pressing it firmly into the corners and up to the top rim.

To parbake the crust, line it with parchment paper and fill with pie weights or uncooked dry beans. Bake for 10 minutes, remove the pie weights and parchment, and return the crust to the oven for 8 to 10 more minutes, until dry and lightly colored. Fill and bake as directed in the recipe.

If you're blind-baking the crust for an unbaked filling, bake as above, but until golden, 25 to 30 minutes, and fill as directed in the recipe.

Notes

- *Grind rolled oats in a food processor to make oat flour. See Flours in Pantry Notes (page 4) for directions.*
- *Add 1 tablespoon sugar to the flours and salt for a sweetened dessert crust.*

Mayonnaise

GF | DF | V

One of the five mother sauces as categorized by Auguste Escoffier, the father of modern French cuisine, mayonnaise is a simple emulsion of oil and vinegar. The egg yolk is the emulsifier, or binding agent, that holds the oil and vinegar in stasis. The larger the egg yolk, the more oil it can hold. If you are using small or medium eggs, decrease the oil by a couple of tablespoons to avoid breaking, or splitting, the mayonnaise.

Makes 1 (scant) cup

Ingredients

1 large egg yolk

1 teaspoon Dijon mustard

¾ cup neutral-tasting vegetable oil, such as sunflower, safflower, or grapeseed oil

1 tablespoon white wine vinegar or lemon juice, plus additional

½ teaspoon kosher salt, plus additional

Method

In a medium nonreactive stainless-steel, glass, or ceramic bowl, whisk together the egg yolk and Dijon mustard. Continue whisking briskly while you pour a very slow stream of the oil into the bowl, just a few drops at a time to start. As you add more, you can increase the speed of the stream, slowing again as you near the last of the oil. The more oil you add, the thicker the mayonnaise will get—to a point; watch it closely to ensure it doesn't break (see Notes).

Once the oil is incorporated, stir in the vinegar or lemon juice and the salt. Allow it to sit for 5 minutes, taste, and adjust seasonings as required.

Cover and store in the fridge for up to 3 days. Use to make Deviled Egg with Tarragon (page 64), Fish Fried in Batter with Tartar Sauce (page 171), or Asparagus Mayonnaise (page 62).

Notes

- An emulsification such as mayonnaise always comes together better when all of the ingredients are at room temperature. If possible, take the egg out of the refrigerator and separate it about an hour before you intend to start.

- Keep the leftover egg white in a sealed container for up to 1 week in the refrigerator. Whisk it with water as a wash for pastry or bread, like German Brötchen (page 224).

- To keep the bowl steady, twist a tea towel into a rope, then form it into a circle on the counter and rest the bowl in the center. This will help keep the bowl from moving while you whisk.

- If the emulsion breaks, it will appear thin and curdled instead of thick and smooth. Dribble 2 teaspoons warm water down the side of the bowl while whisking briskly. Continue to whisk for 2 minutes. If still thin and runny, discard and begin the recipe again.

Vegan Cream

GF | DF | V | VGN

A vegan alternative for everything from mayonnaise to whipping cream. Experiment with different nuts and seeds to achieve different-flavored creams. Soak a date with the nuts to make sweet cream for desserts such as Cranachan with Brian and Jenny (page 249), or stir nutritional yeast and lemon juice into basic cream to make the savory cream used in the filling for Jackfruit Potpie (page 181).

Makes about 1 cup

Ingredients

1 cup raw nuts or seeds, such as cashews, sunflower seeds, pine nuts, almonds, or hazelnuts

1 Medjool date, pit removed (for a sweet cream, optional)

Pinch of kosher salt

1 tablespoon nutritional yeast (for a savory cream, optional)

1 teaspoon lemon juice (for a savory cream, optional)

Method

In a medium bowl of tepid water, soak the cashews and the date (if a sweet cream is desired) for 10 to 12 hours. Strain and discard the water.

In a blender, combine the cashews and date (if using), with ½ cup tepid water and the salt. Blend until smooth, 2 to 5 minutes, depending on your blender's strength and speed, scraping down the sides as needed, and adding more water, if necessary, for your desired thickness.

If making a savory cream, stir in the nutritional yeast and lemon juice. Taste and adjust the seasonings.

Store covered in the fridge for up to 5 days.

Notes

- *Cashew cream is the most well-known version, but you can use almost any raw nut or seed to make a plant-based cream.*

- *While a high-speed blender is faster, it is not necessary. An average blender, given a little extra time, will produce a smooth, light dairy-free cream. Even a food processor will work with nuts soaked for at least 10 hours; however, you must scrape down the sides often for best results.*

- *Alternatively, instead of using a date, stir maple syrup or agave to taste into unsweetened cream for a sweet dollop on your desserts.*

Chapter 2

❧

Breakfast

Shirred Eggs in Butter

Mrs. Figg's Flapjacks

Heart of Palm Frittata

Johnnycake

White's Sugared Morning Buns

Jenny's Breakfast Crumble

Simon Fraser's Grits with Honey

SHIRRED EGGS IN BUTTER

"I'll be back from France by the end of March at the latest," he said, adding gently, "I shall be on the first ship that sails for the Colonies in the new year, Hal. And I'll bring Henry back." Alive or dead. Neither of them spoke the words; they didn't need to.

"I'll be here when you do," Hal said at last, quietly. Grey put his hand over his brother's, which turned at once to take his. It might look frail, but he was heartened at the determined strength in Hal's grasp.

They sat in silence, hands linked, until the door opened and Arthur—now fully dressed—sidled in with a tray the size of a card table, laden with bacon, sausages, kidneys, kippers, shirred eggs in butter, grilled mushrooms and tomatoes, toast, jam, marmalade, a huge pot of fragrantly steaming tea, bowls of sugar and milk—and a covered dish which he set ceremoniously before Hal, this proving to be filled with a sort of nasty thin gruel.

—*An Echo in the Bone*, chapter 24, "Joyeux Noël"

GF | DF(a) | V

These baked eggs are an easy, hands-free main, ideal for a weekend breakfast or brunch. Prepare them before your guests arrive, and put them into the hot oven just as everyone sits down at the table. Once you've poured the coffee and served up the sides, like the Potato Fritters from OK1, the eggs will be ready.

Serves 4

Ingredients

4 teaspoons butter

4 large eggs

4 teaspoons whipping cream

4 teaspoons finely shredded cheese, such as Parmesan or cheddar

Kosher salt and freshly ground pepper to taste

Scallions (white and light green parts) or parsley, finely chopped, for garnish

Method

Move the oven rack to the middle rung and heat the oven to 350°F. Brush four ovenproof ramekins (see Notes) with 1 teaspoon butter each.

Crack 1 egg into each ramekin and top with 1 teaspoon each of the cream and cheese. Season with salt and pepper and bake until the egg whites are just set and the yolks are still slightly runny, 10 to 14 minutes. Garnish with the scallions and serve immediately.

Serve with German Brötchen (page 224) and Beans Baked with Bacon and Onion (page 215) to enjoy breakfast for dinner, Lord John–style.

Notes

- *To make this recipe dairy-free, substitute an equal amount of dairy-free margarine for the butter and plant-based milk for the whipping cream.*
- *For best results, use small 4-ounce (125-milliliter) ovenproof ramekins.*

Mrs. Figg's Flapjacks

Jenny had had a bite with Marsali and the children but declared herself equal to dealing with an egg, if there might be one, so I sent Mrs. Figg to see whether there might, and within twenty minutes we were wallowing—in a genteel fashion—in soft-boiled eggs, fried sardines, and—for lack of cake—flapjacks with butter and honey, which Jenny had never seen before but took to with the greatest alacrity.

"Look how it soaks up the sweetness!" she exclaimed, pressing the spongy little cake with a fork, then releasing it. "Nay like a bannock at all!" She glanced over her shoulder, then leaned toward me, lowering her voice. "D'ye think her in the kitchen might show me the way of it, if I asked?"

—*Written in My Own Heart's Blood*, chapter 6, "Under My Protection"

GF(a) | DF(a) | V | VGN(a)

Light, sweet pancakes that soak up honey, or maple syrup, like tasty little breakfast sponges. Leftovers freeze well and can be reheated in the toaster for breakfast on the go.

Makes 1 dozen 4- to 5-inch pancakes

Ingredients

2 cups all-purpose flour

¼ cup sugar

2 teaspoons baking powder

½ teaspoon kosher salt

Pinch of freshly grated nutmeg (optional)

1½ cups whole milk

2 large eggs

¼ cup (½ stick) butter, melted

Method

Heat a griddle or pan over medium-low heat while you mix the batter.

In a large bowl, whisk together the flour, sugar, baking powder, salt, and nutmeg (if using). In a separate bowl, beat the milk, eggs, and melted butter. Add the wet ingredients to the dry, whisking until just combined. The batter will be slightly lumpy.

Increase the heat under the griddle to medium. Drop ¼ cup of the batter onto the hot, ungreased pan for each flapjack, and cook until bubbles appear on the tops and the bottoms are golden. Flip and cook until golden on the other side.

Serve hot with butter and honey, maple syrup, Fraser Strawberry Jam from OK1, or Brandied Peaches (page 298) and whipped cream for an Outlandishly extravagant weekend breakfast.

Notes

- *To make this recipe gluten-free, substitute your favorite commercially prepared gluten-free all-purpose flour. See Flours in Pantry Notes (page 4) for more information.*

- *To make this recipe dairy-free, substitute plant-based milk for the whole milk, and melted vegan margarine for the butter.*

- *For vegans, use plant-based milk and melted refined coconut oil instead of whole milk and butter. For the eggs, substitute 1 mashed small, overripe banana, 2 tablespoons unsweetened applesauce, or one of the Egg Substitutes for Baking in Pantry Notes (page 4). Ensure the sugar is vegan, and avoid serving these with honey, which is not.*

Heart of Palm Frittata

Grey's plan to speak to the governor at breakfast was foiled, as that gentleman sent word that he was indisposed. Grey, Cherry, and Fettes all exchanged looks across the breakfast table, but Grey said merely, "Fettes? And you, Captain Cherry, please." They nodded, a look of subdued satisfaction passing between them. He hid a smile; they loved questioning people.

The secretary, Dawes, was present at breakfast but said little, giving all his attention to the eggs and toast on his plate. Grey inspected him carefully, but he showed no sign, either of nocturnal excursions or of clandestine knowledge. Grey gave Cherry an eye. Both Fettes and Cherry brightened perceptibly. For the moment, though, his own path lay clear.

He needed to make a public appearance, as soon as possible, and to take such action as would make it apparent to the public that the situation was under control—and would make it apparent to the maroons that attention was being paid and that their destructive activities would no longer be allowed to pass unchallenged.

—A Plague of Zombies

GF | V

Traditionally, a frittata is a versatile, sometimes last-minute egg dish made with whatever you happen to have in the kitchen. Hearts of palm make a good new-world pantry staple that Lord John would have likely come across in eighteenth-century Jamaica. Their gentle crunch and nutty flavor taste a little like artichokes crossed with water chestnuts, and, combined with a soft goat cheese, make for a deliciously textured vegetarian main.

Make this ahead of time and serve it at room temperature or chilled for breakfast with leftover toasted Cuban Flauta (page 226), or serve it warm with Salad Greens with Vinegar (page 205) for a light dinner.

Serves 6

Ingredients

1 large bunch (1 pound or 450 grams) fresh mature spinach (see Notes), or 10 ounces (300 grams) frozen spinach, defrosted

2 teaspoons kosher salt, plus additional

12 large eggs

½ cup whole milk

½ teaspoon freshly ground pepper, plus additional

¼ cup extra-virgin olive oil

1 can (14 ounces or 398 milliliters) hearts of palm, drained, halved lengthwise, and sliced ½ inch thick

2 garlic cloves, minced or grated

4 ounces (115 grams) goat cheese

3 scallions (white and light green parts), halved lengthwise and sliced thinly on the diagonal

Method

Move the rack to the top-middle rung and heat the oven to 350°F. In a large bowl, prepare an ice bath by combining about 2 quarts (2 liters) cold water with a tray of ice cubes.

If using fresh spinach, in a large pan or stockpot, bring 1 inch of salted water to a boil. Add the spinach to the pot and cover briefly until the leaves start to wilt, about 15 seconds. Uncover and stir the spinach a few times before covering the pot for another 45 seconds. Immediately drain and plunge into the ice bath until cool.

Wring dry the freshly steamed or defrosted spinach in a clean dish towel and chop roughly. In a large bowl, beat the eggs; whisk in the milk, 2 teaspoons salt, and ½ teaspoon pepper.

In a 10- to 12-inch cast-iron or other heavy, ovenproof pan, heat the oil over medium-high heat until shimmering. Add the hearts of palm and cook, stirring often, until just golden, 4 to 5 minutes. Add the chopped spinach and garlic, and stir until fragrant, about 30 seconds. Pour in the egg mixture and swirl the pan to distribute the eggs and filling evenly over the surface. Reduce the heat to low and shake the pan gently, tilting it slightly while lifting up the edges of the frittata with a wooden or silicone spatula so that the eggs run underneath.

Cook, gently shaking the pan occasionally, until the edges have set, 4 to 5 minutes. Remove from the heat, break up the goat cheese into large chunks, and scatter them over the frittata; top with the scallions. Transfer the pan to the oven and cook until the middle is just set and no longer jiggles, 10 to 15 minutes.

Slide the frittata onto a platter and, when ready to serve, slice into wedges. Keep leftovers in the fridge for up to 3 days for an instant and tasty snack full of nutritious fuel for your next adventure.

Notes

- *Dairy gives a frittata its essential creaminess. Plant-based milks, even creams, don't have enough richness; if you are avoiding cow's milk, consider using goat's milk if available.*

- *Mature spinach with stems provide the body for this frittata. If you prefer, or can only find, baby spinach, blanch twice the amount to ensure you have enough once it's been cooked down.*

- *Anna's Tester Tip: "I prefer fresh spinach, usually saving frozen for a hurry-up crustless quiche or frittata. It is definitely worth the extra step of blanching fresh. The flavor of the spinach was much more prominent."*

JOHNNYCAKE

Jamie awoke to the smell of frying meat and sat up straight in bed, forgetting his back.

"Lord have mercy," said Mrs. Hardman, looking over her shoulder. "I haven't heard a noise like that since the last time my husband, Gabriel, killed a pig." She shook her head and returned to her cookery, pouring batter into an oiled cast-iron spider that sat in the coals, smoking and spitting in a baleful sort of way.

"I beg your pardon, ma'am—"

"Silvia is my name, Friend. And thine?" she asked, raising one brow at him.

"Friend Silvia," he said through clenched teeth. "My name is Jamie. Jamie Fraser." He'd raised his knees in the involuntary jerk that brought him upright, and now he wrapped his arms around them and laid his sweating face against the worn quilt that covered them, trying to stretch his recalcitrant back. The effort shot pain down his right leg and caused an instant sharp cramp in his left calf muscle, which made him grunt and pant until it let go.

"I'm pleased to see thee sit up, Friend Jamie," Silvia Hardman remarked, bringing him a plate filled with sausage, fried onions, and johnnycake. "Your back is some better, I collect?" She smiled at him.

—*Written in My Own Heart's Blood,* chapter 13,
"Morning Air Awash with Angels"

GF | DF(a) | V | VGN(a)

Johnnycakes are unleavened cornmeal flatbreads also known by a myriad of regional names, including corn cake, hoe cake, mush bread, and shawnee cake, to name just a few. Many historians believe the name is a natural derivation from what is possibly their original name, journey cakes, so called because they could be easily carried on long trips. Others believe the word is a derivative of a native name for corn cakes, *jonakin,* and that the colonists anglicized them to "johnnycakes" over time.

Makes 1 dozen small flat cakes

Ingredients

1 cup whole milk

1 tablespoon butter, plus additional for
  frying

1¼ cups cornmeal

1 tablespoon sugar

½ teaspoon baking powder

1 teaspoon kosher salt

1 large egg, lightly beaten

Method

Heat a griddle or pan over medium-low heat while you mix the batter.

In a small saucepan, heat the milk and the butter to a simmer over medium heat, stirring occasionally to prevent scorching.

In a medium bowl, combine the cornmeal, sugar, baking powder, and salt. Pour the milk in a steady stream into the dry ingredients and whisk into a smooth, lump-free batter. Whisk in the beaten egg. Rest the batter for 10 minutes.

Increase the heat under the griddle to medium. Brush the pan generously with butter and drop the batter in large, mounded tablespoonfuls. Fry two or three at a time until golden brown on both sides, 4 to 5 minutes total.

These are best enjoyed hot from the pan with butter and syrup as for pancakes, or like bread with butter and jam. For a deliciously savory dinner, add ¼ cup shredded cheese and a sliced scallion to the batter, and serve them alongside the Lamb Cutlets with Spinach (page 138).

Notes

- *To make this recipe dairy-free, substitute plant-based milk for the whole milk and refined coconut oil or vegan margarine for the butter.*

- *For vegan diets, make the above substitutions and use an egg substitute for baking (see Pantry Notes, page 4) in place of the egg.*

- *Keep the johnnycakes warm on a baking sheet in a 250°F oven for up to an hour before serving.*

WHITE'S SUGARED MORNING BUNS

Grey spent the next morning in a drafty room in Whitehall, enduring the necessary tedium of a colonels' meeting with the Ordnance Office, featuring a long-winded address by Mr. Adams, First Secretary of the Ministry of Ordnance. Hal, pleading press of business, had dispatched Grey in his place—meaning, Grey thought, manfully swallowing a yawn, that Hal was likely either still at home enjoying breakfast, or at White's Chocolate House, wallowing in sugared buns and gossip, whilst Grey sat through bum-numbing hours of argument over powder allocations. Well, rank had its privileges.

—Lord John and the Brotherhood of the Blade, chapter 2,
"Not a Betting Man"

V

White's Chocolate House opened in London's affluent Mayfair district in 1693 and was owned by Francesco Bianco, an Italian immigrant commonly known as Frank White. The club had gained such a notorious reputation as a gambling house by the early eighteenth century that Jonathan Swift referred to White's as "the bane of half the English nobility."

White's moved to its current location on St. James Street in 1778, and continues today as the oldest gentleman's club in London, widely considered to be the most exclusive private club in the world. These delicious but labor-intensive morning buns are unabashedly modern, the butter-rich brioche and sweet filling reflecting the club's history of debauchery and decadence.

Makes 1 dozen buns

Ingredients

3¼ cups all-purpose flour

2 teaspoons instant yeast

⅔ cup whole milk, lukewarm

3 large eggs, lightly beaten

2 tablespoons granulated sugar

1 teaspoon kosher salt

1¾ cups (3½ sticks) butter, diced, at room temperature, plus additional for greasing

Vegetable oil, for brushing

½ cup dark brown sugar, lightly packed

¼ cup honey

2 teaspoons cinnamon

1½ teaspoons vanilla extract

4 ounces (115 grams) white baking
    chocolate, coarsely chopped

1 to 2 tablespoons coarse sugar,
    for sprinkling

Method

In the bowl of a stand mixer, combine ½ cup of the flour and the yeast. Stir in the milk until well combined. Cover and set aside on the counter for 30 minutes, or until the sponge is bubbling and falls when the bowl is tapped on the counter.

Add the eggs and mix with the paddle attachment on medium speed until smooth, about 3 minutes. In another bowl, combine the remaining 2¾ cups flour, the granulated sugar, and the salt. Add the dry ingredients to the wet and mix on low speed until all the ingredients are well combined, 2 to 3 minutes. Rest the dough for 10 minutes.

Change to the dough hook attachment. With the mixer on medium, add 1 cup (2 sticks) butter, one-third at a time, and mix until well incorporated before adding more, about 3 minutes. When all the butter has been added, mix for another 5 minutes, scraping down the bowl and hook as needed. The dough will be smooth and very soft.

Line a baking sheet with parchment paper and move the dough to the baking sheet. Form it into a thick rectangle about 8 x 10 inches. Lightly brush or spray the top of the dough with oil and cover with plastic wrap. Chill and let rise in the refrigerator for at least 4 hours and up to 24.

Cream together ½ cup plus 2 tablespoons of the butter, the brown sugar, 3 tablespoons of the honey, the cinnamon, and the vanilla. Cover and set aside on the counter.

Leaving it on the parchment, roll the dough out to a slightly larger 10 x 14-inch rectangle. Spread the filling evenly across the top of the dough, leaving a ½-inch border along one long edge. Sprinkle the white chocolate evenly across the filling. Starting with the opposite long edge, roll the dough into a tight log, pinching the edge to seal the seam. Trim about ½ inch off of each side to neaten the edges. Cut the log in half crosswise, then into quarters. Cut each quarter into three equal pieces for a total of twelve.

Brush a muffin pan with butter. Fill the pan with the rolls, spiral side up. Cover with plastic and proof on a draft-free counter until almost doubled in size, 1 to 2 hours.

Move the rack to the middle rung and heat the oven to 375°F.

Bake the buns until golden, 25 to 30 minutes. In a small pan, melt the remaining 2 tablespoons butter and stir in the remaining 1 tablespoon honey. Brush the tops of the baked buns generously with the honey butter and sprinkle with coarse sugar. Cool in the pan for 20 minutes before removing to a rack to finish cooling.

Serve warm or at room temperature, alongside a cup of Cocoa with the MacKenzies (page 284). Store leftovers in a sealed bag for an extra day. Warm gently in the oven to refresh.

Note

- *You can also proof the buns in the refrigerator for 12 to 24 hours. Remove them from the fridge about an hour before you plan to bake them.*

JENNY'S BREAKFAST CRUMBLE

Jenny had sent my medicine chest from Chestnut Street and with it the large parcel of herbs from Kingsessing, which had been delivered there the night before. With the forethought of a Scottish housewife, she'd also included a pound of oatmeal, a twist of salt, a package of bacon, four apples, and six clean handkerchiefs.

Also a neat roll of fabric with a brief note, which read:

> *Dear Sister Claire,*
> *You appear to own nothing suitable in which to go to war. I suggest you borrow Marsali's printing apron for the time being, and here are two of my flannel petticoats and the simplest things Mrs. Figg could find amongst your wardrobe.*
> *Take care of my brother, and tell him his stockings need darning, because he won't notice until he's worn holes in the heel and given himself blisters.*
>
> *Your Good-sister,*
> *Janet Murray*

—*Written in My Own Heart's Blood*, chapter 47,
"Something Suitable in Which to Go to War"

GF | DF | V(a) | VGN(a)

This naturally gluten- and dairy-free apple crumble with bacon streusel, inspired by Jenny's emergency travel rations, is a deliciously sweet and salty way to start the day. See the Notes at the bottom of the recipe for adaptions to make this vegetarian- and vegan-friendly as well.

Makes one 9-inch square pan

Ingredients

1 to 2 teaspoons vegetable oil, plus additional for greasing

4 large baking apples, such as Gala,

Honeycrisp, or Fuji (about 2 pounds or 900 grams)

6 tablespoons brown sugar, unpacked

1 teaspoon cinnamon

½ teaspoon kosher salt

1½ cups rolled oats

4 slices fatty bacon, diced (see Notes)

Method

Move the rack to the middle rung and heat the oven to 375°F. Brush a 9 x 9-inch pan or 9-inch ovenproof skillet with vegetable oil.

Peel, core, and chop the apples. Combine the apples in the prepared pan with 2 tablespoons of the brown sugar, the cinnamon, and salt.

Pulse ½ cup of the oats in a food processor until ground into a flour. In a medium bowl, combine the oat flour with the remaining 1 cup rolled oats, the remaining ¼ cup brown sugar, and the diced bacon. Using your fingertips, rub the bacon into the oats until the topping comes together in moist clumps. This uses hand strength and can take several minutes. If the streusel still looks too dry, mix in 1 to 2 teaspoons vegetable oil. Sprinkle the topping over the apples in an even layer.

Bake until light golden, 30 to 40 minutes. Cool slightly in the rack before serving warm with a spoonful or two of yogurt or cream.

Keep leftovers in the refrigerator for up to 5 days.

Notes

- *To make this recipe for vegetarians and vegans, substitute ⅓ cup refined coconut oil or vegan margarine for the bacon, and work it into the oats with your fingertips. Serve it with sweetened Vegan Cream (page 20).*

- *The smaller you dice the bacon, the easier it will be to rub the fat into the topping.*

Simon Fraser's Grits with Honey

William wished he hadn't accepted the brigadier's invitation to breakfast. If he had contented himself with the lean rations that were a lieutenant's lot, he would have been hungry, but happy. As it was, he was on the spot—blissfully filled to the eyes with fried sausage, buttered toast, and grits with honey, for which the brigadier had developed a fondness—when the message had come from General Burgoyne. He didn't even know what it had said; the brigadier had read it while sipping coffee, frowning slightly, then sighed and called for ink and quill.

"Want a ride this morning, William?" he'd asked, smiling across the table.

Which is how he'd come to be at General Burgoyne's field headquarters when the Indians had come in. Wyandot, one of the soldiers said; he wasn't familiar with them, though he had heard that they had a chief called Leatherlips, and he did wonder how that had come about. Perhaps the man was an indefatigable talker?

—*An Echo in the Bone,* chapter 55, "Retreat"

GF | DF(a) | V | VGN(a)

Corn was introduced to the first colonists at the time of their earliest arrival by natives all down the Eastern Shores of Maryland, Virginia, and Delaware. The new inhabitants, and generations to come after, enjoyed stone-ground corn cooked up into creamy, rib-sticking fare. It's an easy feat to conjure an image of the brigadier general, a Scot, happily digging into his corn porridge smothered in butter and honey, an echo of the oat parritch in his Highland home of Balnain.

Serves 4

Ingredients

2 tablespoons butter

1 cup stone-ground grits or hominy grits

1 cup whole milk

Kosher salt and freshly ground pepper to taste

Honey, for serving

Method

In a medium saucepan, bring 3 cups water and 1 tablespoon of the butter to a boil over high heat. Gradually whisk in the grits in a steady stream. Reduce to medium-low and simmer gently, stirring often, until the water is absorbed and the grits are thickened, about 15 minutes. Stir in ½ cup of the milk and simmer, partially covered and stirring occasionally to keep the grits from sticking, 10 minutes. Stir in the remaining ½ cup milk and simmer, partially covered and stirring occasionally, until the liquid is absorbed and the grits are thick and tender, 30 to 35 minutes more. Stir in the remaining tablespoon butter and season to taste with salt and pepper.

Serve hot, passing the honey at the table. If you prefer a savory breakfast, top your grits with a knob of butter and serve alongside Shirred Eggs in Butter (page 24).

Notes

- *To make this recipe dairy-free, substitute extra-virgin olive oil or refined coconut oil for the butter, and plant-based milk or thinned Vegan Cream (page 20) for the whole milk.*
- *To make this recipe vegan, make the above substitutions and replace the honey with maple syrup or your favorite sweetener.*
- *White grits are made from white corn, while yellow grits are made from yellow corn. Hominy grits are made from corn that has been treated in a lye or other alkali solution to soften and remove the outer hull. Any of the three can be used in this recipe.*
- *Spread any still-warm leftover grits about 1 inch thick onto a parchment-lined or greased plate. Reheat the next day under the broiler or in a buttered frying pan on the stove.*

Chapter 3

Soup

Annie MacDonald's Chicken Noodle Soup

The kitchen door burst open and Mandy scampered out, clutching Mr. Polly, a stuffed creature who had started out life as a bird of some kind, but now resembled a grubby terry-cloth bag with wings.

"Soup, Mama!" she shouted. "Come eat soup!" And soup they ate, Campbell's Chicken Noodle made from the can, and cheese sandwiches and pickles to fill the cracks.

Annie MacDonald was not a fancy cook, but everything she made was edible, and that was saying a good deal, Brianna thought, with memories of other meals eaten around dying fires on soggy mountaintops or scraped as burnt offerings out of an ashy hearth. She cast a glance of deep affection at the gas-fired Aga cooker that kept the kitchen the coziest room in the house.

—*An Echo in the Bone,* chapter 34, "Psalms, 30"

GF(a) | DF

Garlic and ginger add flavor and warmth to an old-fashioned soup chock-full of vegetables and egg noodles. Untraditional, but not so shocking as a MacDonald serving up anything made by a Campbell. Annie's ancestors killed in the Glencoe Massacre of 1692 would at least have demanded a tester to taste for poison.

Serves 6

Ingredients

2 medium leeks, halved lengthwise (white and light green parts)

2 garlic cloves, halved

1-inch piece fresh ginger, quartered

1 teaspoon whole peppercorns

2 bay leaves

2 fresh rosemary sprigs

4 large chicken legs (about 2 pounds or 900 grams)

3 tablespoons extra-virgin olive oil

2 medium celery stalks, diced

1 large carrot, diced or shredded

1 teaspoon kosher salt, plus additional

½ teaspoon freshly ground pepper, plus additional

½ cup dry white wine or sherry

5 ounces (150 grams) dry egg noodles (about 2½ cups)

Method

Thinly slice the leeks on a diagonal and rinse them thoroughly in a bowl of cold water. Scoop out the leeks with your hands or a slotted spoon, leaving the silt and sand behind. Shake dry in a clean dishcloth or salad spinner. Enclose the garlic, ginger, peppercorns, bay leaves, and rosemary in a piece of cheesecloth or a large tea ball to make a bouquet garni.

Place the chicken legs in a stockpot and cover with 3 quarts (3 liters) cold water. Bring to a boil over high heat, boil for 1 minute, and reduce the heat to medium-low. Skim the scum off the surface with a slotted spoon. Submerge the bouquet garni under the chicken in the pot and simmer gently until the chicken is tender, 45 minutes. Remove the chicken to a plate to cool. Strain and reserve the broth.

Clean the pot and heat the olive oil over medium heat. When the oil is shimmering, add the leeks, celery, carrot, and the salt and pepper. Cook until the vegetables are softened, about 5 minutes. Increase the heat to medium-high and continue to cook until the vegetables are lightly golden. Deglaze the pan with the wine and stir until the pan is almost dry.

Add the reserved broth to the pot, bring to a boil, and reduce to a simmer for 15 minutes. Discard the chicken skin and shred the meat from the bones. Reserve the bones to make stock (see Notes). Add the chicken meat and egg noodles to the pot and simmer for 15 more minutes. Season to taste.

Serve hot, with a slice of Dottie's Millet Loaf (page 228) and Rachel Murray's Dill Pickles (page 294) to "fill the cracks." Store leftovers in the fridge for up to 5 days or in the freezer for up to 3 weeks.

Notes

- *To make this soup gluten-free, substitute gluten-free pasta for the egg noodles.*
- *There is plenty of goodness left in those bones after being simmered for only 45 minutes. Pull as much meat from the bones and tendons as you can because it's frugal, but also because meat on the bones makes a stock cloudy instead of the crystal-clear liquid you want.*

An Echo in the Bone Broth

He picked up the letter and read it over again. And again. Set it down and gazed at it for several minutes with narrowed eyes, thinking.

"I'm damned if I believe it," he said aloud, at last. "What the devil are you up to, Willie?"

He crumpled the letter, and taking a candlestick from a nearby table with a nod of apology, set fire to the missive. The steward, observing this, instantly produced a small china dish, into which Grey dropped the flaming paper, and together they watched the writing blacken into ash.

"Your soup, my lord," said Mr. Bodley, and waving the smoke of conflagration gently away with a napkin, placed a steaming plate before him.

—*An Echo in the Bone,* chapter 14, "Delicate Matters"

GF | DF

A frequent stop for Lord John when he is in London, the Society for the Appreciation of the English Beefsteak is a fictional club based on real clubs of the time. One of the most well-known was the Sublime Society of Beef Steaks, later known as the Beefsteak Club. Its early members were required to sign an oath and were rewarded with "Beef and Liberty." Although the club folded in 1867, a modern incarnation from the late twentieth century is in operation on Irving Street in London, still staunchly secretive and open to men only.

Serves 6

Ingredients

2 pounds (900 grams) beef short ribs (about 3 large)

1 tablespoon dark brown sugar

5 pounds (2.25 kilograms) beef bones with marrow

1 cinnamon stick

1 tablespoon coriander seeds

1 tablespoon fennel seeds

1 teaspoon whole peppercorns

3 whole allspice berries

3 whole cloves

2 medium white onions, peeled and halved

2 medium carrots, halved lengthwise

2 garlic cloves, halved lengthwise

2-inch piece fresh ginger, halved
   lengthwise

2 bay leaves

Kosher salt to taste

Mushroom Catsup (page 307) or
   Worcestershire sauce to taste

1 small savoy cabbage,
   finely shredded

1 pound (450 grams) tenderloin, thinly
   sliced across the grain (see Notes)

1 large carrot, thinly sliced on the bias

1 small sweet onion, such as Vidalia,
   thinly sliced

12 fresh basil leaves, for garnish

12 fresh mint leaves, for garnish

4 scallions (white and light green parts),
   thinly sliced, for garnish

Method

Move the rack to the top-middle rung and heat the oven to 400°F.

Sprinkle the short ribs sparingly with the brown sugar and arrange, meat side up, on a large rimmed baking sheet. Roast until browned, about 45 minutes.

In a large stockpot, cover the marrow bones with cold water by 1 inch. Bring to a boil over high heat, and boil 5 minutes to loosen the impurities from the bones. Drain and discard the water, rinsing the bones until they are clean of blood and scum. Clean the stockpot, return the bones to it, and set aside.

Heat a cast-iron pan over low heat, add the cinnamon stick, coriander, fennel, peppercorns, allspice, and cloves. Toast, shaking the pan occasionally, until they begin to release their aroma and brown just slightly, 2 to 6 minutes. Pour the toasted spices into the center of a large square (15 inches) of cheesecloth or muslin.

Increase the heat to medium-high and add the onions, carrots, garlic, and ginger, cut sides down, to the cast-iron pan. Char until dark brown, 2 or 3 minutes for the garlic, 7 or 8 minutes for the rest. Do not burn. Add to the spices in the cheesecloth square, along with the bay leaves. Gather up the corners and tie closed with kitchen twine.

Stack the roasted short ribs on top of the marrow bones in the stockpot, add the sachet of spices and aromatics, cover with cold water by about 4 inches, and bring to a boil over high heat. Reduce to medium-low and simmer very gently, skimming away impurities from the top of the broth as needed. Do not stir. Check the tenderness of the short ribs after 3 to 4 hours of simmering. When ready, remove them from the broth with tongs. Rest until cool enough to handle and pull out the bone. Peel away and discard any fat or gristle, cut across the grain into ½-inch slices, and refrigerate.

Continue to cook the broth at a very low simmer for a total of 7 or 8 hours. Remove the sachet and, using a ladle, strain the broth through three layers of cheesecloth or muslin.

To serve, heat the broth over medium-high heat, but do not boil. Season with salt and mushroom catsup to taste. Arrange the cabbage in the bottom of the serving bowls and top with the sliced raw tenderloin, carrot, onion, and add 2 or 3 slices of short rib. Ladle the broth over the vegetables. Garnish with the basil and mint, tearing the leaves and scattering them into the bowls along with the scallions.

Serve immediately with John Grey's Yorkshire Pudding (page 213) for dipping—a meal worthy of the Beefsteak Club in any century. To store, chill the broth quickly in an ice bath and keep in the refrigerator for up to 5 days or freeze for up to 3 weeks.

Notes

- *Freeze the tenderloin for 2 to 3 hours until it is firm but not solid. With a sharp knife, slice the partially frozen meat thinly against the grain.*

- *Add rice noodles to the bottom of the bowl, or a soft-boiled or poached egg on top, for an even heartier soup.*

- *Fish sauce can also be used instead of the mushroom catsup or Worcestershire sauce.*

- *Reuse the marrow bones at least once more for a weaker, but still substantial, stock for soups and sauces. No harm in throwing the short rib bones in the pot either.*

LEEK AND POTATO SOUP

"Melton said you'd had a bad time since Germany." Quarry ushered him to the dining room and into a chair with an annoying solicitude, all but tucking a napkin under Grey's chin.

"Did he," Grey replied shortly. How much had Hal told Quarry—and how much had he heard on his own? Rumor spread faster in the army than it did among the London salons.

Luckily, Quarry seemed disinclined to inquire after the particulars—which probably meant he'd already heard them, Grey concluded grimly.

Quarry looked him over and shook his head. "Too thin by half! Have to feed you up, I suppose." This assessment was followed by Quarry's ordering—without consulting him—thick soup, game pie, fried trout with grapes, lamb with a quince preserve and roast potatoes, and a broccoli sallet with radishes and vinegar, the whole to be followed by a jelly trifle.

—Lord John and the Haunted Soldier

GF | DF(a) | V | VGN(a)

There are two main classifications of soup in traditional French cuisine: clear soups, such as bouillon and consommé, and thick soups, including bisques and purees like this one of leek and potato. When ready, a thick soup should coat the back of a spoon thoroughly, without stepping over the line into a thick paste.

Serves 6

Ingredients

3 medium leeks (1 pound or 450 grams)
   (white and light green parts only)

3 tablespoons butter

1 garlic clove, minced or grated

1 teaspoon kosher salt,
   plus additional

2 medium yellow potatoes (1 pound or
   450 grams), peeled and diced

½ cup whipping cream

½ teaspoon ground white pepper, plus
   additional

2 to 3 teaspoons lemon juice

Snipped fresh chives, for garnish

Method

Thinly slice the leeks on a diagonal and rinse them thoroughly in a bowl of cold water. Scoop out the leeks with your hands or a slotted spoon, leaving the grit behind. Shake dry in a clean dishcloth or salad spinner.

In a large saucepan, melt the butter over medium heat. When bubbling, add the leeks, garlic, and salt; sweat for 5 minutes. Decrease the heat to medium-low and cook until the leeks are tender, about 15 minutes, stirring occasionally.

Add the potatoes and 1 quart (1 liter) water, increase the heat to medium-high, and bring to a boil. Reduce the heat to low, cover, and gently simmer until the potatoes are soft, about 30 minutes.

Turn off the heat and puree the mixture with an immersion blender until smooth. Stir in the cream, white pepper, and lemon juice. Taste and adjust the seasonings, if required. Sprinkle with chives and serve immediately with a plate of Bacon Savories (page 68) on the side.

Store leftovers in the fridge for up to 5 days.

Note

- *To make this recipe dairy-free and vegan, substitute extra-virgin olive oil for the butter, and savory Vegan Cream (page 20) for the whipping cream. Alternatively, make the soup with an equal amount of Quick Vegetable Stock (page 12) instead of water. Thin with extra stock instead of cream; taste, season, and serve as directed.*

SCOTCH BROTH AT CRANESMUIR

McEwan looked up suddenly and smiled at her.

"It will take a little time," he murmured. "Relax, if you can."

In fact, she could. For the first time in twenty-four hours, she wasn't hungry. For the first time in days, she was beginning to thaw out completely—and for the first time in months, she wasn't afraid. She let out her breath and eased her head back on Roger's shoulder. He made a low humming noise in his throat and took a firmer hold, settling himself.

She could hear Mandy telling Jem a disjointed story about Esmeralda's adventures, in the back room where the landlady had taken them to eat their soup and bread. Sure that they were safe, she gave herself up to the elemental bliss of her husband's arms and the smell of his skin.

—*Written in My Own Heart's Blood,* chapter 109, "Frottage"

GF(a) | DF | V(a) | VGN(a)

Recipes for Scotch broth appeared in cookbooks for the first time in the latter part of the eighteenth century, though variations of this thick, hearty, stew-like soup had been cooking in cast-iron kettles across the Highlands for hundreds of years before that. If you can't find lamb, use beef; more farmers in the Highlands had cattle than sheep before Culloden, so you won't lose any authenticity.

Serve it with Bannocks at Carfax Close from OK1 for a Scots meal almost as old as time.

Serves 6 to 8

Ingredients

2 large leeks (1 pound or 450 grams) (white and light green parts only)

2 pounds (900 grams) lamb flank, breast, or shank

½ cup split peas

½ cup barley

2 medium carrots, shredded

1 cup diced turnip or rutabaga

2 cups finely shredded kale or savoy cabbage

2 teaspoons kosher salt, plus additional

Fresh chopped parsley, for garnish

Method

Thinly slice the leeks on a diagonal and rinse them thoroughly in a bowl of cold water. Scoop out the leeks with your hands or a slotted spoon, leaving the grit behind. Shake dry in a clean dishcloth or salad spinner.

In a large pot, cover the lamb with 2 quarts (2 liters) cold water and bring to a boil over high heat. Allow to boil 1 minute, then skim the scum from the surface. Reduce the heat to medium-low and add the split peas, barley, half the leeks, and half the carrots. Simmer until the peas and barley are tender, about 1 hour.

Add the remaining leeks and carrots, as well as the turnip and 2 cups hot water. Simmer until the turnip is tender, about 30 minutes.

Remove the lamb, discard any bones and gristle, shred the meat, and return it to the pot. Stir in the kale and salt. Taste, and adjust with more salt as needed.

Garnish with the parsley and serve hot. Leftovers will keep in the fridge for up to 5 days or in the freezer for up to a month. Add a little more water if needed when reheating.

Notes

- *To make this recipe gluten-free, substitute rice or your favorite gluten-free grain for the barley.*

- *To make it vegan, omit the lamb and increase the amounts of split peas and barley to 1 cup each. For even more flavor, substitute Quick Vegetable Stock (page 12) for the water. Stir in a spoonful of Mushroom Catsup (page 307) or vegan Worcestershire sauce near the end for a boost of plant-based umami.*

- *If you prefer to use beef, choose a similar tough cut, such as flank, shin, shank, or blade. Beef will result in a milder tasting soup.*

- *Most early recipes for Scotch broth call for 2 tablespoons salt to be added at the end, but I added only a tablespoon to ours when all was said and done; start with less and add more to taste.*

Savannah Clam Chowder

"Luckily, we hadna started up L'Oignon yet," she said, answering Jamie's look. "It's only been printing up handbills and broadsheets and the odd religious tract. I think it will be all right," she said bravely, but she reached to touch Félicité's dark head, as though to reassure herself.

We had the clams made into chowder—rather a watery chowder, as we had very little milk, but we thickened it with crumbled biscuit, and there was enough butter—and were setting the table for supper when Fergus and Ian came clattering up the stairs, flushed with excitement and full of news.

—*Written in My Own Heart's Blood*, chapter 129, "Invasion"

GF(a) | DF(a)

Look out, Boston and Manhattan, this deceptively simple recipe produces a home-style chowder with deep, sophisticated flavor. I suggest serving the biscuits alongside, rather than in, the bowl. Like most chowders and stews, it's even tastier the next day.

Serves 6

Ingredients

4 pounds (1.8 kilograms) fresh clams, such as cherrystone or Manila, scrubbed (see Notes)

8 ounces (225 grams) salt pork, diced

1 large onion, diced

2 celery stalks, diced

1 garlic clove, minced or grated

1 tablespoon chopped fresh thyme leaves

¼ to ½ teaspoon cayenne pepper

¼ cup all-purpose flour

2 pounds (900 grams) yellow potatoes, such as Yukon Gold, peeled and diced

2 bay leaves

2 cups light cream

Kosher salt and freshly ground pepper to taste

Method

In a Dutch oven or other large, heavy pot, bring the clams and 2 cups water to a boil, covered, over high heat. Cook until the clams just open, 4 to 8 minutes, dis-

carding any that do not open. Transfer the clams to a large bowl with a slotted spoon. Strain and reserve the clam broth, adding water to equal 6 cups. When the clams are cool enough to handle, pull the meat from the shells. Discard the shells and chop large clams into bite-size pieces.

Add the salt pork to the clean and dry Dutch oven. Heat over medium heat and render the fat until the salt pork is golden and just crisp, 10 to 12 minutes. Transfer the salt pork with a slotted spoon to a small bowl. Pour off the excess fat, leaving ¼ cup in the pan. Add the onion and celery. Cook, stirring often, until the onion is translucent, about 5 minutes.

Stir in the garlic, thyme, and cayenne until fragrant, about 30 seconds. Sprinkle in the flour and stir for 2 minutes to cook off the starch. Add the reserved broth, potatoes, and bay leaves. Bring to a simmer over medium heat and cook until the potatoes are tender, about 20 minutes.

Discard the bay leaves and stir in the reserved clam meat, salt pork, and cream. Heat gently until piping hot, but do not boil. Season with salt and pepper to taste.

Serve hot with a fresh batch of Mrs. Bug's Buttermilk Drop Biscuits from OK1 for a hearty lunch. Add Salad Greens with Vinegar (page 205) to make it dinner.

Store leftovers in the fridge for up to 3 days. Do not freeze.

Notes

- *To make this chowder gluten-free, substitute brown rice flour for the all-purpose.*
- *To make this recipe dairy-free, instead of light cream, use a batch of savory Vegan Cream (page 20), thinned to the consistency of light cream.*
- *Fresh clams make the best chowder, but they're not always available. Substitute two 10-ounce (295-gram) cans of clam meat and 1½ quarts (1.5 liters) bottled clam juice, and begin with the second step.*
- *Clam's brininess varies greatly; taste every pot before seasoning.*
- *Bacon will add a smokiness to your chowder, but I love to change up the taste by using salt pork in some of my soups. Choose whichever one suits your taste and render it slowly, starting in a cold pan to prevent sticking.*

SLOW COOKER HOT PEASE PORRIDGE

The men had lain on their arms all night, by Sir Henry's orders. While one didn't actually lie on a musket and cartridge box, there was something about sleeping with a gun touching your body that kept you alert, ready to rouse from sleep in nothing flat.

William had no arms to lie on, and hadn't needed rousing, as he hadn't slept, but was no less alert for the lack. He wouldn't be fighting, and deeply regretted that—but he would be out in it, by God.

The camp was a-bustle, drums rattling up and down the aisles of tents, summoning the soldiers, and the air was full of the smells of baking bread, pork, and hot pease porridge.

—Written in My Own Heart's Blood, chapter 68,
"Go Out in Darkness"

GF | DF | V(a) | VGN(a)

A protein-filled soup, with or without the ham hock, that should be more at home on the breakfast table in these days of high-protein diets. It has been a favorite of mine since early childhood, when I would ask for a bowl of leftover soup in the morning, while my older brothers rolled their eyes and made retching noises over their cereal.

What was soup just after cooking will be a thick, almost solid, porridge after a night in the fridge. Add water as needed when reheating.

Serves 6, with leftovers

Ingredients

1 pound (450 grams) split peas

1 large smoked ham hock (about 2 pounds or 900 grams)

1 cup diced onion

1 cup diced celery

1 cup diced carrot

2 garlic cloves, grated or minced

2 bay leaves

Kosher salt and freshly ground pepper to taste

Method

In a 5- or 6-quart (5- to 6-liter) slow cooker, combine the split peas, ham hock, onion, celery, carrot, garlic, and bay leaves. Cover with 10 cups (2.5 liters) water and cook on low for 6 to 8 hours, or on high for 4 to 5 hours.

Remove the ham hock to a plate and cool slightly. Discard the bay leaves. Shred the ham and return to the soup. Season to taste with salt and pepper before serving with a plate of Cheese Savories (page 66) on the side.

Store leftovers in the fridge for up to 5 days or in the freezer for up to 1 month.

Notes

- *To make the soup vegan, omit the ham hock and substitute Quick Vegetable Stock (page 12) for the water. Stir in a spoonful of Mushroom Catsup (page 307) for a boost of plant-based umami.*

- *If you prefer, cook the soup in a large pot on the stove; bring to a boil over medium-high heat, reduce to low, partially cover, and cook for 3 to 4 hours, stirring occasionally to prevent scorching.*

Chapter 4

Appetizers

Asparagus Mayonnaise

From the Chu Diary:

> Thursday, June 4
> 9:00—bath
> 10:00—body groomer (ouch)
> 11:00—hairdresser
> 1:00—measurements, Madame Alexander's, eau-de-nil ball gown
> 3:00—promenade in Hyde Park with Sir Robert Abdy, Bt.
> 8:00—supper party, Lady Wilford

Note: Lady Wilford's party well supplied. Two engagements for next week, and a promising conversation with the Marquess of Tewksbury about hocus-pocus in House of Lords.

Note: Also met Duke of Beaufort at supper, chatted briefly over asparagus mayonnaise. Asked me to ride with him in Rotten Row next Tuesday. Declined on grounds that I have no horse, only to have him offer me one. Accepted. How hard can it be?

—*A Fugitive Green*, chapter 5, "Strategy and Tactics"

GF | DF | V | VGN(a)

A simple, elegant, make-ahead appetizer that can be served plated at the table or alongside other finger food, such as Mushroom Pâté (page 77) and Vegan Sausage Rolls (page 75), at a more stand-up cocktail party.

Serves 6 as a plated appetizer

Ingredients

24 to 36 asparagus spears, depending on size

Kosher salt

1 cup Mayonnaise (page 18)

½ garlic clove, grated or minced

½ teaspoon smoked paprika

Freshly ground pepper to taste

Lemon wedges, for garnish

Method

To prepare the asparagus, hold a single stalk in your hands and gently bend it, looking for the natural break point. Snap each stalk (usually somewhere just below the middle) and reserve the woody ends for another use (see Notes).

Prepare an ice bath by filling a large bowl with cold water and a tray of ice cubes.

In a large pan, bring ½ inch of water to a boil. Add a pinch of salt to the water, then add half the asparagus. Simmer, uncovered, until it is fork-tender, as quickly as 1 minute for slender asparagus, and up to 5 to 6 minutes for large, thick stalks. When done, plunge the asparagus into the ice bath until completely cool, 3 to 5 minutes. Repeat with the other half of the asparagus. Drain the cooled asparagus and gently blot dry with a clean tea towel. Store, covered, in the fridge until ready to serve, up to 2 days.

In a small bowl, stir together the mayonnaise, garlic, and smoked paprika until smooth. Taste and adjust the seasonings, if required.

Serve, plating 4 to 6 spears of asparagus per person. Season with salt and pepper, and garnish with a dollop of mayonnaise and wedge of lemon. Alternatively, arrange the spears on a large serving dish and serve the mayonnaise in a small bowl for dipping.

Notes

- *To make this recipe vegan, substitute store-bought vegan mayonnaise or savory Vegan Cream (page 20) for the mayonnaise.*
- *Use the ends of the asparagus for your next batch of Quick Vegetable Stock (page 12), which makes a great base for asparagus soup.*
- *Janet Lee's Tester Tip: "I am so excited about this mayo! I don't usually eat much mayo because I have a sensitivity to soybean and canola oils, and now I can make my own. Going to try with olive oil later in the week. I used grapeseed for this one. Amazing!"*

DEVILED EGG WITH TARRAGON

"Whether you choose to call yourself the Duke of Pardloe, the Earl of Melton, or plain Harold Grey, you're still a peer. You can't be tried by anything save a jury of your peers—to wit, the House of Lords. And I didn't really require Washburn to tell me that the odds of a hundred noblemen agreeing that you should be either imprisoned or hanged for challenging the man who seduced your wife to a duel, and killing him as a result, is roughly a thousand to one—but he did tell me so."

"Oh." Hal hadn't given the matter a moment's thought but if he had would likely have reached a similar conclusion. Still, he felt some relief at hearing that the Honorable Lawrence Washburn, KC, shared it.

"Mind you—are you going to eat that last slice of ham?"

"Yes." Hal took it and reached for the mustard pot.

Harry took an egg sandwich instead. "Mind you," he repeated, mouth half full of deviled egg and thin white bread, "that doesn't mean you aren't in trouble."

—*A Fugitive Green,* chapter 2, "Cold Honey and Sardines"

GF(a) | DF | V

Boiled whole eggs heavily seasoned with pepper were a popular appetizer in ancient Rome, and recipes for stuffed eggs, the yolks smashed with cheese, raisins, and herbs, first appeared in the fifteenth century. It's not until the late eighteenth century that the word *devil*, as applied to food, appears, referring to a highly seasoned dish.

By the nineteenth century, it was in common use as a noun, meaning something cooked with hot condiments such as mustard and cayenne pepper, and straightforwardly derives from its association with the devil, who resides in the fiery depths of hell.

Makes 12 deviled eggs or 8 tea sandwiches

Ingredients

6 large eggs

3 to 4 tablespoons Mayonnaise (page 18)

1 teaspoon Dijon mustard

1 teaspoon finely chopped capers

1½ teaspoons finely chopped
    fresh tarragon leaves

Pinch of cayenne pepper

Kosher salt and freshly ground pepper
    to taste

1 tablespoon minced fresh chives or
    parsley, for deviled egg garnish

Butter or vegan margarine,
    for sandwiches

Thinly sliced white bread,
    for sandwiches

Chopped watercress or shredded iceberg
    lettuce, for sandwiches

Method

Prepare an ice bath by filling a large bowl with cold water and a tray of ice cubes. In a medium saucepan, lay the eggs in a single layer and cover with cold water by at least 1 inch. Bring to a boil over medium-high heat, then remove from the heat, cover, and let sit in the hot water for 10 minutes. Drain and cool in an ice bath.

Peel the eggs. Using a sharp knife, slice the eggs in half lengthwise.

FOR DEVILED EGGS: Carefully scoop out the yolks into a small bowl; cover and refrigerate the empty egg-white halves. Mash the yolks with a fork and stir in the mayonnaise, mustard, capers, tarragon, and cayenne until smooth. Taste and season with salt and pepper. Fill each egg-white half with 1 heaping teaspoon of the yolk mixture, rounding and smoothing the tops with a spoon. Garnish each with a sprinkling of minced fresh chives and serve.

FOR TEA SANDWICHES: Mash the egg whites together with the yolks, mayonnaise, mustard, capers, and tarragon, adding a little extra mayonnaise as needed to make the mixture smooth; season to taste. Butter the bread slices and spread the egg mixture on half of them. Top each with a thin layer of watercress for color and crunch, and the remaining slices of bread. Slice into halves or thirds and serve.

Cover and refrigerate leftovers for up to 2 days.

Notes

- *To make gluten-free sandwiches, use slices of your favorite gluten-free bread.*
- *The fresher the eggs, the harder they are to peel. Try to use at least week-old eggs. If what you have are farm fresh, roll the drained eggs around in a bowl to crack most of the shells before submerging in the ice bath.*
- *Capers are salty; taste the mixture before adding additional salt.*

CHEESE SAVORIES

They sat now sprawled in chairs before the fire, awaiting dinner, surrounded by a prostrate pack of heavily breathing dogs, their patience sustained by a plate of savories and a decanter of excellent brandy. A spurious sense of peace prevailed, but Grey was not fooled.

"Have you quite lost your mind, Stephan?" he inquired politely.

Von Namtzen appeared to consider the question, inhaling the aroma of his brandy.

"No," he said mildly, exhaling. "Why do you ask?"

"For one thing, your servants are terrified. You might have killed that groom, you know. To say nothing of breaking your own neck."

—*Lord John and the Brotherhood of the Blade,* chapter 26,
"Drinking with Dachshunds"

GF | V

These were created as *Outlander Kitchen*'s first on-purpose gluten-free recipe, and I am proud of the delicious, versatile bites of cheesy goodness. Serve them alongside Bacon Savories (page 68) and Deviled Egg with Tarragon (page 64), and watch your Outlander-themed, gluten-free buffet disappear.

Makes about 3 dozen

Ingredients

1 cup almond meal

¼ cup gluten-free flour, such as brown rice flour, cornmeal, or finely ground oats (see Notes)

1 teaspoon sugar

½ teaspoon kosher salt

⅛ to ¼ teaspoon cayenne pepper

5 ounces (150 grams) hard cheese, such as aged cheddar or Gruyère, shredded (about 1½ cups)

5 ounces (150 grams) soft, unripened cheese, such as Boursin or goat cheese

Method

In a large bowl, mix together the almond meal, flour, sugar, salt, and cayenne to taste; stir in the cheddar. Break up the soft cheese into pieces and add to the bowl, mixing with your hands, squeezing and kneading the dough together.

On the counter, lay down a piece of plastic wrap at least 24 inches long. Form the mixture into an 18-inch log on top of the wrap and roll it up tightly in the plastic. Twist the ends of the wrap in opposite directions until very tight and secure with tape if necessary. Freeze the log until firm, about 1 hour.

Move the rack to the middle rung and heat the oven to 350°F. Line a baking sheet with parchment paper.

Unwrap the chilled cheese log and slice it into ½-inch-thick rounds. Space about 1 inch apart on the parchment-lined baking sheet and bake until golden on the bottom, 20 to 25 minutes.

Cool on the pan and serve. Store leftovers in an airtight container for up to 3 days.

Notes

- *Different flours result in different textures and tastes in the final product. Brown rice flour results in a soft cookie, while those made with cornmeal have a slight crunch. Oat flour savories have a pleasant, earthy flavor that pairs well with soup. All-purpose flour also works, for those of us who have no gluten worries.*

- *Make the dough log up to 2 weeks ahead of time. On the day you plan to serve them, defrost the log on the counter briefly, then slice and bake as instructed.*

BACON SAVORIES

"Wasn't that Lord Melton?" Bernard Adams, who was short of sight, squinted dubiously toward the end of the room where Hal had made his escape. "I wanted to speak with him, regarding the extravagance of his request for . . ."

Grey drained another glass, listening to the tall clock in the corner chiming midnight, and thought how pleasant it would be to turn into a pumpkin and sit inert at Adams's feet, impervious to the man's blather.

Instead, he fixed his eyes on the mole to the right of Adams's mouth, nodding and grimacing periodically as he worked his way methodically through three more glasses of champagne and a plate of bacon savories.

—*Lord John and the Brotherhood of the Blade*, chapter 16,
"In Which an Engagement Is Broken"

GF | DF

These addicting small bites are *Outlander Kitchen*'s eighteenth-century version of rumaki, a retro appetizer from the 1950s and '60s, first made popular in Polynesian tiki bars and restaurants. It's impossible to stop at just one, especially when served with a tasty tropical libation like Whisky and Coconut Milk (page 277).

Makes about 3 dozen one-bite appetizers

Ingredients

2 cans (8 ounces or 227 milliliters each) whole water chestnuts, drained

2 teaspoons Mushroom Catsup (page 307) or Worcestershire sauce

½ teaspoon mustard powder

1 pound thin-sliced (450 grams) bacon

¼ cup sugar

Method

In a small bowl, combine the water chestnuts, mushroom catsup, and mustard powder. Cover and marinate in the fridge for 2 to 4 hours.

Move the rack to the upper-middle rung and heat the oven to 425°F. Line a rimmed baking sheet with parchment.

Cut the bacon slices crosswise into thirds. Roll a water chestnut in the sugar and wrap in bacon. Place it seam side down on the prepared baking sheet and repeat with the remaining water chestnuts, sugar, and bacon.

Roast in the oven until the bacon is browned and crisped, 25 to 30 minutes. Serve hot or at room temperature. Pair these with Mr. Willoughby's Coral Knob and Mushroom Pasties from OK1 for an appetizer table everyone will love.

Note

- *Bacon-wrapped cheese-stuffed olives were a very close second to the water chestnuts. Also delicious are bacon-wrapped radishes, turnip wedges, and Brussels sprout halves—and the list goes on!*

Mocktopus with Tomatoes and Olives

Before Grey could sort out a coherent response to this statement, the door opened suddenly and a sweet-faced black girl with a yellow scarf round her head and an enormous battered tin tray in her hands sidled through it.

"*Señores*," she said, curtsying despite the tray, and deposited it on the desk. "*Cerveza, vino rústico, y un poco comida: moros y cristianos*"—she unlidded one of the dishes, loosing a savory steam—"*maduros*"—that was fried plantains; Grey was familiar with those—"*y pulpo con tomates, aceitunas, y vinagre!*"

"*Muchas gracias, Inocencia,*" Malcolm said, in what sounded like a surprisingly good accent. "*Es suficiente.*" He waved a hand in dismissal, but instead of leaving, she came round the desk and knelt down, frowning at his mangled leg.

"*Está bien,*" Malcolm said. "*No te preocupes.*" He tried to turn away, but she put a hand on his knee, her face turned up to his, and said something rapid in Spanish, in a tone of scolding concern that made Grey raise his brows. It reminded him of the way Tom Byrd spoke to *him* when he was sick or injured—as though it were all his own fault, and he therefore ought to submit meekly to whatever frightful dose or treatment was being proposed—but there was a distinct note in the girl's voice that Tom Byrd's lacked entirely.

—*Besieged*

GF | DF | V | VGN

From *pulpo con tomates, aceitunas, y vinagre* comes Mocktopus with Tomatoes and Olives. This marinated vegetable salad is full of bright, fresh flavor and absolutely no octopus. Standing in for an eight-armed, suckered sea beast are king oyster mushrooms, found in Asian groceries and some urban supermarkets. When grilled, their tender chewiness is a delicious substitute everyone can enjoy.

Serves 6

Ingredients

5 tablespoons extra-virgin olive oil

2 tablespoons sherry vinegar or
   red wine vinegar

½ teaspoon kosher salt, plus additional

¼ teaspoon freshly ground pepper,
   plus additional

¾ pound (340 grams) king oyster mushrooms (about 4 large)

½ pound (225 grams) cherry tomatoes

1 cup mixed olives, drained

2 teaspoons chopped fresh oregano

1 garlic clove, grated or minced

¼ teaspoon crushed red pepper flakes

Method

Heat the grill on high or, alternatively, heat a grill pan on the stove over medium-high heat.

In a large bowl, whisk together the olive oil, vinegar, salt, and pepper. Cut the mushrooms in half lengthwise, and brush them liberally all over with the oil and vinegar. Grill until tender with grill marks, 10 to 12 minutes. Toss the tomatoes in the oil and vinegar, and grill until they just start to burst their skins, about 5 minutes.

Chop the grilled mushrooms into bite-size pieces. Toss in the bowl with the oil and vinegar, along with the grilled tomatoes, olives, oregano, garlic, and red pepper flakes. Season to taste with salt and pepper, and refrigerate for at least 2 hours to allow the flavors to meld.

Serve with a fresh loaf of Cuban Flauta (page 226) to soak up the juices, followed by Cuban Black Beans and Rice (page 194) for an OK2 vegan Cuban feast.

Note

• *If you prefer to make the salad with octopus in place of the mushrooms, butcher and clean a small octopus, following an instructional video online, if needed. Cover and simmer the octopus arms and body in salted water with chopped onion and garlic until tender, about 90 minutes. When cool enough to handle, remove and discard the skin from the octopus. Season with salt and pepper, and grill on high for 3 to 4 minutes, weighing the arms down for the best grill marks and caramelization. Cut the octopus into bite-size pieces and toss in the bowl with the tomatoes, olives, and dressing. Refrigerate as directed before serving.*

Sardines on Toast for Lady Joffrey

"Lord John!" A clear voice hailed him, and he looked round to find his friend, Lucinda, Lady Joffrey, smiling at him, a small leather-bound book in one hand. "How do you do, my dear?"

"Excellently well, I thank you." He made to kiss her hand, but she laughed and drew him in, standing on tiptoe to kiss his cheek instead.

"I crave a favor, if you please," she whispered in his ear, and came down on her heels, looking up at him, expectant of his consent.

"You know I can deny you nothing," he said, smiling. She reminded him always of a partridge, small, neat, and slightly plump, with a kind, soft eye. "What is your desire, Lady Joffrey? A cup of punch? Sardines on toast? Or had you in mind something more in the way of apes, ivory, and peacocks?"

—*Lord John and the Brotherhood of the Blade,* chapter 5, "Genius and Sub-Genius"

GF(a) | DF

Atlantic sardines, aka European pilchards, are small, oily fish related to herring. Caught off the British and French coasts, in the Mediterranean Sea, and off the Atlantic coast of North America, sardines are high in B vitamins, a good source of omega-3 fatty acids, and low in contaminants such as mercury.

Lady Joffrey's sardines would have been fresh; the first sardine canning factory was founded in Brittany in 1880. Canned sardines are my choice here because of their widespread availability and shelf stability—a quick nutritious snack is only a trip to the pantry away.

Serves 6

Ingredients

6 slices bread, such as white, whole-wheat, or rye

3 tablespoons chopped fresh parsley

Finely grated zest and juice of 1 lemon

2 tablespoons extra-virgin olive oil

1 garlic clove, grated or minced

1 small red chile, deseeded and minced

3 cans (3 ounces or 120 grams) sardines in oil, drained

Method

Toast the bread lightly. In a small bowl, mix together the parsley and lemon zest; set aside.

In a large pan, heat the olive oil over medium-high heat. When the oil is shimmering, add the garlic and red chile; stir until fragrant, about 30 seconds. Add the sardines and heat through until warm, about 2 minutes per side. Add the lemon juice to the pan and toss lightly.

Divide the fish among the toast, drizzle with the warm oil, and garnish with the parsley and lemon zest. Serve immediately.

Notes

- *To make this recipe gluten-free, replace the bread with slices of your favorite gluten-free loaf.*
- *No red chiles? Substitute ¼ to ½ teaspoon crushed red pepper flakes.*

VEGAN SAUSAGE ROLLS

Fergus had brought me a sausage roll and a cannikin of coffee—real coffee, for a wonder. "Milord will send for you shortly," he said, handing these over. "Is he nearly ready?" The food was warm and fresh—and I knew it might be the last I got for some time—but I barely tasted it. "Have I time to dress Lord John's eye again?" The pervading air of haste was clearly perceptible to me, and my skin had started twitching as though I were being attacked by ants.

—*Written in My Own Heart's Blood,* chapter 71, *"Folie à Trois"*

GF(a) | DF | V | VGN

From Rolls with Pigeon and Truffles and Sarah Woolam's Scotch Pies in OK1, to Benedicta's Steak and Mushroom Pie (page 93) and Jerry MacKenzie's Time-Traveling Pasties (page 106) here in OK2, *Outlander Kitchen* has a lot of recipes for meat wrapped in pastry.

These vegan rolls are a satisfying and delicious change for the good. If you're short on time, buy a sheet of frozen vegan puff pastry instead of making the short crust.

Makes eighteen 2-inch rolls

Ingredients

2 tablespoons refined coconut oil or extra-virgin olive oil

2 medium onions, julienned

1 teaspoon kosher salt, plus additional

1 cup chopped walnuts

2 tablespoons aged sherry vinegar or red wine vinegar

1 cup cooked black beans

1 cup cooked millet

2 tablespoons nutritional yeast (optional)

½ teaspoon crushed red pepper flakes

½ recipe Vegan Short Crust Pastry (page 13)

All-purpose flour, for dusting

Nondairy milk, for brushing

Method

In a medium pan, heat the oil over medium heat. When the oil is shimmering, add the onions and salt. Sauté until light golden, 10 to 15 minutes, stirring occasionally and reducing the heat, if necessary, to prevent the onions from burning. Move the onions to the edge of the pan and add the walnuts to the center. Toast the nuts for 2 to 3 minutes, stirring constantly. Pour in the vinegar and mix well.

Combine the onions and walnuts with half the black beans in the bowl of a food processor. Pulse six to eight times until well mixed. Transfer to a large bowl and stir in the remaining black beans, the millet, nutritional yeast (if using), and red pepper flakes. Season to taste with salt, if necessary.

Move the rack to the middle rung and heat the oven to 425°F. Line a baking sheet with parchment paper.

On a lightly floured board, roll out the pastry into a 10 x 18-inch rectangle about ¼ inch thick. Cut the pastry in half lengthwise so that you have two pieces measuring 5 x 18 inches. Form half the filling into a log about 1 inch in diameter along the long edge of the pastry closest to you. Brush the opposite edge sparingly with water and roll the sausage in the pastry, leaving about a ½-inch overlap. Pinch the join firmly closed, then roll the seam to the counter and rock the pastry gently to flatten and even out the join. Repeat with the remaining filling and pastry.

Brush the tops and sides of the pastry with the nondairy milk. Using a sharp knife, cut each pastry log into nine 2-inch pieces, and place them seam side down on the lined baking sheet. Bake until golden brown, 22 to 25 minutes.

Cool at least 15 minutes on a rack before serving with a batch of vegan Scotch Broth at Cranesmuir (page 52) for a filling lunch or dinner.

Store leftovers in the fridge for up to 2 days. Warm slightly in a 300°F oven to recrisp the pastry.

Notes

- *To make this recipe gluten-free, substitute a sheet of frozen gluten-free puff pastry and use your favorite gluten-free flour mix for rolling.*
- *Freeze the sliced, unbaked rolls for up to 2 weeks. Thaw overnight in the fridge before baking as directed.*
- *Aged sherry vinegar, although more expensive, adds deeper, more sophisticated flavor than its less costly counterparts.*
- *No millet? Use an equal amount of cooked rice or your favorite grain.*

Mushroom Pâté

"Wait, will you?" I said crossly, putting my hand over the bottle's open mouth. "I haven't any idea how strong this stuff is. You won't do me any good by killing me with opium."

It cost me something to say so; my instinct was to drain the bottle forthwith, if it would stop the beastly pain. That nitwit Spartan who allowed the fox to gnaw his vitals had nothing on me. But, come right down to it, I didn't want to die, either of gunshot, fever, or medical misadventure. And so Dottie borrowed a spoon from Mrs. Macken, who watched in grisly fascination from the door while I took two spoonfuls, lay down, and waited an interminable quarter of an hour to judge the effects.

"The marquis sent all sorts of delicacies and things to aid your recovery," Dottie said encouragingly, turning to the basket and starting to lift things out by way of distraction. "Partridge in jelly, mushroom pâté, some terrible-smelling cheese, and—"

—*Written in My Own Heart's Blood,* chapter 83, "Sundown"

GF | DF | V | VGN

Despite being purely plant based, this mushroom faux gras will satisfy even the staunchest meat eater, and would most definitely have passed the marquis's approval. Enjoy it on Pumpkin Seed and Herb Oatcakes from OK1, with a glass of sparkling white wine and your favorite friends.

Makes about 3 cups

Ingredients

¾ cup green lentils

1 cup shelled walnuts

¼ cup extra-virgin olive oil

¼ pound (115 grams) button mushrooms, cleaned and sliced

2 medium shallots, julienned

2 garlic cloves, grated or minced

1 tablespoon brandy

3 tablespoons chopped fresh parsley

2 tablespoons lemon juice

1 tablespoon capers

1 tablespoon fresh thyme leaves

1½ teaspoons kosher salt,
  plus additional

½ teaspoon freshly ground black pepper,
  plus additional

⅛ to ¼ teaspoon cayenne pepper

Method

In a medium saucepan, cover the lentils generously with water. Bring to a boil, then reduce the heat to a simmer, cover, and cook until tender, 15 to 20 minutes. Drain and pour into the bowl of a food processor.

In a medium frying pan over low heat, toast the walnuts until fragrant, about 5 minutes. Add them to the food processor and wipe out the pan. Return the pan to the stove, increase the heat to medium, and add the oil. When the oil is shimmering, add the mushrooms and shallots, stirring occasionally until the mushrooms have released their water and everything is soft and cooked without color. Stir in the garlic and brandy, and stir until fragrant, about 30 seconds. To the food processor with the walnuts, add the parsley, lemon juice, capers, thyme, salt, pepper, and cayenne. Process until very smooth, 2 to 3 minutes. Cool; taste and adjust the seasonings.

Transfer to a serving bowl and refrigerate for at least an hour to give the flavors time to blend. Serve with toast points, crackers, or the oatcakes suggested above.

Refrigerate leftovers up to 3 days or freeze for up to 2 weeks.

Chapter 5

Beef

Ragout of Beef with Oysters

Steak with Wild Mushrooms and Onion Confit

Ropa Vieja

Benedicta's Steak and Mushroom Pie

Ragout of Beef with Oysters

Hal turned at once for the door, not looking back. And just as well, Grey thought, seeing the hasty exchange of gestures and glances between the general and his stepson—horrified annoyance from the former, exemplified by rolling his eyes and a brief clutching of the shabby wig; agonized apology by the latter—an apology extended wordlessly to Grey, as Percy Wainwright turned to him with a grimace.

Grey lifted one shoulder in dismissal. Hal was used to it—and it was his own fault, after all.

"We are fortunate in our timing," he said, and smiled at Percy. He touched Wainwright's back, lightly encouraging him toward the door. "It's Thursday. The Beefsteak's cook does an excellent ragout of beef on Thursdays. With oysters."

—*Lord John and the Brotherhood of the Blade*, chapter 1,
"All in the Family"

GF(a) | DF(a)

Although beef ragout appeared on the menu every Thursday at the Beefsteak, *Outlander Kitchen*'s beef ragout is a celebratory feast made for special occasions. Bottom round is an inexpensive cut full of flavor; a long braise in red wine and ale results in fork-tender beef, and the oysters give the dish a last spike of umami that will cause your guests to exclaim with delight.

This recipe is inspired by the ingredients for "Beef Alamode" in *The Art of Cookery Made Plain and Easy*, first published in England in 1747 by Mrs. Hannah Glasse, but it turned out to be very different in the end.

Serves 6 to 8

Ingredients

3 to 4 pounds (1.25 to 2 kilograms) bottom round, cut into 6 to 8 pieces

2 teaspoons kosher salt, plus additional

1 teaspoon freshly ground pepper, plus additional

6 tablespoons all-purpose flour

¼ cup extra-virgin olive oil

1 cup porter or dark ale

1 cup red wine

6 ounces (170 grams) salt pork,
    cut into 2 pieces

1 large onion, quartered

¼ lemon

4 tinned anchovies, drained

6 bay leaves

6 fresh parsley sprigs

6 fresh thyme sprigs

2 garlic cloves, halved

12 whole peppercorns

6 whole cloves

2 tablespoons butter

8 oysters, shucked

Chopped fresh parsley, for garnish

Method

Season the bottom round pieces with the salt and pepper and dredge in 4 tablespoons of the flour.

In a Dutch oven or large, heavy pot, heat 2 tablespoons of the olive oil over medium-high heat. When the oil is shimmering, arrange half of the beef pieces in the pan and brown on all sides, 5 to 8 minutes total. Move the beef to a plate, add the remaining 2 tablespoons oil to the pan, and repeat with the remaining beef. Transfer the beef to a plate and remove the pot from the heat.

Pour the ale, wine, and 1 cup water into the pot, stirring up the brown bits. Be careful; the liquid will boil instantly, and the steam is intense. When the flash boil dies down, return the beef and any accumulated juices to the pot, along with the salt pork, onion, lemon, anchovies, bay leaves, parsley, thyme, garlic, pepper-corns, and cloves. Return the pot to medium-high heat. Bring to a boil, reduce to low, and cover. Cook, stirring occasionally, until the beef is tender, about 2 hours. Remove the beef and the salt pork. Tent lightly with foil while you make the sauce.

Strain and reserve the liquid; discard the solids. Return the liquid to the pot and simmer briskly until reduced to about 3 cups, 10 to 15 minutes. Reduce the heat to low. Mash together the butter and the remaining 2 tablespoons flour and stir into the reduced braising liquid for added richness and shine.

Return the beef and salt pork to the pan and roughly shred the meat with two forks. Poke the oysters in among the beef and cook for a further 5 minutes. Taste and adjust the seasonings if necessary.

Garnish with the parsley and serve hot, with John Grey's Yorkshire Pudding (page 213) and Sautéed Turnip Greens (page 220).

Notes

- *To make this recipe gluten-free, replace the all-purpose flour with brown rice flour or your favorite gluten-free flour mix.*

- *To make this recipe dairy-free, replace the butter with vegan margarine or additional olive oil.*

- *Substitute a quarter of a Preserved Lemon (page 10), flesh still attached, for the fresh lemon for even more flavor.*

STEAK WITH WILD MUSHROOMS
AND ONION CONFIT

They sat quietly while the steak—accompanied by a heap of wild mushrooms, garnished with tiny boiled onions and glistening with butter—was served. Hal watched, smelled, made the appropriate noises of appreciation to Mr. Bodley, and asked for a bottle of good Bordeaux. All this was purely automatic, though; his mind was in the library, on the night of the ball.

"I didn't want you to be hurt." He could still see the look on her face when she'd said it, and he believed her now just as much as he had then, the firelight glowing in her eyes, on her skin, in the folds of her green dress. "Shall I prove it?"

And she had, after all, proved it. A violent shiver ran through him at the memory.

—*A Fugitive Green*, chapter 17, "Red Wax and Everything"

GF

Choose wild mushrooms in season from your local farmers' market for the best flavor here, though farmed oyster mushrooms and shiitakes are available year-round at many supermarkets. If button mushrooms are more to your budget, pick up a few shiitakes to give the sauce an umami boost, and you'll have a delicious, decadent dinner.

Pearl onions are available in the produce section in autumn. Cipollini are harder to find, but they're especially mild and sweet. Shallots are a reliable year-round choice. The leftover onion confit oil is wonderful in Rice Pilaf (page 208) and the Heart of Palm Frittata (page 28).

Serves 6

Ingredients

¾ pound (340 grams) pearl onions, cipollini onions, or shallots, peeled and halved if large

1 to 1½ cups extra-virgin olive oil

3 tablespoons butter, softened

1 tablespoon Prepared Horseradish (page 309) or store-bought

2 teaspoons minced fresh parsley

4 teaspoons kosher salt, plus additional

1½ teaspoons freshly ground pepper, plus additional

3 thick-cut (at least 1-inch-thick) rib eye or New York strip steaks (about 2½ pounds or 1.1 kilograms)

1 pound (450 grams) wild mushrooms, wiped clean, stems trimmed or removed if woody, coarsely chopped

2 garlic cloves, minced or grated

1 cup Quick Vegetable Stock (page 12) or beef stock

½ cup full-bodied red wine, such as Merlot or Cabernet

Vegetable oil, for brushing

Method

In a small saucepan, cover the pearl onions with olive oil and heat over medium heat until just bubbling. Reduce to medium-low and cook until fork-tender, about 30 minutes, stirring occasionally and reducing the heat if the onions begin to brown. Strain the onions, pressing down on them gently, and reserve the flavored confit oil.

While the onions cook, in a small bowl, mash together the butter, horseradish, parsley, and a pinch each of salt and pepper. Set aside.

Season the steaks liberally on all sides with 1 tablespoon salt and 1 teaspoon pepper. If cooking the steaks to medium or beyond on the stove, move the rack to the middle rung and heat the oven to 400°F. If cooking rare to medium-rare steaks, or grilling them, there is no need for the oven.

Heat ¼ cup of the confit onion oil in a large pan over medium heat. When the oil is shimmering, add the mushrooms and the remaining 1 teaspoon salt and ½ teaspoon pepper. Cook, stirring occasionally, until they have released their water and are golden brown, 10 to 12 minutes. Add the garlic and stir until fragrant, about 30 seconds.

Deglaze the pan with the stock and red wine, and simmer briskly until the sauce is reduced to a glaze on the mushrooms. Move the mushrooms to the sides of the pan and arrange the confit onions in the middle. Turn the heat off and cover to keep warm.

Heat two large, heavy pans over medium heat for at least 5 minutes. Increase the heat to medium-high and brush both skillets lightly with vegetable oil. When the oil smokes, add the steaks to the pans, pressing down firmly with your fingertips to seal the steak to the pan's surface. Cook, untouched, until a dark crust forms on the underside, about 5 minutes. Flip and, if cooking to rare or medium-rare, continue to cook on the stovetop until an instant-read thermometer reads 120°F for rare or 130°F for medium-rare. For medium and well-done, roast in the oven to the desired doneness, 140°F for medium, and 150° for well-done. Alternatively, cook the steaks outside on the grill to your desired doneness.

Rest the steaks on a board, tented lightly with aluminum foil, for 5 minutes. Slice on the diagonal and divide the steak among the plates. Top with the mushrooms and confit onions, and finish with a knob of the horseradish butter. Share any collected juices from the steaks around the plates and serve.

Store leftovers in the fridge for up to 3 days. Store leftover confit oil in the fridge, covered, for up to 1 month.

Notes

- *Short on time? Skip the confit and slice a medium onion to cook along with the wild mushrooms. Make the horseradish butter while the steaks rest.*

- *For more tenderness and flavor, try dry-brining your steaks before cooking. Season as instructed in the recipe, then arrange the steaks in a single layer on a rack set in a pan to catch any drips. Refrigerate, uncovered, at least overnight and up to 72 hours. Remove from the fridge an hour before cooking to take the chill off the meat. This technique also works well with many other cuts of meat, including William's Spatchcocked Turkey (page 101), as a preparation for roasting or grilling.*

Ropa Vieja

"That smells good," he said, walking up beside her. "What is it?"

"Cassava bread," she said, turning to him and raising an eyebrow. "And *platanos* and *ropa vieja*. That means 'old clothes,' and while the name is quite descriptive, it's actually very good. Are you hungry? Why do I bother asking?" she added before he could answer. "Naturally you are."

"Naturally," he said, and was, the last vestiges of seasickness vanishing in the scents of garlic and spice. "I didn't know you could speak Spanish, Mother."

"Well, I don't know about speaking, so much," she said, thumbing a straggle of graying blond hair out of her left eye, "but I gesture fluently. What are you doing here, John?"

—*Besieged*

GF | DF

Ropa vieja originated in southern Spain and the Canary Islands, a Spanish archipelago off the coast of northwest Africa. Named because its strips of tender beef and peppers resemble laundry hanging on the line, colonizers brought the recipe with them to the New World, and generations of Cubans have transformed the dish, making it their own.

Serves 6 to 8

Ingredients

2 pounds (900 grams) brisket or flank steak, cut into 4 pieces

1 large carrot, chopped

6 large garlic cloves, crushed

½ bunch fresh flat-leaf parsley

2 bay leaves

2 teaspoons whole peppercorns

1½ teaspoons whole allspice berries

2 large red bell peppers

3 whole cloves

2 teaspoons whole cumin seeds, toasted (see Pantry Notes)

1 teaspoon kosher salt, plus additional

¼ cup extra-virgin olive oil

1 large yellow onion, julienned

1 large green bell pepper, seeds and ribs removed, and julienned

1 can (28 ounces or 796 milliliters) crushed tomatoes

½ cup dry white wine

2 tablespoons tomato paste

2 tablespoons capers

2 fresh oregano sprigs, leaves finely chopped, for garnish

Method

In a large saucepan or Dutch oven, combine the beef, carrot, 3 of the garlic cloves, the parsley, bay leaves, 1 teaspoon of the peppercorns, and 1 teaspoon of the allspice with 6 cups cold water. Bring to a boil over high heat, reduce to a simmer, and cook, covered, for 1½ to 2 hours, until the beef is tender.

Move the rack to the top rung of the oven and turn the broiler to high. Arrange the red bell peppers on a baking sheet and broil until they are softened and blackened all over, turning occasionally, 6 to 10 minutes. Enclose the roasted peppers in a paper bag until cool enough to handle; peel, deseed, and slice them into strips. Set aside.

Remove the pan from the heat and allow the beef to cool in the broth. When cool enough to handle, shred the beef by hand and set it aside. Strain the broth and set aside 1 cup. Store the remaining broth for a future use (see Notes).

Use a mortar and pestle to mash the remaining 3 garlic cloves, 1 teaspoon peppercorns, and ½ teaspoon allspice with the cloves, cumin, and salt into a paste.

In a large skillet over medium heat, heat the oil until shimmering. Add the onion and green bell pepper and sauté, stirring occasionally, until soft and deep golden, 12 to 15 minutes. Add the garlic-spice paste to the skillet and stir constantly until fragrant, about 2 minutes.

Stir in the reserved 1 cup beef broth, the shredded beef, crushed tomatoes, wine, and tomato paste. Bring to a simmer, then reduce to low heat and cook gently, covered, for 20 minutes.

Just before serving, stir in the roasted red peppers and capers. Adjust the seasoning to taste, and garnish with chopped oregano before serving hot with Cuban Black Beans and Rice (page 194).

Keep leftovers refrigerated for up to 5 days.

Notes

- *Flank steak is traditional but can be chewy after hours of cooking. Brisket is better suited to the cooking method and results in a fork-tender dish.*

- *Store the leftover broth in the fridge for up to 5 days or freeze for up to 1 month. Use it in Steak with Wild Mushrooms and Onion Confit (page 85), add it to a pot of Scotch Broth at Cranesmuir (page 52), or simply season with salt and enjoy its soothing warmth.*

BENEDICTA'S STEAK AND MUSHROOM PIE

"Have you eaten, Johnny?" she asked, flipping the fan open again.

"No," he said, suddenly recalling that he was starving. "I hadn't the chance."

"Well, then." The Countess waved one of the footmen over, selected a small pie from his tray, and handed it to her son. "Yes, I saw you talking to Lady Mumford. Kind of you; the dear old thing dotes upon you."

Dear old thing. Lady Mumford was possibly the Countess's senior by a year. Grey mumbled a response, impeded by the pie. It was steak with mushrooms, delectable in flaky pastry.

"Whatever were you talking to Joseph Trevelyan so intently about, though?" the Countess asked, raising her fan in farewell to the Misses Humber. She turned to look at her son, and lifted one brow, then laughed. "Why, you've gone quite red in the face, John—one might think Mr. Trevelyan had made you some indecent proposal!"

"Ha ha," Grey said, thickly, and put the rest of the pie into his mouth.

—*Lord John and the Private Matter,* chapter 5,
"Eine Kleine Nachtmusik (A Little Night Music)"

GF(a) | DF

One of *Outlander Kitchen*'s most popular and time-tested recipes, this pie has a home-made filling of beef and mushrooms in a rich gravy and is topped with store-bought puff pastry. A smart compromise for the time-crunched, multitasking cook in the twenty-first century.

You can also top it with a batch of Vegan Short Crust Pastry (page 13) for a purely homemade pie.

Serves 6

Ingredients

2 pounds (900 grams) beef sirloin or
    top round, cut into 1-inch cubes
2 teaspoons kosher salt, plus additional

1½ teaspoons mustard powder
½ teaspoon freshly ground pepper, plus
    additional

2 slices bacon, diced

2 tablespoons vegetable oil, plus
    additional

1 large onion, diced

¾ pound (340 grams) button
    mushrooms, cleaned and sliced

2 garlic cloves, minced or grated

¼ cup all-purpose flour

12 ounces (355 milliliters) dark,
    low-hops beer, such as a chocolate
    porter or stout

1 tablespoon Mushroom Catsup
    (page 307) or Worcestershire sauce

3 cups Quick Vegetable Stock (page 12)
    or beef stock

2 teaspoons fresh thyme leaves

1 bay leaf

1 large egg

1 sheet puff pastry (10 to 12 ounces,
    or 285 to 340 grams)

Method

Toss the cubed steak with the salt, mustard powder, and pepper.

In a large pan over medium heat, crisp the bacon, being careful not to overbrown it. Use a slotted spoon to remove the bacon to a plate lined with paper towels. Add enough vegetable oil to the pan to yield 2 tablespoons of fat.

Increase the heat to medium-high and brown the beef in batches, about 5 minutes per batch. Transfer the beef to a plate, add another 2 tablespoons oil to the pan, and sauté the onion and mushrooms until soft and translucent, 5 to 7 minutes. Add the garlic and cook until fragrant, about 30 seconds, then stir in the flour and cook for 2 minutes, stirring constantly.

Deglaze the pan with the beer and mushroom catsup, stirring well. Add the stock, reserved beef and bacon, thyme, and bay leaf. Stir well and bring to a boil.

Reduce to a simmer, partially cover, and cook until the beef is tender and the gravy shiny and thick, about 1 hour. Season to taste, then remove from the heat and cool slightly while you prepare the pastry. Remove the bay leaf.

Move the rack to the upper-middle rung and heat the oven to 400°F. Whisk the egg with 1 teaspoon water.

Arrange six 8-ounce (240-milliliter) ovenproof ramekins on a baking sheet lined with parchment paper, and divide the beef mixture evenly among them.

Roll out the puff pastry to about an ⅛-inch thickness and, with a SHARP knife, cut squares large enough to generously cover the ramekins. Lay the puff pastry tops across the filled ramekins, press gently to adhere to the edge of the dishes, then brush the tops with the egg wash. Use a sharp knife to poke a small hole in the top of each and bake until golden, 30 to 35 minutes. Rest 5 to 10 minutes before serving.

Alternatively, pour the filling into a 13 x 9-inch baking pan and top with a single sheet of puff pastry. Increase the baking time to 35 to 40 minutes. Rest 15 minutes before serving.

Serve with Salad Greens with Vinegar (page 205). Store leftovers in the fridge for up to 3 days.

Notes

- *To make this recipe gluten-free, replace the all-purpose flour with brown rice flour, whisking it in after the beef has simmered and just before you remove the pan from the heat. Substitute gluten-free beer or red wine for the beer, and ensure the puff pastry is also gluten-free.*

- *For a vegan pie, try the Jackfruit Potpie (page 181).*

Chapter 6

※◈◎

Poultry

Coq au Vin

William's Spatchcocked Turkey with Bread Salad

Jerry MacKenzie's Time-Traveling Pasties

Frogs' Legs Provençal (Chicken Wings)

Chicken and Cornmeal Stew

The Cheerful Chicken's Poulet au Miel (Chicken in Honey)

Coq au Vin

"John!" she cried, beaming at sight of him. "There you are! I was so hoping you'd come home in time."

"In time for what?" he asked, with a sense of foreboding.

"To sing, of course." She skipped down the stairs and seized him affectionately by the arm.

"We're having a German evening—and you do the lieder so well, Johnny!"

"Flattery will avail you nothing," he said, smiling despite himself. "I can't sing; I'm starving. Besides, it's nearly over, surely?" He nodded at the case clock by the stair, which read a few minutes past eleven. Supper was almost always served at half-past.

"If you'll sing, I'm sure they'll wait to hear you. Then you can eat afterward. Aunt Bennie has the most marvelous collation laid on—the biggest steamed pudding I've ever seen, with juniper berries, and lamb cutlets with spinach, and a coq au vin, and some absolutely disgusting sausages—for the Germans, you know. . . ."

—*Lord John and the Private Matter,* chapter 5,
"Eine Kleine Nachtmusik (A Little Night Music)"

GF(a) | DF

Traditionally, coq au vin was made using an aged cockerel. The whole bird, including its comb, was thrown into the pot and cooked for a long time in wine, which helped to tenderize the old, stringy meat.

As with most stews and braises, this version using chicken legs tastes even better the next day. Refrigerate it in its pan, then warm it gently in the oven before serving, and let the full, rich aroma rejuvenate you after a hard day's work or a long night singing the lieder.

Serves 4 to 6

Ingredients

6 whole chicken legs, skinned
   (see Notes)

1½ teaspoons kosher salt
½ teaspoon freshly ground pepper

1 tablespoon extra-virgin olive oil, plus additional

3 strips thick-cut bacon, cut crosswise into ¼-inch strips

¾ pound (340 grams) button mushrooms, halved

1 large onion, julienned

2 garlic cloves, grated or minced

1 tablespoon tomato paste

3 tablespoons brandy

2 tablespoons all-purpose flour

1 cup Quick Vegetable Stock (page 12) or chicken stock

1 cup full-bodied red wine, such as Cabernet or Merlot

2 fresh thyme sprigs

2 bay leaves

1 to 2 tablespoons chopped fresh parsley

Method

Season the chicken with the salt and pepper. In a large, heavy pan, heat the oil over medium-high heat until shimmering. Add the bacon and fry until crisp, 5 to 6 minutes. Remove the bacon with a slotted spoon and drain on paper towels. Brown the chicken pieces in the remaining fat, about 4 minutes per side. Fry the chicken in two batches, if necessary, to avoid overcrowding the pan. Remove to a plate.

Reduce the heat to medium and place the mushrooms and onion in the pan, adding another tablespoon or two of oil if the pan is dry. Cook until the onion is softened and translucent, 5 to 7 minutes. Add the garlic and tomato paste, and stir for 1 minute. Deglaze the pan with the brandy, scraping up the brown bits from the bottom of the pan. Reduce the heat to medium-low, arrange the chicken pieces on top of the vegetables, pour over any accumulated juices, cover, and simmer for 15 minutes.

Remove the cover and sprinkle in the flour. Turn everything at least once and stir gently to incorporate the flour into the liquid in the pan. Add the reserved bacon, the stock, wine, thyme, and bay leaves. Increase the heat to medium-high and bring to a boil. Partially cover the pan, reduce the heat to medium, and simmer gently for 30 more minutes.

Garnish the chicken with the chopped parsley and serve immediately with Rice Pilaf (page 208) or Tobias Quinn's Colcannon (page 200).

Refrigerate any leftovers for up to 3 days.

Notes

- *To make this recipe gluten-free, substitute brown rice flour or your favorite gluten-free flour mix for the all-purpose flour, continuing with the recipe as instructed.*

- *Use a paper towel or clean dishcloth to grab the chicken skin at the top of the thigh and peel it down to the bottom of the leg. A quick yank at the end should easily remove the skin in one piece.*

WILLIAM'S SPATCHCOCKED TURKEY WITH BREAD SALAD

William was with Sandy Lindsay, talking about the best way to cook a turkey—one of Lindsay's scouts having just brought him one—when the letter arrived. It was likely William's imagination that a dreadful silence fell upon the camp, the earth shook, and the veil of the temple was rent in twain. But it was very shortly apparent that something had happened, nonetheless.

There was a definite change in the air, something amiss in the rhythms of speech and movement among the men surrounding them. Balcarres felt it, too, and stopped in his examination of the turkey's outspread wing, looking at William with eyebrows raised.

"What?" said William.

"I don't know, but it isn't good." Balcarres thrust the limp turkey into his orderly's hands and, snatching up his hat, made for Burgoyne's tent, William on his heels.

—*An Echo in the Bone,* chapter 59, "Battle of Bennington"

The best and most efficient way to an evenly cooked, moist turkey with crisp skin is to spatchcock it, or remove its backbone, and roast it spread flat on the pan. For an easier holiday meal, prepare the bread salad, spatchcock the turkey, and make the stock for the gravy in the morning, so that the majority of the work is done before your guests arrive.

Serves 8 to 10

Ingredients

2 tablespoons dried cranberries

2½ tablespoons white wine vinegar

2 tablespoons sliced almonds

1 large day-old peasant-style bread loaf (see Notes)

½ cup extra-virgin olive oil

Kosher salt and coarsely ground pepper

3 garlic cloves, thinly sliced

1 bunch scallions (white and light green parts), thinly sliced on the diagonal

1 whole turkey (12 to 14 pounds or 5.5 to 6.5 kilograms), neck and giblets reserved

3 large onions, chopped

1 lemon, cut into 8 wedges, or
    2 Preserved Lemons (page 10),
    each cut into quarters
12 fresh thyme sprigs
2 teaspoons minced fresh rosemary

2 bay leaves
¼ cup (½ stick) butter
¼ cup all-purpose flour
6 cups arugula leaves or baby greens
    (mustard, kale, chard, etc.)

Method

Soak the cranberries in 1 tablespoon of the white wine vinegar and 1 tablespoon hot water. In a small, heavy pan over medium-low heat, toast the almonds until they're just beginning to turn golden, 3 to 5 minutes. Set both aside.

Move the rack to the top rung and turn on the oven's broiler. Closely trim most of the crust off the bread, saving it to use for breadcrumbs in another recipe. Tear the loaf into bite-size pieces and toss in a large bowl with 2 tablespoons of the olive oil. Spread the bread onto a baking sheet and briefly broil until lightly toasted, 3 or 4 minutes. Return the bread to the bowl.

Whisk ¼ cup of the olive oil with the remaining 1½ tablespoons white wine vinegar. Season with salt and pepper. Drizzle 2 tablespoons of this dressing over the bread and toss.

In a small skillet, heat 1 tablespoon of the olive oil over medium heat. When the oil is shimmering, add the garlic and scallions. Cook, stirring constantly, until softened but not browned, about 2 minutes. Add to the bread and fold in. Drain the cranberries and fold them in along with the almonds. Taste the bread and add a little more dressing, salt, and pepper, if necessary. Toss well, cover, and refrigerate until about 30 minutes before serving time.

Pat the turkey dry with paper towels and place it breast side down on the cutting board. Using poultry shears, make a cut along one side of the backbone, starting where the thigh meets the tail. Cut your way around the thigh joint and continue up the backbone until you've snipped through every rib bone and completely split the turkey up through the neck. Use your hands to spread the turkey open slightly.

Repeat the cut up the other side of the backbone, making sure to keep your fingers out of the way of the blades. Use a clean dish towel or rag to keep a hold of the bird and prevent it from slipping. Turn the bird over so it's breast side up, and press down firmly with both hands on the breasts until the breast bone snaps and the bird lies (almost) flat on the cutting board.

Move the rack to the lower rung and heat the oven to 450°F. Line a large rimmed baking sheet or broiler pan with aluminum foil and scatter 2 of the chopped onions, the lemon wedges, and thyme sprigs over the surface. Place a wire rack on top.

Rub the surface of the turkey all over with the remaining 1 tablespoon olive oil. Mix together 5 teaspoons salt, 1 teaspoon pepper, and the rosemary, and season the turkey liberally inside and out. Arrange the turkey on top of the rack, breast side up, so that it does not overhang the edges. Tuck the turkey's wing tips behind the back.

Put the turkey in the oven and reduce the temperature to 425°F. Roast, rotating the pan once or twice, until an instant-read thermometer inserted into the deepest part of the thigh, without touching the bone, registers 165°F, 70 to 80 minutes.

While the turkey roasts, roughly chop the neck, backbone, and giblets. Add them to a large saucepan, cover with water by 2 inches, and bring to a boil over high heat. After it has boiled for 1 minute, reduce the heat to a simmer and skim the surface with a slotted spoon. Add the remaining chopped onion and the bay leaves and simmer for 45 minutes. Strain and discard the solids. Skim any fat from the stock's surface.

Remove the turkey from the oven and transfer the rack to a new baking sheet. Rest at room temperature for 20 to 30 minutes before carving.

Strain the collected juices from the baking sheet, drizzle half over the bread salad, and toss well. Transfer to a 9 x 13-inch baking dish and cover lightly with foil. Put into the oven that is now turned off but still hot for 15 minutes.

In a large pot over medium heat, melt the butter. Stir in the flour and cook, stirring constantly, until the flour is light golden, about 3 minutes. Whisk in 1 quart (1 liter) of the reserved stock in a thin, steady stream, whisking constantly to avoid lumps. Pour in the remaining half of the pan juices, bring to a gentle boil, reduce to a simmer, and cook until thickened and slightly reduced, about 10 minutes. Season to taste with salt and pepper and cover to keep the gravy warm.

Return the bread to the salad bowl and toss with the arugula and remaining vinaigrette. Season to taste.

Carve and serve the turkey with the bread salad and gravy for a lighter version of your next holiday meal. Start the evening with an Iced Negus (page 274) and close with a slice of Argus House Chocolate Cake (page 252) for everyone.

Store leftovers in the fridge for up to 5 days. Be sure to make a batch of Hot Broth at Castle Leoch (Brown Chicken Stock) from OK1 using the remains of the carcass.

Notes

- *To make the bread salad vegan, ensure the bread is vegan. Prepare as directed, up to dressing the salad and refrigerating. When ready to serve, instead of using the pan juices, heat ½ cup seasoned Quick Vegetable Stock (page 12), pour it over the salad, and toss. Heat, toss with the arugula, and serve with Sautéed Turnip Greens (page 220) and Honey-Roasted Butternut Squash from OK1 for a complete meal.*

- *Watch an instructional video or two online about how to spatchcock a bird before you begin. If you're new to the method, the smaller bones of a chicken are easier for a first timer to cut through, and it's just as delicious with the bread salad as its bigger cousin. Reduce the cooking time to 40 to 50 minutes.*

- *A large loaf of bread torn into bite-size pieces equals approximately 6 cups. Choose a lighter, less dense bread with lots of air holes. The denser the bread, the heavier and chewier the bread salad.*

Jerry MacKenzie's Time-Traveling Pasties

He licked his lips at the smell. Hot pastry, steaming, juicy meat. There was a row of fat little pasties ranged along the sill, covered with a clean cloth in case of birds, but showing plump and rounded through it, the odd spot of gravy soaking through the napkin.

His mouth watered so fiercely that his salivary glands ached and he had to massage the underside of his jaw to ease the pain.

It was the first house he'd seen in two days. Once he'd got out of the ravine, he'd circled well away from the mile-castle and eventually struck a small cluster of cottages, where the people were no more understandable, but did give him some food. That had lasted him a little while; beyond that, he'd been surviving on what he could glean from hedges and the odd vegetable patch. He'd found another hamlet, but the folk there had driven him away.

—A Leaf on the Wind of All Hallows

DF | V(a) | VGN(a)

Pasties are the handheld descendants of large, medieval English meat pies. From the Old French *paste,* which referred to a filled pie baked without a dish, the most enduring pasty of all is that from Cornwall, filled with chipped beef, potatoes, swedes (also known as rutabaga or yellow turnip), and onion, and granted protected status by the European Commission in 2011. There are centuries of literary evidence of pasties and their spread across Britain. Chaucer mentioned them in *The Canterbury Tales,* and records from thirteenth-century Norwich describe pastry makers accused of reheating three-day-old pasties for sale as fresh.

Makes 6

Ingredients

4 cups all-purpose flour, plus
    additional for dusting
Kosher salt
¾ cup lard or (1½ sticks) butter
2 large eggs

1 medium leek, halved lengthwise
    (white and light green parts
    only)
1 pound (450 grams) boneless, skinless
    chicken thighs, diced

1 medium potato, diced

1 medium turnip, diced

1 medium carrot, shredded

¼ cup fresh parsley, large stems removed and chopped

½ teaspoon freshly ground pepper

Method

In a large bowl, mix the flour with 2 teaspoons salt, leaving a well in the center. In a small pan, melt the lard. Pour it into the well with 1 cup warm water and 1 of the eggs. Mix by hand into a dough, then knead on a lightly floured counter until it forms a smooth ball, 3 to 4 minutes. Wrap in plastic and chill in the fridge for at least 60 minutes and up to 24 hours.

Thinly slice the leek halves and rinse them thoroughly in a bowl of cold water. Scoop out the leeks with a slotted spoon, leaving the silt and sand behind. Shake dry in a clean dishcloth or salad spinner.

In a large bowl, combine the leeks with the chicken, potato, turnip, carrot, parsley, 1½ teaspoons salt, and the pepper.

On a lightly floured counter, roll out half the pastry. Turn and loosen the dough occasionally as you continue to roll it into a round that is an even ⅛ inch thick. Cut three 7-inch circles from the dough.

Pile one-sixth of the filling onto the center of each circle. Wet the top edge of the pastry sparingly with water, and bring the top and bottom up to meet above the filling. Press the edges firmly together and crimp to seal well (see Notes). With a sharp knife, make a slit in the top of each pie to vent steam. Repeat with the remaining pastry and filling to make another three pasties. Wrap and refrigerate the filled pies for at least 30 minutes and up to overnight.

Move the rack to the upper-middle rung and heat the oven to 400°F. Line a baking sheet with parchment paper.

Lightly beat the remaining egg with 1 teaspoon water. Brush the pasties sparingly with the egg wash and bake on the prepared baking sheet until golden brown, rotating the sheet halfway through, 35 to 45 minutes. Cool at least 10 minutes on a wire rack.

Serve hot or cold. Store cooked pasties in the fridge for up to 3 days.

Notes

- *To make vegetarian and vegan pasties, omit the chicken and replace with an extra leek, small potato, and carrot. Toss the filling with 2 tablespoons extra-virgin olive oil or walnut oil before proceeding with the recipe, substituting the Vegan Short Crust Pastry (page 13), which uses coconut oil, making it more delicate than one made with butter or lard. Handle gently when crimping.*

- *To crimp, roll and press the edge of the dough under itself as you work left to right (opposite for left-handers). Find instructional videos online.*

- *Freeze unbaked pasties for up to 2 weeks. Cook from frozen as instructed, allowing a few extra minutes for the pies to cook through.*

Frogs' Legs Provençal
(Chicken Wings)

Frog legs of that size really did look quite like chicken drumsticks. And tasted very like, too, dredged in flour and egg with a little salt and pepper and fried.

"Why is it that the meat of strange animals is so often described as tasting like chicken?" Rachel asked, neatly snaring another leg out from under her husband's reaching hand. "I've heard people say that of everything from catamount to alligator."

"Because it does," Ian answered, raising a brow at her and stabbing his fork into a platter of catfish chunks, similarly coated and fried.

—*Written in My Own Heart's Blood,* chapter 128, "Gigging Frogs"

GF | DF

Inspired by a classic recipe for frogs' legs from Provence, these easy, garlicky, crisp-roasted wings tossed in lemon make for spectacularly delicious twenty-first-century snacking when arranged alongside Mr. Willoughby's Coral Knob and Beer-Battered Corn Fritters from OK1 on the game-day buffet table.

Serves 6

Ingredients

3 to 4 pounds (1.4 to 1.8 kilograms) chicken wings, split

2 teaspoons kosher salt

½ teaspoon freshly ground pepper

¼ cup (½ stick) butter

2 garlic cloves, grated or minced

1½ teaspoons mustard powder

½ teaspoon crushed red pepper flakes

2 tablespoons fresh lemon juice

2 tablespoons chopped fresh parsley

Method

In a large bowl, toss the wings with the salt and pepper and set aside on the counter for 30 minutes. Move a rack to the upper-middle rung and heat the oven to 425°F.

In a small saucepan, melt the butter and stir in the garlic, mustard powder, and red pepper flakes until smooth. Pour over the seasoned chicken and toss to combine.

Arrange the wings on a parchment-lined, rimmed baking sheet that is just large enough to fit them all.

Roast until golden on all sides, about 45 minutes, turning once or twice.

Pour the wings and any butter from the baking sheet into a large bowl and toss with the lemon juice and parsley. Serve immediately with an ice-cold beer or glass of white wine.

Keep leftovers in the fridge for up to 3 days.

Note

- *Alternatively, prepare chicken drumsticks as described for the wings, then roast at 375°F until golden, 60 to 70 minutes, turning once or twice.*

CHICKEN AND CORNMEAL STEW

"By your leave, ma'am," he said, and without waiting for my leave, picked up the sack and pulled out a dead chicken. The neck flopped limp, showing the large, bloody hole through its head where an eye—well, two eyes—had once been. His scarred mouth pursed in a soundless whistle and he looked sharply up at Jamie. "You do that a-purpose?" he asked.

"I always shoot them through the eye," Jamie replied politely. "Dinna want to spoil the meat."

A slow grin spread over Colonel Morgan's face, and he nodded. "Come with me, Mr. Fraser. Bring your rifle."

We ate that night at Daniel Morgan's fire, and the company—filled with chicken stew—raised cups of beer and hooted to toast the addition of a new member to their elite corps. I hadn't had a chance of private conversation with Jamie since Morgan's abduction of him that afternoon, and rather wondered what he made of his apotheosis. But he seemed comfortable with the riflemen, though he glanced now and then at Morgan, with the look that meant he was still making up his mind.

—An Echo in the Bone, chapter 61,
"No Better Companion than the Rifle"

GF | DF(a)

Anyone who has been camping knows there is no food more delicious than that cooked over an open fire after a day spent in the fresh air working up an appetite. And while most of us will prepare this quick, one-pot stew over the stove instead of a campfire, it's as much a comfort after a hard day at the office as it would have been to a company of Morgan's Riflemen after their march to Saratoga.

Serves 6

Ingredients

1½ pounds (680 grams) boneless, skinless chicken breast

1 teaspoon kosher salt, plus additional

½ teaspoon freshly ground pepper, plus additional

1 teaspoon fennel seeds, toasted (see
    Pantry Notes, page 5)
1 teaspoon coriander seeds, toasted (see
    Pantry Notes, page 5)
¼ cup (½ stick) butter
2 medium onions, diced
1 large carrot, diced

2 medium celery stalks, diced
¼ teaspoon crushed red pepper flakes
1 quart (1 liter) Quick Vegetable Stock
    (page 12) or chicken stock
½ cup cornmeal
1 tablespoon finely chopped fresh
    rosemary or parsley, for garnish

Method

Season the chicken breasts with the salt and pepper. Grind the fennel and coriander seeds in a mortar and pestle or a spice grinder; set aside.

In a Dutch oven or heavy saucepan, melt the butter over medium-low heat. When the butter is bubbling, add the chicken to the pan and cook until light golden on both sides, 10 to 12 minutes total, reducing the heat if the butter begins to burn. Transfer the chicken to a cutting board and rest 5 minutes before cutting it into ½-inch cubes.

Increase the heat to medium-high, add the vegetables to the pan, and use the water they release to scrape up any brown bits from the pan's surface. Add the fennel, coriander, and red pepper flakes, and cook, stirring occasionally, until the onions are translucent, 5 to 7 minutes.

Add the stock and bring to a boil. Add the cornmeal in a thin stream, stirring constantly, until well incorporated. Stir in the chicken and any juices. Reduce the heat to low and cook, stirring occasionally, until the vegetables are tender and the cornmeal is cooked and thick, 20 to 25 minutes. Season to taste with salt and pepper and garnish with chopped rosemary.

Serve hot. Store leftovers in the fridge for up to 5 days.

Notes

- *To make this stew dairy-free, substitute extra-virgin olive oil or walnut oil for the butter.*
- *Rhiannon's Tester Tip: "I am not a fan of fennel, so I was wary. I was pleasantly surprised. That's one of the reasons I love doing this   trying things I would normally avoid."*

The Cheerful Chicken's Poulet au Miel (Chicken in Honey)

D'eglise, looking pleased with the new job, left Ian and Jamie at a large tavern called *Le Poulet Gai,* where some of the other mercenaries were enjoying themselves—in various ways. The Cheerful Chicken most assuredly did boast a brothel on the upper floor, and slatternly women in various degrees of undress wandered freely through the lower rooms, picking up new customers with whom they vanished upstairs.

The two tall young Scots provoked a certain amount of interest from the women, but when Ian solemnly turned his empty purse inside out in front of them—he having put his money inside his shirt for safety—they left the lads alone.

—Virgins

GF | DF

Le Poulet Gai may not be a child-friendly establishment, but the whole family will love their signature dish: sweet and sticky honey-mustard roasted chicken. Serve with a green salad and a batch of Corn Muffins from OK1 for an easy weeknight meal everyone will devour.

Serves 4 to 6

Ingredients

1 tablespoon extra-virgin olive oil, plus additional for greasing

½ cup heather honey

¼ cup Dijon mustard

1 tablespoon red wine vinegar

1 teaspoon minced fresh thyme

1 teaspoon kosher salt

½ teaspoon freshly ground pepper

3 pounds (1.4 kilograms) bone-in, skin-on chicken pieces

Method

Move the rack to the upper-middle rung and heat the oven to 375°F. Brush the bottom and sides of a ceramic or glass baking dish generously with olive oil.

In a large bowl, stir together the honey, mustard, oil, vinegar, thyme, salt, and pepper until well combined. Toss the chicken pieces in the sauce to coat well.

Arrange the chicken in the prepared dish, skin side down, and pour any remaining sauce over it. Roast for 30 minutes, flip the chicken pieces, and return the dish to the oven until the chicken is cooked through, the skin is browned, and the sauce has thickened, about 30 minutes more. Remove from the oven, tent lightly with foil, and rest 10 minutes.

Serve, passing the sauce at the table. Keep leftovers covered in the fridge for up to 3 days.

Notes

- *Cut up a whole chicken into 10 pieces, or use all thighs, breasts, legs, or wings, if you prefer.*
- *No heather honey? Substitute clear liquid honey.*
- *Leftovers make delicious chicken salad, especially when you stir a bit of the leftover sauce in with the mayonnaise.*

Chapter 7

❧ ⌘ ⌥

Pork

Ham Steaks with Raisin and Mustard Sauce

Pork Tenderloin with Cider Sauce and German Fried Potatoes

The White Sow's Crispy Pork Belly and Apple Slaw

Gail Abernathy's Brats and Sauerkraut

Ham Steaks with Raisin and Mustard Sauce

"I thought you were dead," I said abruptly. "What did you mean, you thought I was dead?" He opened his mouth to answer but was interrupted by Phaedre, who came to serve us, smiling pleasantly.

"I get you something, sir, ma'am? You wanting food? We've a nice ham today, roast taters, and Mrs. Symonds's special mustard 'n raisin sauce to go along of it."

"No," Mr. Christie said. "I—just a cup of cider, if ye please."

"Whisky," I said. "A lot of it."

Mr. Christie looked scandalized, but Phaedre only laughed and whisked off, the grace of her movement attracting the quiet admiration of most of the male patrons.

"Ye haven't changed," he observed. His eyes traveled over me, intense, taking in every detail of my appearance. "I ought to have known ye by your hair."

—*An Echo in the Bone*, chapter 19, "Ae Fond Kiss"

GF | DF

This mustard-and-raisin sauce combines the essence of older, more traditional recipes with modern techniques to lighten the taste and simplify the preparation. A delicious, low-labor dish that comes together in a matter of minutes. Serve with Tobias Quinn's Colcannon (page 200) for a hearty meal full of comfort.

Serves 6

Ingredients

3 tablespoons chopped golden raisins

1 tablespoon red wine vinegar

⅓ cup extra-virgin olive oil

¼ cup Dijon mustard

2 teaspoons honey

1 teaspoon minced fresh rosemary

Pinch of cayenne pepper or paprika

½ teaspoon kosher salt

2 to 3 pounds (1 to 1.4 kilograms) ham, cut into ½-inch slices, or 4 large ham steaks

2 tablespoons butter (optional)

Method

In a small ramekin or bowl, soak the golden raisins in the red wine vinegar and 2 tablespoons hot water for 10 minutes.

In the bowl of a small food processor, combine the soaked raisins and their liquid, the olive oil, mustard, honey, rosemary, cayenne, and salt. Pulse until relatively smooth. Alternatively, use an immersion blender to bring the sauce together, or finely mince the raisins and rosemary and combine with the rest of the ingredients by hand. Refrigerate until ready to serve.

Fry the ham slices in batches in the butter over medium-high heat, keeping them warm in a low-heat oven. Alternatively, cook the ham on a grill or under the broiler in the oven. Whichever method you choose, ensure they are warmed through. The deeper the grill marks and color on the steak, the better the flavor.

Serve hot or cold with the sauce on the side. Keep leftovers in the fridge for up to 3 days.

Notes

- *Any raisin or currant will do, although darker fruit may affect the color of the finished sauce.*
- *The mustard sauce recipe doubles easily and makes a sweet, aromatic accompaniment for a whole holiday ham.*

Pork Tenderloin with Cider Sauce and German Fried Potatoes

He was quartered with several other British officers in one of three large farmhouses near the canal, a place called Hückelsmay. Despite the aura of suppressed tension, the atmosphere in the house was welcoming, the air filled with the scent of fried potatoes and roast pork, warm with smoke and conviviality.

Grey forced himself to eat a little, mostly for Tom's sake, and then went to sit in a corner, where he could avoid having to talk to people.

—Lord John and the Brotherhood of the Blade,
chapter 28, "Hückelsmay"

GF | DF(a)

Another favorite from OutlanderKitchen.com, this savory, fork-tender tenderloin with cider sauce pairs perfectly with crispy potatoes for a meal that will leave the whole family satisfied.

Serves 6

Ingredients

2 pounds (900 grams) small white potatoes, scrubbed clean

2 large pork tenderloins (about 3 pounds or 1.4 kilograms total)

12 fresh sage leaves, chopped

2 garlic cloves, halved

1½ teaspoons kosher salt, plus additional

½ teaspoon freshly ground pepper, plus additional

5 tablespoons extra-virgin olive oil

1½ cups apple cider (see Notes)

¼ cup apple cider vinegar

1 fresh thyme sprig (optional)

2 tablespoons honey

3 tablespoons butter, plus additional

4 slices thick-cut bacon, cut crosswise into ¼-inch strips

1 medium onion, julienned

Method

Move the rack to the upper-middle position and heat the oven to 400°F.

In a large pot, cover the potatoes with water by about 1 inch. Cover the pot and bring to a boil. Reduce to a simmer and steam the potatoes until tender, about 20 minutes. Drain and transfer them to a plate. When cool enough to handle, peel and cut them into ½-inch slices.

Remove the silver skin from the tenderloins and cut each into three or four pieces on the diagonal.

Combine the sage, garlic, salt, and pepper in a mortar and pestle or small food processor. Pound and mash, or pulse, into an almost-smooth paste. Stir in 2 tablespoons of the olive oil.

In a large bowl, rub the pork pieces with the herb paste until evenly coated. In a large, heavy pan over medium-high, heat 1 tablespoon of the olive oil until shimmering, add the pork, in batches if necessary to avoid overcrowding the pan. Sear until golden on all sides, 4 to 5 minutes total.

Transfer the pork to a roasting pan and roast until the internal temperature reaches 145°F, 15 to 18 minutes. Remove from the oven and tent with foil to keep warm.

While the pork cooks, return the large, heavy pan to medium-high heat and add the cider, vinegar, and thyme (if using), scraping up the brown bits. Simmer briskly until the liquid reduces to 1 cup, about 10 minutes. Reduce the heat to low, stir in the honey to dissolve, and finish with 1 tablespoon of the butter. Whisk until smooth and season to taste with salt and pepper. Pour into a small saucepan, reduce the heat, and keep warm, stirring occasionally.

Wipe out the pan and add the bacon. Fry over medium heat until the fat is mostly rendered, about 5 minutes. Add the onion to the pan and fry until both are lightly browned, another 5 minutes. Remove from the pan with a slotted spoon.

Add the remaining 2 tablespoons oil and 2 tablespoons butter to the pan. When bubbling, add a single layer of potatoes to the pan. Season generously with salt and pepper, and add the remaining potatoes on top of the first layer with another sprinkle of salt and pepper. Reduce the heat to medium-low and cook, untouched, until golden brown, 10 to 15 minutes. Turn them over as best you can without stirring, and increase the heat to medium. Cook until golden, adding more butter if necessary to facilitate browning. Return the onion and bacon mix to the pan, seasoning everything with salt and pepper to taste.

Serve the pork and potatoes piping hot, passing the cider sauce at the table.

Store leftovers in the fridge for up to 3 days.

Notes

- *To make this recipe dairy-free, replace the butter with additional olive oil.*

- *An artisanal dry, alcoholic (hard) cider works best, but you can also use your choice of non-alcoholic (soft) cider.*

- *German bacon,* Bauchspeck, *is traditional for this dish. Find it in German delicatessens and online.*

The White Sow's Crispy Pork Belly and Apple Slaw

Ian stiffened suddenly, and Jamie turned his head sharp to see what the matter was. He couldn't see anything, but then caught the sound that Ian had heard. A deep, piggish grunt, a rustle, a crack. Then there was a visible stirring among the blackened timbers of the ruined house, and a great light dawned.

"Jesus!" he said, and gripped Ian's arm so tightly that his nephew yelped, startled. "It's under the Big House!"

The white sow emerged from her den beneath the ruins, a massive cream-colored blotch upon the night, and stood swaying her head to and fro, scenting the air. Then she began to move, a ponderous menace surging purposefully up the hill.

Jamie wanted to laugh at the sheer beauty of it.

—*An Echo in the Bone,* chapter 2, "And Sometimes They Aren't"

GF | DF

Dry-brined pork belly is roasted until succulent and tender, then sliced and crisped in the pan. The light slaw with sliced apple is a perfect foil to the rich roasted fat of the pork belly. The pork must be brined overnight, so start a day, or two, before you intend to serve.

Serves 4 as a main course or 6 as an appetizer

Ingredients

1 tablespoon kosher salt, plus additional

2 teaspoons sugar

½ teaspoon freshly ground pepper, plus additional

2 pounds (900 grams) pork belly, skin removed

½ small green cabbage, shredded (about 3 cups)

¼ small purple cabbage, shredded (about 1 cup)

1 medium carrot, shredded (about ½ cup)

3 scallions (white and light green parts), sliced thinly on the diagonal

½ teaspoon caraway seeds (optional)

3 tablespoons extra-virgin olive oil
    or vegetable oil
2 tablespoons red wine vinegar
    or apple cider vinegar
1 tablespoon honey

1 teaspoon Dijon mustard
1 small tart green apple, cored
    and julienned
Chopped fresh cilantro or mint,
    for garnish

Method

In a small bowl, combine the salt, sugar, and pepper. Rub the pork liberally with the dry brine, cover, and refrigerate overnight.

Move the rack to the middle rung and heat the oven to 450°F.

Place the pork belly, fat side up, in a parchment-lined cast-iron skillet or small roasting pan and roast for 30 minutes. Reduce the heat to 275°F and cook until tender but not falling apart, 1½ to 2 hours more.

Remove from the oven and transfer to a rack to cool completely. Wrap it tightly in plastic and refrigerate until chilled through—at least 4 hours and up to 2 days.

In a medium bowl, combine the cabbages, carrot, scallions, and caraway seeds (if using).

In a small bowl, whisk together the oil, vinegar, honey, and mustard. Season to taste with salt and pepper. Pour over the cabbage salad and toss well. Cover and refrigerate for at least 1 hour and up to 6 hours.

Slice the cold pork belly crosswise into ½-inch slices. Heat a heavy skillet over medium-high and fry the pork belly until crisp on both sides, 5 to 7 minutes.

Just before serving, add the apple to the slaw and toss; garnish with chopped cilantro. Serve, dividing the slaw among the plates and piling the crispy pork slices on top. If serving as a main, add a slice of Corn Bread (page 232) to complete the plate.

Store leftovers in the fridge for up to 2 days.

Note

- *To make the slaw vegan, use red wine vinegar and substitute agave or vegan sugar for the honey. Serve with Cuban Black Beans and Rice (page 194).*

Gail Abernathy's Brats and Sauerkraut

Dr. Joseph Abernathy pulled into his driveway, looking forward to a cold beer and a hot supper. The mailbox was full; he pulled out a handful of circulars and envelopes and went inside, tidily sorting them as he went.

"Bill, bill, occupant, junk, junk, more junk, charity appeal, bill, idiot, bill, invitation . . . hi, sweetie—" He paused for a fragrant kiss from his wife, followed by a second sniff of her hair. "Oh, man, are we having brats and sauerkraut for dinner?"

"You are," his wife told him, neatly snagging her jacket from the hall tree with one hand and squeezing his buttock with the other. "I'm going to a meeting with Marilyn. Be back by nine, if the rain doesn't make the traffic too bad. Anything good in the mail?"

"Nah. Have fun!"

—*Written in My Own Heart's Blood,* chapter 46,
"Baby Jesus, Tell Me . . ."

GF(a) | DF | V(a) | VGN(a)

Bratwurst comes from the Old German *brät,* meaning "finely chopped meat," and *wurst,* meaning "sausage." The first documented recipe comes from the city of Nuremberg in 1313. As centuries passed, different regions developed their own unique recipes, which emigrants brought with them to America.

Serves 6

Ingredients

¼ cup vegetable oil

10 to 12 bratwurst sausages

2 medium onions, julienned

2 garlic cloves, grated or minced

2 cups Quick Vegetable Stock (page 12) or chicken stock

2 teaspoons caraway seeds

1 teaspoon mustard powder

1 to 1½ quarts (1 to 1.5 liters) Minnie's Sauerkraut (page 292) or store-bought sauerkraut, drained

2 tablespoons chopped fresh dill, for garnish

Method

In a large pan, heat 2 tablespoons of the oil over medium heat. When the oil is shimmering, add the bratwurst and brown on all sides, 6 to 8 minutes total. Transfer to a platter.

Add the remaining 2 tablespoons oil and the onions to the same pan and cook, stirring occasionally, until golden, about 10 minutes. Add the garlic and stir until fragrant, 30 seconds. Add the stock, caraway seeds, mustard powder, sauerkraut, and the browned bratwurst; simmer, uncovered, for 45 minutes.

Garnish with the dill and serve on German Brötchen (page 224) rolls with spicy yellow mustard, or with boiled potatoes to complete the meal.

Notes

- *If preparing for someone who follows a gluten-free diet, ensure the bratwurst are gluten-free.*
- *Substitute pale ale for the stock for a different, but equally delicious, take on this recipe, ensuring it is gluten-free, if necessary.*
- *To make this recipe vegan, use vegan bratwurst-style sausages instead of pork.*

Chapter 8

❧

Lamb

Gigot d'Agneau (Leg of Lamb)

Lamb Stew

Lamb Cutlets with Spinach

Gigot d'Agneau
(Leg of Lamb)

"Aye," she said, looking resigned, and took both pot and bottle. It probably wasn't the worst thing she'd ever done as a mother. I gave her instructions regarding the boiling of bedding and strict advice about soap and religious hand-washing, wished her well, and left, feeling a strong urge to scratch my own bottom.

This faded on the walk back to the Higginses' cabin, though, and I slid into the pallet beside Jamie with the peaceful sense of a job well done.

He rolled over drowsily and embraced me, then sniffed.

"What in God's name have ye been doing, Sassenach?"

"You don't want to know," I assured him. "What do I smell like?" If it was just garlic, I wasn't getting up. If it was feces, though . . .

"Garlic," he said, luckily. "Ye smell like a French *gigot d'agneau*." His stomach rumbled at the thought, and I laughed—quietly.

"I think the best you're likely to get is parritch for your breakfast."

"That's all right," he said comfortably. "There's honey for it."

—*Written in My Own Heart's Blood,* chapter 142, "Things Coming into View"

GF | DF

The tradition of eating lamb on Easter has its roots in Passover observances before the birth of Christianity, and roasted lamb has been the centerpiece of the pope's Easter dinner since the ninth century. Following is the recipe for a traditional French Easter leg of lamb. Because it requires little preparation or active cooking, it makes for a relatively easy holiday meal.

Serves 6 to 8

Ingredients

7- to 8-pound (3- to 3.75-kilogram) leg of lamb, hip bone removed and retained, trimmed to a light layer of fat

2 garlic cloves, each cut into 4 slivers

2 tablespoons extra-virgin olive oil

2 tablespoons kosher salt, plus additional

1 tablespoon minced fresh rosemary

1 teaspoon freshly ground pepper, plus additional

2 large onions, julienned

2 large carrots, chopped

4 celery stalks, chopped

2 cups chicken or beef stock

1 teaspoon lemon juice

Method

Remove the meat from the refrigerator 2 hours before you plan to roast it.

Move the rack to the middle rung and heat the oven to 500°F.

With the point of a small knife, make eight small, deep incisions along the length of the leg and insert a sliver of garlic into each. In a small bowl, combine the olive oil, salt, rosemary, and pepper. Rub the leg with the mixture and place it, fat side up, and the hip bone on a rack set in a roasting pan.

Roast, uncovered, for 20 minutes. Reduce the heat to 375°F, scatter the onions, carrots, and celery around the meat, and continue to roast, uncovered and without basting, until an instant-read thermometer inserted in the fleshiest part of the leg reads 125°F for medium-rare, about 60 to 70 minutes longer (see Notes). Remove to a plate, tent with foil, and rest 15 to 20 minutes.

Add the stock to the roasting pan and bring it to a boil over medium-high heat. Boil briskly for 3 to 4 minutes, scraping the bottom of the pan to loosen all the roasting juices and browned bits. Reduce the sauce by half, about 10 minutes, and then strain it, pressing down on the vegetables with a spoon to extract all their juices. Discard the vegetables and hip bone. Skim the sauce of most of its surface fat, season with salt and freshly ground pepper to taste, and stir in the lemon juice.

Serve with the sauce, accompanied by green beans and Fergus's Roasted Tatties from OK1, for the Outlander version of a traditional Easter Sunday dinner. Refrigerate leftovers for up to 3 days in the refrigerator.

Notes

- *Resting a roast results in juicier meat and allows for carryover cooking that increases the internal temperature of a roast by 5 to 10°F, so that by the time you are ready to serve, this roast will be at 135°F—a perfect medium-rare.*

- *A leg of lamb is at its best when medium-rare, but if you prefer medium, cook it to an internal temperature of 130 to 135°F, and for medium-well 145°F. Rest as above.*

- *Use leftover lamb to make the Shepherd's Pie in OK1.*

Lamb Stew

Ian sat on the floor, bent over, holding his eye and breathing through his mouth in short gasps. After a minute, he straightened up. His eye was puffing already, leaking tears down his lean cheek. He got up, shaking his head slowly, and put the bench back in place. Then he sat down, picked up his cup and took a deep gulp, put it down and blew out his breath. He took the snot-rag Jamie was holding out to him and dabbed at his eye.

"Sorry," Jamie managed. The agony in his hand was beginning to subside, but the anguish in his heart wasn't.

"Aye," Ian said quietly, not meeting his eye. "I wish we'd done something, too. Ye want to share a bowl o' stew?"

—Virgins

GF(a) | DF | V(a) | VGN(a)

A quick stew made with ground meat with a healthy dose of spice. Veggies and lentils round out the flavor for a delicious meal in just over 30 minutes.

Serves 4 to 6

Ingredients

1 teaspoon vegetable oil

1 pound (450 grams) ground lamb

1½ teaspoons kosher salt, plus additional

1½ teaspoons freshly toasted and ground cumin seed (see Pantry Notes, page 5)

1 teaspoon freshly toasted and ground coriander seed (see Pantry Notes, page 5)

½ teaspoon freshly ground pepper, plus additional

1 medium onion, julienned

1 can (28 ounces or 796 milliliters) diced tomatoes

1 bottle (12 ounces or 330 milliliters) amber or dark ale

1 medium potato, peeled and chopped

1 large carrot, sliced ½ inch thick on the diagonal

⅓ cup green lentils

¼ cup chopped fresh cilantro or parsley, for garnish

Method

In a large skillet, heat the oil over high heat until just smoking. Add the lamb to the pan, breaking it up with your hands to spread it out a bit. Mix together the salt, cumin seed, coriander seed, and pepper, and sprinkle it over the lamb. Add the onion and allow the meat to brown, untouched, until dark golden, about 5 minutes.

Toss everything together with a spatula and, when the lamb is no longer pink, add the tomatoes, ale, potato, carrot, and lentils; stir to combine and bring to a boil. Reduce to low, cover, and cook at a gentle simmer until the vegetables are tender, 20 to 30 minutes. Add salt and pepper to taste.

Garnish each serving with a sprinkling of cilantro and serve on top of Rice Pilaf (page 208) or Tobias Quinn's Colcannon (page 200).

Store leftovers in the fridge for up to 5 days or freeze for up to 2 weeks.

Notes

- *To make this recipe gluten-free, substitute gluten-free beer, red or white wine, or stock for the ale. All will give the stew a unique flavor.*
- *To make this stew vegetarian and vegan, replace the ground lamb with store-bought vegan ground round.*
- *Change up the vegetables in the same way. This stew is equally delicious with peas and potatoes, or with parsnip and turnip, and so on. Adjust the cooking times as required.*
- *Darcy's Tester Tip: "I loved toasting and grinding my own spices for this. What a huge, flavorful difference!"*

LAMB CUTLETS WITH SPINACH

"If you'll sing, I'm sure they'll wait to hear you. Then you can eat afterward. Aunt Bennie has the most marvelous collation laid on—the biggest steamed pudding I've ever seen, with juniper berries, and lamb cutlets with spinach, and a coq au vin, and some absolutely disgusting sausages—for the Germans, you know . . ."

Grey's stomach rumbled loudly at this enticing catalog of gustation. He still would have demurred, though, had he not at this moment caught sight of an elderly woman with a swatch of ostrich plume in her tidy wig, through the open double doors of the drawing room.

The crowd erupted in applause, but as though the lady sensed his start of recognition, she turned her head toward the door, and her face lighted with pleasure as she saw him.

—*Lord John and the Private Matter,* chapter 5,
"Eine Kleine Nachtmusik (A Little Night Music)"

GF | DF

Thick, meaty chops or sirloin medallions topped with a fresh, entirely possible (although unlikely) eighteenth-century salsa verde.

Serves 6

Ingredients

6 boneless lamb sirloin medallions
   or thick-cut boneless loin chops
   (about 3 pounds or 1.4 kilograms)
2 teaspoons kosher salt, plus additional
¾ teaspoon freshly ground pepper,
   plus additional
1 cup spinach leaves, packed

½ cup chopped fresh mint
⅓ cup chopped fresh parsley
Zest and juice of 2 lemons
1 teaspoon crushed red pepper flakes
2 garlic cloves, chopped
½ cup extra-virgin olive oil
Vegetable oil, for the grill

Method

Remove the lamb from the refrigerator 1 hour before cooking. Pat it dry with paper towels and season it with the salt and pepper.

In the cup of a food processor or blender, puree the spinach, mint, parsley, lemon zest, red pepper flakes, garlic, and olive oil until smooth, scraping down the sides as needed. Transfer to a bowl and season to taste with salt and pepper.

Heat the grill on high for 15 minutes. Brush or wipe the grill lightly with vegetable oil and cook the meat, turning every 2 minutes, until well browned and beginning to char, about 8 to 14 minutes, depending on the desired doneness. A thermometer inserted into the thickest part should read 120°F for medium-rare, 130°F for medium, 140°F for medium-well. Transfer the lamb to a plate and tent lightly with aluminum foil. Rest for 10 to 15 minutes.

Stir 1 tablespoon of the lemon juice into the spinach salsa verde; taste and adjust the seasoning with salt, pepper, and more lemon juice, if required.

Serve the lamb chops with salsa verde. This is a delicious spring feast when served with Broccoli Sallet with Radishes and Vinegar (page 198) and Rice Pilaf (page 208).

Notes

- *The lamb can also be cooked on a grill pan over high heat on the stove.*
- *Jennifer's Tester Tip: "When I couldn't find lamb cutlets, the butcher suggested butterflied shoulder. It was amazing."*

Chapter 9

❧

Game

Rabbit Stew with Onions

Game Pie

Lord John's Lunchbox

Hunter's Venison Pie with Sweet Potato and Parsnip Mash

The Old Fox's Roast Haunch of Venison

RABBIT STEW WITH ONIONS

Jamie and Hamish did not return for supper, leading me to suppose that the loo must be going well for them. Things were going reasonably well for me, too; Mrs. Kebbits, the militia wife, did feed Ian and myself, and very hospitably, with fresh corn dodgers and rabbit stew with onions. Best of all, my sinister visitor didn't return.

—*An Echo in the Bone*, chapter 67, "Greasier than Grease"

GF | V(a)

A light, white-wine braise gives this dish a sophisticated modern twist to elevate it from its battlefield origins in Mrs. Kebbits's kettle. Ask the butcher to cut the rabbit into pieces for you if you're feeling squeamish.

Serves 4

Ingredients

1 rabbit (2½ to 3 pounds or 1.1 to 1.4 kilograms), cut into 6 to 8 pieces

1½ teaspoons kosher salt, plus additional

½ teaspoon white pepper, plus additional

Boiling water

½ ounce (15 grams) dried mushrooms, such as porcini or morel

¼ cup extra-virgin olive oil

1 pound (450 grams) sweet onions (about 2), such as Vidalia, cut into ½-inch wedges

2 garlic cloves, grated or minced

1 cup white wine

1 cup Quick Vegetable Stock (page 12) or chicken stock

4 fresh thyme sprigs

⅓ cup whipping cream

6 large basil leaves, for garnish

Method

Move the rack to the upper-middle rung and heat the oven to 325°F. Pat the rabbit pieces dry and season with salt and pepper. In a small bowl, pour just enough boiling water over the dried mushrooms to cover. Soak for 5 minutes, then lift the mushrooms from the water with a fork to leave the grit at the bottom of the dish. Chop coarsely, discarding the soaking water.

In a large Dutch oven or heavy ovenproof pan, heat 2 tablespoons of the olive oil over medium-high heat. When the oil is shimmering, add the rabbit pieces in batches and fry until browned on both sides, 6 to 8 minutes total. Transfer to a plate.

Reduce the heat to medium, add the remaining 2 tablespoons olive oil to the pan, and sauté the onions with a large pinch of salt until soft and light golden, 15 to 20 minutes. Add the reconstituted mushrooms and garlic and stir until fragrant, about 1 minute. Add the rabbit pieces, white wine, stock, and thyme. Bring to a boil, scraping up the brown bits from the bottom of the pan. Cover and braise in the oven until the rabbit is fork-tender, 75 to 90 minutes.

Transfer the rabbit to a serving plate, tent with foil, and rest for 15 minutes. Stir the cream into the braising pan with the onions and heat to a slow boil over medium-high. Reduce to medium-low and simmer until the sauce is reduced and coats the back of a spoon, 10 to 15 minutes. Season to taste with salt and pepper.

Pour the sauce and onions over the rabbit pieces. Garnish with the basil, tearing it with your hands and scattering it on top.

Serve immediately with Spoon Bread from OK1 to soak up the sauce.

Notes

- *For a vegetarian version, grill slices of smoked tofu and add them to the sautéed onions with the white wine, stock, and thyme. Braise for 15 minutes, then stir in the cream and finish as instructed.*

- *Skinless, bone-in chicken thighs are an easily procured substitute for the rabbit.*

- *White pepper means no black flecks in the finished sauce. However, if black pepper is what you have, use that.*

GAME PIE

He had employed Mrs. Figg, a nearly spherical black woman, as cook, on the assumption that she could not have gained such a figure without having both an appreciation of good food and the ability to cook it. In this assumption he had been proved right, and not even that lady's uncertain temperament and taste for foul language made him regret his decision, though it did make him approach her warily. Hearing his news, though, she obligingly put aside the game pie she was making in order to assemble a tea tray.

—An Echo in the Bone, chapter 73,
"One Ewe Lamb Returns to the Fold"

From the time of the Romans through to the Victorians, game pies have been the centerpiece of wealthy tables for hundreds of years. *Outlander Kitchen'*s version is a large, unabashedly meaty pie filled with duck, rabbit, and venison and encased in a rich, savory crust.

Serves 12

Ingredients

2 duck legs (about 1 pound or
    450 grams)

1 rabbit (2½ to 3 pounds or
    1.1 to 1.4 kilograms), cut into
    6 pieces

Kosher salt

2 cups duck or chicken stock
    (see Notes)

4 cups all-purpose flour

6 tablespoons lard or butter

6 tablespoons duck fat or butter
    (see Notes)

2 large eggs

1 pound (450 grams) venison sausage,
    removed from its casing
    (see Notes)

6 ounces (170 grams) bacon, minced

8 large fresh sage leaves, minced

1 tablespoon minced fresh rosemary

Freshly ground black pepper

½ teaspoon cayenne pepper

1 tablespoon gelatin

Method

Season the duck and rabbit generously with salt and arrange them in a Dutch oven or other heavy ovenproof pot with a lid. Add the stock and bring to a boil over medium-high heat. Reduce to a simmer and cover, cooking until the meat is tender. The rabbit saddle and forelegs will cook first, 45 to 60 minutes; the legs and duck will take at least 90 minutes and up to 2 hours. Remove the pieces as they are cooked, set aside, and pull the meat from the bones when cool enough to handle. Strain the stock through three layers of cheesecloth. Set aside 2 cups of stock and reserve the rest for another use.

In a large bowl, mix the flour with 2 teaspoons salt, leaving a well in the center. In a small pan, melt the lard and duck fat. Pour it into the well along with 1 cup warm water and 1 of the eggs. Mix by hand into a dough, then knead on the counter until it forms a smooth ball, 3 to 4 minutes. Wrap and chill in the fridge for at least 60 minutes and up to 24 hours.

Move the rack to the middle rung and heat the oven to 350°F.

Cut off one-fourth of the pastry and set it aside. Roll out the rest into a large circle with a ¼-inch thickness. Line a 9- or 10-inch springform pan with the dough, pressing it firmly into the corners of the pan and ensuring it reaches well up the sides, ideally to the top. Patch any holes or cracks with pastry scraps.

In a large bowl, use your hands to thoroughly mix together the duck and rabbit meat, uncooked venison sausage, bacon, sage, rosemary, 1 teaspoon salt, 2 teaspoons black pepper, and the cayenne. Fill the pastry with the meat mixture, gently pressing it into the corners without packing it down and smoothing the top level.

Roll out the remaining piece of dough to a circle with a ¼-inch thickness. Beat the remaining egg with 1 teaspoon water and paint the top of the crust. Reserve the egg wash. Lay the rolled-out dough on top of the pie and crimp to seal. Cut a ½-inch hole in the center.

Bake for 30 minutes. Lower the heat to 325°F and bake for another 90 minutes.

Remove the pie from the oven and remove the springform pan's side. Paint the tops and sides of the pie with the egg wash and return it to the oven until golden, another 15 to 20 minutes. Cool on a rack for at least 2 hours.

When the pie is cool, pour ½ cup of the reserved stock into a small bowl and sprinkle the gelatin over the surface. Whisk the gelatin into the stock and rest for 5 minutes. In a medium saucepan, bring the remaining 1½ cups stock to a simmer.

Pour in the gelatin mixture, stir for a minute, and remove from the heat. Cool 15 minutes.

Use a funnel to slowly and carefully pour the gelatinized stock through the hole in the top of the crust until the space between the cooked meat and the underside of the crust is filled. Quickly mop up any spills on the top crust.

Cool on the counter for another hour. Carefully move the pie to the refrigerator and chill several hours, preferably overnight. Serve cold or at room temperature.

Notes

- *Use the leftover stock to make Rabbit Stew with Onions (page 142).*
- *The thriftiest option is to purchase a whole duck. Use the breasts for Lord John's Lunchbox (page 148) and the fat you render from those breasts, along with the legs, as well as the stock you make from the duck's carcass, for this pie.*
- *Jason and Jen's Tester Tip: "To make a quick venison sausage, mix together 1 pound (450 grams) ground venison, 1½ teaspoons kosher salt, ¾ teaspoon onion powder, ¾ teaspoon paprika, ¼ teaspoon ground pepper, ⅛ teaspoon ground allspice, and ⅛ teaspoon ground nutmeg. Rest in the refrigerator for at least 60 minutes before proceeding with the recipe."*

Lord John's Lunchbox

He was aware—as most of the merrymakers were not—of the mollies among the crowd. Some dressed as women, others in their own male garb surmounted by outlandish masks, finding each other by glance and grimace, by whatever alchemy of flesh enabled body to seek body, freed by disguise of their usual constraints.

More than one gay blade glanced at him, and now and then one jostled him in passing, a hand brushing his arm, his back, lingering an instant on his hip, the touch a question. He smiled now and then, but walked on.

Feeling hungry, he turned in to a supper table, bought a box, and found a place on the nearby lawn to eat. As he finished a breast of roast fowl and tossed the bones under a bush, a man sat down beside him. Sat much closer than was usual.

He glanced warily at the man, but did not know him, and deliberately looked away, giving no hint of invitation.

—Lord John and the Haunted Soldier

GF | DF

Crisp roast duck breast with a marmalade sauce and an optional drop of whisky, all on a bed of German potato salad. It's Lord John in a box! Delicious served warm on the table, or cold, as a picnic lunch. The potato salad is vegan.

Serves 2 for dinner or 4 for lunch

Ingredients

2 boneless duck breasts (1¼ to 1½ pounds or 500 to 680 grams)

1½ pounds (680 grams) small waxy potatoes, scrubbed and halved

Kosher salt and freshly ground pepper

1 small onion, julienned

¼ cup extra-virgin olive oil

¼ cup apple cider vinegar

2 tablespoons chopped fresh dill

1 cup duck or chicken stock (see Notes)

½ teaspoon crushed red pepper flakes

3 tablespoons Seville Orange Marmalade (page 301) or store-bought marmalade

1 tablespoon scotch whisky
   (optional)
1 to 3 teaspoons lemon juice

2 scallions (white and light green parts),
   thinly sliced on the diagonal, for
   garnish

Method

Remove the duck breasts from the refrigerator 1 hour before you plan to start cooking. Move the rack to the center rung and heat the oven to 400°F.

Place the potatoes in a large pot with 1 inch of water and a pinch of salt. Cover and bring to a boil. Reduce to a simmer and steam the potatoes until fork-tender, 15 to 20 minutes. Drain; keep the potatoes in the pot. Add the onion, olive oil, vinegar, and dill, and toss well, crushing the potatoes slightly. Season to taste with salt and pepper. Cover to keep warm.

Pat the duck breasts dry with paper towels. Using a sharp knife, score the skin of the duck breasts on the diagonal at ½-inch intervals, ensuring you cut only the skin, not the meat. Turn the duck breast and score the skin diagonally in the other direction, making a crisscross pattern. Season generously with salt and pepper.

Heat a cast-iron or other heavy ovenproof pan over medium-low heat for 5 minutes. Add the duck breasts to the pan, skin side down, and cook, untouched, until the fat is rendered and the skin is crisp and golden, 8 to 12 minutes. Flip the breasts over and cook for another minute.

Transfer the pan to the oven and cook until medium-rare, 155°F on an instant-read thermometer inserted into the thickest part of the breast, 6 to 8 minutes. Move the breasts to a cutting board to rest for 5 minutes.

Pour all but 2 teaspoons of the fat through a strainer and reserve for another use (see Notes). Heat the pan over medium-high heat until the fat sizzles. Add the stock and red pepper flakes to the pan and boil to reduce the liquid by half, about 5 minutes. Add the marmalade and the whisky, if using, and boil 1 minute. Remove the pan from the heat and stir in the lemon juice.

To serve immediately, slice the duck on the diagonal into ½-inch-thick slices, arrange on plates on top of the warm potato salad, and spoon the marmalade sauce over the duck. Garnish with the sliced scallions.

To serve cold, refrigerate the cooled, unsliced duck, sauce, and potato salad for up to 2 days. Slice and serve as above.

Notes

- *Store-bought marmalade will benefit from the addition of the whisky.*
- *Use the fat rendered from the duck breasts for Game Pie (page 144).*
- *During the resting period, the temperature of the meat continues to increase by 5 to 10°F. For this recipe, the duck will be approximately 165°F after resting.*

Hunter's Venison Pie
with Sweet Potato and Parsnip Mash

He passed the Free North Church and half-smiled at it, thinking of Mrs. Ogilvy and Mrs. MacNeil. They'd be back, he knew, if he didn't do something about it. He knew their brand of determined kindliness. Dear God, if they heard that Bree had gone to work and—to their way of thinking—abandoned him with two small children, they'd be running shepherd's pies and hot stovies out to him in relays. That mightn't be such a bad thing, he thought, meditatively licking his lips—save that they'd stay to poke their noses into the workings of his household, and letting them into Brianna's kitchen would be not merely playing with dynamite but deliberately throwing a bottle of nitroglycerin into the midst of his marriage.

—*An Echo in the Bone,* chapter 16, "Unarmed Conflict"

GF | DF

Inspired by the traditional Shepherd's Pie in OK1, this recipe tops a hearty mix of venison and vegetables with a dairy-free mash of sweet potatoes and parsnips.

Enjoy it on its own or with a piece of Corn Bread (page 232) on the side.

Serves 6

Ingredients

2 pounds (900 grams) parsnips
  (about 4 large)

5 tablespoons extra-virgin olive oil

Kosher salt and freshly ground pepper

2½ pounds (1.1 kilograms) sweet
  potatoes (3 or 4 medium)

2 pounds (900 grams) ground venison

1 large onion, julienned

1 large russet potato, peeled
  and diced

6 large button mushrooms, cleaned
  and sliced thinly

2 large garlic cloves, grated or minced

1 tablespoon minced fresh rosemary

2 tablespoons tomato paste

½ cup red wine or water

1½ cups beef stock

1 tablespoon Mushroom Catsup
  (page 307) or Worcestershire sauce

3 large egg yolks

1 tablespoon Prepared Horseradish
(page 309) or store-bought, plus
additional

¼ teaspoon freshly grated nutmeg
1 to 2 teaspoons maple syrup (optional)

Method

Move the rack to the middle rung and heat the oven to 400°F. Line a baking sheet with parchment paper.

Peel the parsnips and cut them into 1 x 2-inch lengths. In a large bowl, toss the parsnips with 1 teaspoon of the olive oil. Season lightly with salt and pepper and arrange on the prepared baking sheet along with the whole, unpeeled sweet potatoes. Roast until the vegetables are very tender and a fork pierces them easily, 40 to 50 minutes.

In a large cast-iron pan, heat 2 teaspoons of the olive oil over medium-high heat. When just smoking, add the venison, breaking it up with your hands as you put it into the pan. Season with 1½ teaspoons salt and ½ teaspoon pepper. Cook, untouched, until the bottom is browned, 3 to 4 minutes. Stir the meat, and when it is no longer pink, add the onion, potato, mushrooms, garlic, and rosemary. Cook, stirring occasionally, until the vegetables are softened, 6 to 8 minutes. Add the tomato paste and stir well to combine, about 1 minute. Deglaze the pan with the wine and reduce, scraping up the brown bits, until the pan is almost dry. Add the stock and mushroom catsup, reduce the heat to medium-low, and simmer, uncovered, for 15 minutes. Taste and season with salt and pepper.

Scoop the flesh from the sweet potatoes and, in a large bowl, mash them together with the parsnip sticks, the remaining ¼ cup olive oil, the egg yolks, horseradish, and nutmeg to the desired texture. Taste and adjust the seasoning with salt, additional horseradish, and maple syrup (if needed).

Spoon the mash over the meat in the pan. Bake until the top is golden and the filling is bubbling, 30 to 35 minutes. Rest 10 minutes before serving.

Notes

- *This recipe is a delicious way to use up the leftovers from The Old Fox's Roast Haunch of Venison (page 155). Dice 2 pounds (900 grams) cooked meat as finely as you can and continue with the recipe. If there is leftover gravy, add it to the meat along with the stock.*

- *To make the mash recipe vegan, use ½ cup of Vegan Cream (page 20) in place of the egg yolks.*

The Old Fox's
Roast Haunch of Venison

He would admit that Washington knew what he was about, though; he listened more than he talked, and when he said something, it was to the point. And he did give off an air of relaxed authority, though it was clear the present prospect excited him very much.

His face was pockmarked, big-featured, and far from handsome, but had a good bit of dignity and presence. His expression had become very animated, and he went so far as to laugh now and then, showing very bad, stained teeth. Jamie was fascinated; Brianna had told him they were false, made of wood or hippopotamus ivory, and he had a sudden dislocating recollection of his grandfather: the Old Fox had had a set of teeth made of beechwood. Jamie had thrown them on the fire during an argument at Beaufort Castle—and just for an instant he was there, smelling peat smoke and roasting venison, every hair on his body a-prickle with warning, surrounded by kinsmen who might just kill him.

—Written in My Own Heart's Blood, chapter 10,
"The Descent of the Holy Ghost upon a Reluctant Disciple"

GF | DF

Simon Fraser was the second-born son to the lesser Beaufort Frasers and fought and assaulted his way to the title 11th Lord Lovat. A confirmed Jacobite at heart, he changed allegiances more than once to ensure his survival. His support of Charles Stuart at Culloden earned him a traitor's execution, and the Old Fox was the last man hung, drawn, and quartered on Tower Hill in 1747.

Do not cook a venison haunch past medium. It will be tough.

Serves 6

Ingredients

3- to 4-pound (1.4- to 1.8-kilogram)
  boneless venison haunch
  (see Notes)

4 teaspoons extra-virgin olive oil

1 tablespoon kosher salt,
  plus additional

¾ teaspoon freshly ground pepper, plus additional

1 medium onion, chopped

1 large carrot, chopped

2 celery stalks, chopped

1 Preserved Lemon (page 10), cut into quarters, or ½ fresh lemon

6 bay leaves, preferably fresh

3 ounces (90 grams) sliced pancetta

1 cup red wine

1 cup beef stock

Method

Remove the meat from the refrigerator 1 hour before you plan to roast it.

Move the rack to the top-middle rung and heat the oven to 450°F. Rub the roast with 1 tablespoon of the olive oil and season it with the salt and pepper. In a large bowl, toss the onion, carrot, celery, and lemon with the remaining teaspoon olive oil.

Place the meat in a roasting pan and cook for 20 minutes. Remove from the oven and reduce the heat to 350°F. Place the bay leaves on top of the roast and drape the pancetta over to cover. Scatter the vegetables and lemon around the roast, pour ½ cup of the red wine over them, and return the pan to the oven. Continue to roast until an instant-read thermometer inserted into the thickest part reads 125°F for rare, 130°F for medium-rare, and 135°F for medium. This will take at least 35 minutes and up to 1 hour, depending on your desired doneness. Check the temperature after 30 minutes and every 15 minutes after that. Do not cook the venison past 140°F, or it will be inedibly tough. Remove the pancetta and bay leaves after it comes out of the oven. Lightly tent the roast with aluminum foil and rest for 20 minutes.

While the meat rests, strain the pan juices into a medium saucepan, discarding the solids. Bring to a boil over medium-high heat. Add the beef stock and the remaining ½ cup red wine. Boil gently until reduced by one-third, about 10 minutes. Season to taste, reduce to low, and keep warm.

Carve the roast and arrange it on a platter with the sauce alongside. Serve with Fergus's Roasted Tatties from OK1, buttered peas, and Prepared Horseradish (page 309).

Notes

- *Prepare a bone-in leg roast the same way, keeping in mind that it will take longer to roast than its boneless counterpart. When testing the temperature, ensure the thermometer isn't touching the bone, which will give you an inaccurate reading.*

- *Resting a roast results in juicier meat, and allows for carryover cooking that increases the internal temperature of a roast by 5 to 10°F.*

- *Pancetta is a purposely mild choice. Bacon's smokiness can overpower the natural flavors of venison, especially in a gravy.*

- *Nibble on the crispy pancetta while you make the sauce, or reserve it in the fridge for sandwiches or as "bacon bits" for a salad.*

Chapter 10

❧

Fish and Seafood

Shrimp Confit and Trout in Savoy Cabbage

Coquilles St. Jacques

Crispy Squid in Cornmeal

Herb-Roasted Salmon

Fish Fried in Batter with Tartar Sauce

Shrimp Confit and Trout in Savoy Cabbage

It was the best party that Dorothea Jacqueline Benedicta Grey had ever attended. She had danced with earls and viscounts in the most beautiful ballrooms in London, eaten everything from gilded peacock to trout stuffed with shrimp and riding on an artful sea of aspic with a Triton carved of ice brandishing his spear over all. And she'd done these things in gowns so splendid that men blinked when she hove into view.

Her new husband didn't blink. He stared at her so intently through his steel-rimmed spectacles that she thought she could feel his gaze on her skin, from across the room and right through her dove-gray dress, and she thought she might burst with happiness, exploding in bits all over the taproom of the White Camel tavern. Not that anyone would notice if she did; there were so many people crammed into the room, drinking, talking, drinking, singing, and drinking, that a spare gallbladder or kidney underfoot would pass without notice.

Just possibly, she thought, one or two whole people might pass without notice, too—right out of this lovely party.

—*Written in My Own Heart's Blood,* chapter 94,
"The Sense of the Meeting"

GF | DF

A modern play on trout stuffed with shrimp riding on an artful sea of aspic, which, despite a bevy of modern appliances, would be tough to whip up for a Saturday night dinner party. Assemble the cabbage rolls up to a day ahead to give you more time with your guests as they arrive. Once everyone is seated, have someone pour the wine while you sneak into the kitchen to quickly cook this delicious main.

Serves 6

Ingredients

1 pound (450 grams) large shrimp (30 to 35 per pound), shelled and deveined

1-inch strip of lemon peel

1 bay leaf

1 garlic clove, halved

½ teaspoon crushed red pepper flakes

Extra-virgin olive oil

Kosher salt

6 large savoy cabbage leaves

6 tablespoons capers, drained

¼ cup chopped fresh dill or parsley, plus
    additional sprigs for garnish

Freshly ground pepper to taste

6 boneless, skinless trout fillets
    (4 ounces each)

½ cup white wine

Method

In a medium pan, combine the shrimp, lemon peel, bay leaf, garlic clove, and red pepper flakes. Pour in the olive oil until the shrimp are barely submerged. Cook on the stove's lowest setting until the shrimp are pink, at least 20 minutes; the slower the better. Using a slotted spoon, transfer the shrimp to a plate to cool; strain and reserve the oil, discarding the solids.

Bring a large pot of salted water to a boil. Blanch the cabbage leaves until bright green and tender, about 2 minutes. Remove and gently pat dry with a clean dishcloth.

Chop 2 tablespoons of the capers together with the dill. In a small bowl, combine this with ¼ cup of the cooled shrimp oil and a pinch each of salt and pepper. Season the trout with salt and pepper. Mix the wine with ¼ cup water.

Lay one of the cabbage leaves on a cutting board, vein side down. Trim approximately an inch from the bottom of the vein to remove the thickest portion so that the leaf lies flat. Cut a trout fillet in half crosswise and stack the pieces on the bottom half of the leaf. Spread with a spoonful of the caper mixture and top with 2 of the shrimp. Bring the bottom of the cabbage leaf over the filling, then fold in the sides and roll it closed. Move to a plate, seam side down, and repeat with the remaining leaves and filling, reserving a dozen shrimp for garnish.

In a small pan over medium-low heat, gently reheat the reserved shrimp with 3 tablespoons of the shrimp oil. When heated through, transfer them to a bowl and cover to keep warm. Increase the heat under the pan to high. When almost smoking, add the remaining capers and fry until crispy, tossing a few times, 1 to 2 minutes. Remove from the heat.

Heat a large pan over medium-high. Add 2 tablespoons of the shrimp oil and swirl to coat the bottom of the pan. When the oil is shimmering, place the cabbage rolls in the pan, seam side down. Fry until light golden on the bottom, about 2 minutes. Pour in the wine and water, reduce to medium, and cover. Steam 6 minutes, remove a roll from the pan and gently open the seam to check that the fish is firm and flaky. If not, reroll, return to the pan and steam for another 2 to 3 minutes.

Plate the cabbage rolls, garnishing with the warm shrimp and crispy capers.

Serve with Rice Pilaf (page 208) and your favorite seasonable vegetable, steamed to tender-crisp perfection.

Note

- *Use the leftover shrimp oil for an omelette, drizzled over a stir-fry, or—my favorite—in a batch of shrimp and egg fried rice.*

Coquilles St. Jacques

"Are you ready?" Hal poked his own powdered head in, inquiring.

"As I'll ever be," Grey said, straightening himself. "Tom, you won't forget about the bottles?"

"Oh, no, me lord," Tom assured him. "You can count on me."

"Well, then." He crooked an arm toward his brother, and bowed. "Shall we dance?"

"Ass," said Hal, but tolerantly.

The feast, held in the ancient guildhall, was exactly as Grey had predicted: long, eye-glazingly boring, and featuring course after course of roast pork, boiled beef, gravied mutton, roasted pheasants, sliced ham, braised quail, grilled fish, eggs in aspic and in pies, shellfish in soup, in pastry, and on the half shell, plus sundry savories, syllabubs, and sweets, all served on a weight of silver plate sufficient to purchase a small country and washed down with gallons of wine, drunk in a succession of endless toasts in honor of everyone from Frederick, King of Prussia, King George of England, and Duke Ferdinand down to—Grey was sure—the kitchen cat, though by the time this point in the proceedings was reached, no one was paying sufficient attention as to be sure.

—*Lord John and the Brotherhood of the Blade,* chapter 23, "The Rhineland"

Saint James the Greater, son of Zebedee and Solomon, was a disciple of Jesus and is the patron saint of Spain. His emblem was a scallop shell, and early pilgrims traveling to his shrine each carried a shell to signify their journey. At stops along the way, they were offered what food they could scoop up in their shell. Coquille St. Jacques is French for "Saint James's shell," and also refers to the classic preparation of scallops in cream sauce, traditionally served in a shell.

Serves 4 as a main or 6 as an appetizer

Ingredients

1 pound (450 grams) sea scallops, shelled and cleaned (10 to 20, depending on size)

3 tablespoons butter, plus additional, for greasing

Kosher salt and freshly ground pepper

1 cup fresh white breadcrumbs
(see Notes)

½ cup finely shredded Gruyère cheese

2 tablespoons minced fresh parsley

2 tablespoons extra-virgin olive oil

1 pound (450 grams) cremini or
button mushrooms, stems removed
and discarded, chopped

2 medium shallots, minced

1 small garlic clove, grated or minced

1 fresh thyme sprig

½ cup brandy or white wine

½ cup whipping cream

½ cup Quick Vegetable Stock
(page 12) or chicken stock

1 teaspoon vegetable oil

Method

Move the rack to the top rung and heat the oven to 400°F. Lightly grease 4 or 6 scallop shells or shallow ovenproof bowls with butter and arrange them on a baking sheet lined with parchment paper or a silicone sheet.

Season the scallops generously with salt and pepper. In a small bowl, mix together the breadcrumbs, Gruyère, parsley, olive oil, and ¼ teaspoon salt until all the breadcrumbs are well coated. Set aside.

In a food processor, pulse the mushrooms, shallots, and garlic until finely chopped but not mushy. In a large pan, melt the butter over medium heat until bubbling. Add the mushroom mixture and cook, stirring occasionally, until the mushrooms have released their water and are just starting to brown, 10 to 12 minutes.

Add the thyme and stir 1 more minute. Deglaze the pan with the brandy and reduce until the pan is almost dry, about 2 minutes. Stir in the cream and stock, and simmer briskly until reduced and thickened, 8 to 10 minutes. Remove from the heat, discard the thyme, and season to taste with salt and pepper. Divide the mushroom sauce evenly among the shells and top with the prepared breadcrumbs. Cook in the oven until bubbling and golden brown, about 10 minutes.

Heat a large, heavy pan over medium heat for about 5 minutes. When the pan is hot, increase the heat to high, brush the pan with the vegetable oil, and add the scallops, flat side down. Gently press each scallop into the pan to increase the surface contact and get a good sear. Cook, untouched, until dark golden on one side, 3 to 4 minutes.

Remove the scallops and quickly divide them among the hot shells, nestling the scallops, seared side up, into the mushroom sauce and the breadcrumbs.

Serve immediately, either on their own as an appetizer, or with Salad Greens with Vinegar (page 205), a loaf of bread, and a bottle of your favorite white wine.

Notes

- *There are three types of scallops available in North America. Sea scallops are the largest, followed by smaller bay scallops, and finally calico scallops, whose shells must be steamed open before further preparation.*

- *Bay scallops are too small to sear without turning them rubbery. To substitute bay scallops in this recipe, allow the mushroom cream sauce to cool significantly before mixing in the scallops. Divide among the shells or bowls, top with the breadcrumbs, and bake 5 to 10 minutes longer than directed.*

- *Watch the scallops carefully; you want a good dark sear, but not at the expense of overcooking. They are cooked as they turn opaque, before they become white and rubbery. Don't worry if you think they are slightly undercooked. The heat of the mushroom sauce will continue to cook the scallops as you take everything to the table.*

- *To make fresh breadcrumbs, remove the crusts from day-old or older bread and pulse in a food processor until the crumbs are coarse and evenly sized.*

Crispy Squid in Cornmeal

Lord John and his niece, Dorothea, ate that night at a small ordinary near the shore, whose air was redolent with the luscious scents of baked fish, eels in wine sauce, and small whole squid, fried crisply in cornmeal. John inhaled deeply with pleasure, handed Dottie to a stool, and sat down himself, enjoying the moment of gustatory indecision.

—*Written in My Own Heart's Blood*, chapter 125, "Squid of the Evening, Beautiful Squid"

GF(a) | DF | V(a) | VGN(a)

The plural of *calamaro* (Italian for "squid"), calamari, made its way as a fried appetizer to North America from the Mediterranean in the 1970s. And although most East Coast fishermen used squid only as bait until as late as the 1980s (when it fetched less than ten cents per pound), who's to say an enterprising South Carolinian ordinary owner wasn't serving small whole squid fried in cornmeal two hundred years prior?

Serves 3 or 4 as a main course or 6 as an appetizer

Ingredients

2 quarts (2 liters) peanut oil

1½ pounds (680 grams) whole squid, cleaned and skinned

½ cup cornmeal

½ cup all-purpose flour

Kosher salt and freshly ground pepper

Lemon wedges, for serving

Method

In a large, heavy pot, heat the oil over medium-high heat to 375°F.

Pat the squid dry. If the squid are large, cut the tentacles in half lengthwise. Cut the tubes into ½-inch rings. Set aside.

Pour the cornmeal into a medium bowl and the flour into another. Dredge a handful of the squid in the cornmeal and gently shake off the excess; dredge it in the flour and shake again. Lower the squid into the hot oil. Repeat with another handful and cook two handfuls at a time until light golden, about 1 minute.

Use a slotted spoon to transfer to a paper towel–lined plate. Season immediately with salt and pepper. Repeat until all of the squid is cooked, ensuring the oil temperature returns to 375°F between batches.

Serve immediately with lemon wedges and Tartar Sauce (page 171).

Notes

- *To make this recipe gluten-free, substitute brown rice flour for the all-purpose.*

- *For a vegetarian or vegan twist on this recipe, cut rings from hearts of palm, gently pushing out the soft core of the palm hearts so that they resemble squid rings. Dredge and fry the rings as instructed and serve with tartar sauce made with vegan mayonnaise.*

- *If your squid are uncleaned, watch one or two instructional videos online before you begin.*

HERB-ROASTED SALMON

Captain von Namtzen's sternly handsome face was wreathed in smiles, though Grey saw that it bore the marks of some recent difficulty, the lines between nose and mouth harsher than they had been, hollows beneath the broad cheekbones and the deep-set eyes. He squeezed Grey's hand to express his pleasure at their reacquaintance, and Grey felt a few bones give, though nothing actually cracked.

"I should be so pleased," von Namtzen said. "But I am engaged . . ." He turned, looking vaguely behind him and gesturing toward a well-dressed gentleman who had been standing out of range. "You know Mr. Frobisher? His lordship John Grey," he explained to Frobisher, who bowed.

"Certainly," the gentleman replied courteously. "It would give me great pleasure, Lord John, was you to join us. I have two brace of partridge ordered, a fresh-caught salmon, and a vast great trifle to follow—Captain von Namtzen and I will be quite unequal to the occasion, I am sure."

—*The Scottish Prisoner,* chapter 9, "Eros Rising"

GF | DF(a)

Slow roasting in a moist, gentle heat keeps the salmon tender, and the butter infuses the fish with fresh herb flavor. A dinner-party-worthy meal paired with Broccoli Sallet with Radishes and Vinegar (page 198) and Nettle Rolls from OK1.

Serves 6

Ingredients

¼ cup (½ stick) butter, softened

1 scallion (white and light green parts),
    finely chopped

2 tablespoons chopped fresh parsley

2 tablespoons chopped fresh basil
    or dill

1 tablespoon capers, chopped

Zest of 1 lemon, grated or minced

1 teaspoon kosher salt

½ teaspoon freshly ground pepper

2½-pound (1.1-kilogram) side of
    salmon, skin on

Lemon wedges, for garnish

Method

Move the racks to the middle and lower rungs. Place a pan filled with 1 inch of water on the bottom rack and heat the oven to 275°F.

In a small bowl, use a fork to combine the butter, scallion, parsley, basil, capers, lemon zest, salt, and pepper.

Line a rimmed baking sheet with parchment paper and place the salmon on it, skin side down. Spread the herb butter evenly across the flesh of the salmon. Bake until the salmon is firm and cooked, 40 to 45 minutes. Check for doneness by inserting the tip of your knife in the thickest part of the fish. If the flesh flakes, it is cooked. If not, put it back into the oven for another 5 to 10 minutes, then check again.

Serve immediately, garnished with lemon wedges. Store leftovers in the fridge for up to 2 days.

Notes

- *To make this dish dairy-free, replace the butter with 2 tablespoons extra-virgin olive oil.*
- *To prepare single fillets instead, allow for about 6 ounces (170 grams) per person. The cooking time will be drastically reduced—check for doneness at about 20 minutes.*

FISH FRIED IN BATTER WITH TARTAR SAUCE

There was food in the city, food in abundance, and he paused for a moment of anticipatory bliss on the edge of the market square, deciding between fish fried in batter or a Cornish pasty. He had just stepped forward, money in hand, to the pasty-seller's stall, when he saw the woman look over his shoulder and her face change to a look of horror.

He whirled round and was knocked flat. There were screams and shouts, but these were lost in the mad slobber of Rollo's tongue licking every inch of his face, including the inside of his nose.

He whooped at that and half-sat up, fending off the ecstatic dog.

"A cú!" he said, and hugged the huge, wriggling creature in delight. He seized the dog's ruff in both hands then, laughing at the lolling tongue.

"Aye, I'm glad to see ye, too," he told Rollo. "But what have ye done wi' Rachel?"

—*An Echo in the Bone,* chapter 97, "Nexus"

GF | DF

Everyone loves fish fried in batter! Brown rice flour is naturally gluten-free, and together with cornstarch, it produces a light, crispy batter for fish. Use the remainder of your rice flour for the Press-In Crust (page 17) and to thicken stews such as the filling for Benedicta's Steak and Mushroom Pie (page 93).

Serves 6

Ingredients

1 cup Mayonnaise (page 18)

¼ cup minced gherkins

3 tablespoons minced scallions (white and light green parts)

2 tablespoons chopped capers

2 tablespoons finely chopped fresh dill or parsley

1 tablespoon fresh lemon juice

1 garlic clove, grated

1 teaspoon Dijon mustard

½ teaspoon Mushroom Catsup (page 307) or Worcestershire sauce

Kosher salt and freshly ground black pepper

1½ cups brown rice flour

½ cup cornstarch

1 teaspoon baking powder

1 teaspoon sugar

½ teaspoon cayenne pepper

1½ to 2 pounds (680 to 900 grams) whitefish, such as haddock, cod, or halibut, cut into 6 pieces

Vegetable oil, for frying

½ cup gluten-free beer or club soda

½ cup vodka

Method

In a small bowl, stir together the mayonnaise, gherkins, scallions, capers, dill, lemon juice, garlic, mustard, and mushroom catsup until combined. Taste and season with salt and black pepper. Set the tartar sauce aside.

In a large bowl, combine the brown rice flour, cornstarch, baking powder, sugar, 1 teaspoon salt, and cayenne. Dust the fish pieces in this mixture, shaking off the excess.

In a large, deep pan or Dutch oven, heat 3 inches of oil to 360°F. When the oil is to temperature, stir the beer and vodka into the rice flour mixture until just combined (a few lumps in the batter are fine).

Dip the fish pieces into the batter one at a time, gently shake off the excess, and lower them into the oil. Fry in batches to avoid overcrowding the oil. Fry until both sides are golden, turning once, 5 to 6 minutes total.

Serve with the tartar sauce, malt vinegar, and Matchstick Cold-Oil Fries from OK1 (see Notes).

Notes

- *To make this with all-purpose flour, eliminate the brown rice flour and replace with only ¾ cup of all-purpose flour.*

- *All distilled spirits, including vodka, are considered inherently gluten-free.*

- *To serve these with Matchstick Cold-Oil Fries from OK1, fry the potatoes first and keep them warm in a low (250°F) oven. Check the temperature of the oil with an instant-read thermometer before frying the fish.*

- *Do not make the batter ahead of time; the bubbles of a freshly opened beer (or club soda) result in lighter, crispier fish.*

Chapter 11

Vegetarian and Vegan

Young Ian's Grilled Succotash Salad

Claire's Beans and Sass

Jackfruit Potpie

Asparagus and Gruyère Quiche

Steel-Cut Oat Risotto

Stuffed Vegetable Marrow

Cuban Black Beans and Rice

Young Ian's Grilled Succotash Salad

My own pièce de résistance was stew—which, lacking onions, garlic, carrots, and potatoes, had devolved into a sort of pottage consisting of venison or turkey stewed with cracked corn, barley, and possibly chunks of stale bread. Ian, surprisingly, had turned out to be a passable cook; the succotash and squash pie were his contributions to the communal menu. I did wonder who had taught him to make them, but thought it wiser not to ask.

So far no one had starved, nor yet lost any teeth, but by mid-March, I would have been willing to wade neck-deep in freezing torrents in order to acquire something both edible and green.

Ian had, thank goodness, gone on breathing. And after a week or so had ceased acting quite so shell-shocked, eventually regaining something like his normal manner. But I noticed Jamie's eyes follow him now and then, and Rollo had taken to sleeping with his head on Ian's chest, a new habit. I wondered whether he really sensed the pain in Ian's heart, or whether it was simply a response to the cramped sleeping conditions in the cabin.

—*An Echo in the Bone,* chapter 8, "Spring Thaw"

GF | DF | V | VGN

Originally written for OutlanderKitchen.com, this make-ahead grilled vegetable salad uses corn, zucchini, and tomatoes at their summer best. Great as a side or main-dish salad at your annual backyard barbecue.

Serves 6 as a main dish or 8 to 10 as a side

Ingredients

2 cups frozen lima beans

2 ears of corn, shucked

1 medium zucchini, halved lengthwise

1 medium red onion, halved, root end attached

1 large jalapeño pepper, halved lengthwise and seeded

2 teaspoons vegetable oil

4 medium tomatoes, cored, seeded, and chopped

6 tablespoons extra-virgin olive oil

2 tablespoons red wine vinegar

2 teaspoons Dijon mustard

Zest of 1 lemon, minced or grated

1 garlic clove, minced or grated

1 teaspoon kosher salt, plus additional

½ teaspoon freshly ground black pepper, plus additional

½ cup basil leaves, unpacked

Method

Heat a grill to medium-high heat.

Cook the lima beans according to the package directions. Prepare an ice bath by filling a large bowl with cold water and a tray of ice cubes. Drain and plunge the cooked lima beans into the ice bath to cool rapidly. Drain and add to a large bowl.

Brush the corn, zucchini, onion, and jalapeño with the vegetable oil and grill over medium-high heat, turning occasionally, until softened and lightly charred, 10 to 12 minutes. Cut the kernels from the corn and chop the zucchini and onion into bite-size pieces. Dice the jalapeño. Add all of the grilled veggies and the tomatoes to the bowl with the lima beans.

In a small bowl or a jar with a tight-fitting lid, combine the olive oil, red wine vinegar, Dijon, lemon zest, garlic, salt, and black pepper, and whisk or shake. Add the dressing to the salad and toss well to combine. Cover and refrigerate at least 1 hour and up to 4 hours to allow the flavors to develop.

Season with additional salt and pepper to taste. Tear the basil into the bowl and toss just before serving cold alongside Lamb Cutlets with Spinach (page 138) or your favorite grilled meat. Store leftovers in the refrigerator for up to 3 days.

Notes

- *Not a lima bean fan? Substitute frozen, shelled edamame beans instead.*
- *Preserved Lemons (page 10) adds a wonderful depth to the dressing. Start with the minced peel from half a preserved lemon and add more to taste.*

Claire's Beans and Sass

From my point of view, the most interesting thing about Mr. Oglethorpe's plan—in the course of conversation, it was revealed to me that he'd founded not only Savannah but the whole Province of Georgia—was that each house of a tything was provided with a one-mile tract of farmland outside the city and a five-acre kitchen garden closer in.

"Really," I said, my fingers beginning to itch at the thought of dirt. "Er . . . what do you plant?"

The upshot of this conversation—and many like it—was that I made an arrangement to help with the keeping of the kitchen garden in return for a share of "sass" (as Mrs. Landrum puzzlingly referred to green stuff like kale and turnips), beans, and dried corn, as well as a small plot where I could cultivate medicinal herbs. A secondary consequence of this amiable acquaintance was that Rachel and Ian, whose room was below ours, began referring to their unborn child as Oglethorpe, though this was politely shortened to "Oggy" whenever Mrs. Landrum was in hearing.

—*Written in My Own Heart's Blood,* chapter 126,
"The Oglethorpe Plan"

GF | DF | V | VGN

Believed to have originated in Peru, beans were introduced to Europe in the fifteenth century by Spanish explorers. This simple pot of beans and veggies is full of flavor, and it's especially creamy when made with cannellini beans, a relative of the kidney bean that was originally cultivated in Argentina by Italian immigrants and later taken to Italy, where it is now grown.

Serves 6, with leftovers

Ingredients

2 cups dried white beans, such as navy,
   Great Northern, or cannellini

3 tablespoons extra-virgin olive oil

1 large onion, grated

3 celery stalks, strings discarded, grated

1 medium carrot, shredded

1 garlic clove, grated or minced

¼ to ½ teaspoon cayenne pepper

8 cups Quick Vegetable Stock
(page 12) or water
½ bunch kale or turnip greens
(about ½ pound or 225 grams),
stemmed, leaves shredded

1 teaspoon kosher salt,
plus additional
1 tablespoon minced fresh rosemary

Method

Cover the beans with tepid water by 2 inches and soak overnight. Drain.

In a Dutch oven or other large, heavy pot, heat the olive oil over medium-high heat. When the oil is shimmering, add the onion, celery, carrot, garlic, and cayenne to taste. Cook until the vegetables are soft, stirring occasionally, 5 to 10 minutes. Add the beans and 8 cups stock. Increase the heat to high and bring to a boil. Skim the surface of scum, reduce the heat to low, cover, and simmer gently until the beans are falling apart, about 2 hours.

Uncover, increase the heat to medium, and stir in the kale leaves and salt. Simmer briskly for 15 minutes to reduce the liquid slightly, stirring frequently to avoid scorching. Use a potato masher to mash some of the beans into a paste and stir to thicken the stew. Stir in the rosemary, taste, and adjust the seasonings. Serve hot with Dottie's Millet Loaf (page 228).

Store leftovers in the fridge for up to 5 days or freeze for up to 4 weeks.

Notes

- *Quick-soak method for beans: Cover the dried beans with water by 2 inches and bring to a boil over high heat. Boil for 2 minutes, remove from the heat, and cover for 1 hour. Drain and proceed with the recipe.*

- *2 cups of dried beans equals 6 cups cooked or canned beans. Drain and rinse canned beans well before continuing with the recipe.*

- *Brianne's Tester Tip: "To make grating the onion easier, cut the onion in half, leaving the root end intact. Peel and grate."*

Jackfruit Potpie

She wasn't hungry, but she was empty and, after a moment's indecision, gave in and let him buy her a meat pie from a pie man. The smell of it was so strong and good that she felt somewhat restored just from holding it. She nibbled the crust, felt the rich flood of juice and flavor in her mouth, and, closing her eyes, gave herself over to the pie.

"There, now." Mick, having long since finished his own pie, sat gazing benevolently at her. "Better, is it not?"

"Yes," she admitted. At least she could now think about the matter, rather than drowning in it. And while she hadn't been conscious of actually thinking at any time since leaving her rooms, evidently some back chamber of her mind had been turning things over.

Esmé and Nathaniel were dead. Harold, theoretical Duke of Pardloe, wasn't. That's what it came down to. She could do something about him. And she found that she was determined to do it.

—*A Fugitive Green,* chapter 14, "Notorious Bores"

GF(a) | DF | V | VGN

Jackfruit belongs to the same family as figs and durians. Grown across Southeast Asia, when ripe, it has a sweet, tangy flavor similar to mango. Unripe jackfruit has a neutral taste, and its stringy texture lends itself well as a substitute for pulled meats. It makes a delicious vegan potpie filling mixed with mushrooms, flavored with dark beer, and topped with store-bought frozen pastry.

Serves 4

Ingredients

1 can (17 ounces or 500 milliliters) green jackfruit in water, drained

2 tablespoons extra-virgin olive oil

1 large onion, julienned

1 teaspoon kosher salt, plus additional

1 teaspoon mustard powder

½ teaspoon freshly ground pepper, plus additional

¾ pound (340 grams) button mushrooms, cleaned, stems removed, and sliced

2 garlic cloves, minced or grated

¼ cup all-purpose flour

1 cup dark, low-hop vegan beer, like a chocolate porter or stout (see Note)

1 tablespoon Mushroom Catsup (page 307) or vegan Worcestershire sauce

3 cups Quick Vegetable Stock (page 12)

2 teaspoons fresh thyme

1 bay leaf

1 cup frozen green peas, thawed

½ recipe Vegan Short Crust Pastry (page 13), or 1 sheet vegan puff pastry, thawed

2 tablespoons plant-based milk, for brushing

Method

Move the rack to the upper-middle rung and heat the oven to 400°F. Slice through the core of the jackfruit pieces, cutting them into ¼-inch-thick slices.

In a large pan over medium heat, heat the oil until shimmering. Add the sliced jackfruit, onion, salt, mustard powder, and pepper. Sauté until the onions are soft and translucent and the jackfruit is softened, 5 to 7 minutes. Use the back of a fork or potato masher to break up and shred the jackfruit.

Stir in the mushrooms and cook until they've released their water, about 10 minutes. Add the garlic, stir until fragrant, about 30 seconds, then add the flour and cook for 2 minutes, stirring constantly.

Deglaze the pan with the beer and mushroom catsup, stirring well. Add the stock, thyme, and bay leaf, and bring to a boil. Reduce to a simmer, partially cover, and cook until the beef is tender and the gravy shiny and thick, about 1 hour. Season to

taste, remove from the heat, stir in the peas, and cool slightly while you prepare the pastry.

Arrange four 8-ounce (250-milliliter) ovenproof ramekins on a baking sheet lined with parchment paper, and divide the jackfruit mixture evenly among them.

Roll the pastry out to about an ⅛-inch thickness. With a SHARP knife, cut four squares large enough to generously cover the dishes. Lay the pastry tops across the filled ramekins, press gently to adhere to the edge of the dishes, then brush the tops with the milk. Use a sharp knife to poke a small hole in the top of each and bake until golden, 30 to 35 minutes.

Alternatively, pour the filling into a 9 x 9-inch baking pan and top with a single sheet of pastry. Brush with the milk and increase the baking time to 35 to 40 minutes.

Rest 5 to 10 minutes before serving with Salad Greens with Vinegar (page 205). Store leftovers in the fridge for up to 3 days.

Note

- *To make this recipe gluten-free, substitute brown rice flour for the all-purpose, whisking it in after the jackfruit and mushrooms have simmered and just before you remove the pan from the heat. Substitute vegan/gluten-free beer or vegan red wine for the beer, and ensure the puff pastry is also vegan/gluten-free.*

ASPARAGUS AND GRUYÈRE QUICHE

The feast, held in the ancient guildhall, was exactly as Grey had predicted: long, eye-glazingly boring, and featuring course after course of roast pork, boiled beef, gravied mutton, roasted pheasants, sliced ham, braised quail, grilled fish, eggs in aspic and in pies, shellfish in soup, in pastry, and on the half shell, plus sundry savories, syllabubs, and sweets, all served on a weight of silver plate sufficient to purchase a small country and washed down with gallons of wine, drunk in a succession of endless toasts in honor of everyone from Frederick, King of Prussia, King George of England, and Duke Ferdinand down to—Grey was sure—the kitchen cat, though by the time this point in the proceedings was reached, no one was paying sufficient attention as to be sure.

—*Lord John and the Brotherhood of the Blade*,
chapter 23, "The Rhineland"

GF | V

While the eggs in pies listed above would have been hard-boiled and encased in pastry, I've stretched the fictional food net wide to transform this dish into a fresh, spring-seasonal quiche. A divine way to showcase fresh, local asparagus.

Makes one 9-inch deep-dish quiche

Ingredients

¾ pound (340 grams) asparagus

1 tablespoon extra-virgin olive oil

1 small yellow onion, julienned

Kosher salt and freshly ground pepper

4 large eggs

1 cup light cream

3 ounces (90 grams) Gruyère, shredded (about 1 cup)

1 recipe Press-In Crust (page 17), parbaked as directed

1 teaspoon minced fresh thyme

Method

Move the rack to the middle rung and heat the oven to 375°F.

Gently bend each asparagus stalk, looking for its natural break point (usually somewhere just below the middle), and snap off the woody end of each one; reserve the ends for another use (see Notes). Cut the top halves into ½-inch pieces, leaving the tips whole or slicing them lengthwise in half if they're thick.

Heat the oil in a medium frying pan over medium heat. Add the asparagus, onion, and a pinch each of salt and pepper. Cook, stirring occasionally, until the onion is soft and translucent and the asparagus is bright green, 5 to 7 minutes. Remove from the heat.

In a bowl whisk together the eggs and cream. Season with 1 teaspoon salt and ½ teaspoon pepper.

Sprinkle half of the Gruyère on the parbaked crust. Spread the asparagus and onion mixture evenly on top, scatter the thyme, and pour the egg mixture over that. Sprinkle with the remaining cheese and bake for 20 to 25 minutes, or until the custard is set firm and the top is golden.

Cool on a rack for at least 15 minutes before serving warm or at room temperature with a fresh herb-filled salad tossed with Basic Salad Dressing from OK1.

Notes

- *If gluten is not bad news for you, you can also use the recipe for Vegan Short Crust Pastry (page 13) or my original Short Crust Pastry recipe in OK1.*
- *Use the woody stalks from the asparagus in a batch of Quick Vegetable Stock (page 12).*

STEEL-CUT OAT RISOTTO

He'd last spoken Greek in Ardsmuir prison, trading bits of Aristophanes with Lord John over a makeshift supper of porridge and sliced ham, the rations being short even in the governor's quarters, owing to a storm that had kept regular supplies from being delivered. There had been claret to wash it down with, though, and it had been a cordial evening. He'd taken care of the bits of business that needed to be done on behalf of the prisoners, and then they'd played chess, a long, drawn-out duel that had lasted nearly 'til dawn. Grey had won, at last, and had hesitated, glancing at the battered sofa in his office, clearly wondering whether he might offer Jamie the use of it, rather than send him back to the cells for an hour's sleep before the prisoners rose.

Jamie had appreciated the thought, but it wouldn't do, and he'd set his face impassively, bowed correctly, and bade Lord John good night, himself rapping on the doorframe to summon the dozing guard.

—*The Scottish Prisoner*, chapter 24, "Clishmaclaver"

GF | DF(a) | V | VGN(a)

During our 2013 boat trip exploring the Caledonian Canal from Inverness to Fort William, My Englishman and I ate this dish docked beside Invergarry Castle on Loch Oich, where it is said that Bonnie Prince Charles sheltered for a night after his defeat at Culloden. It's rib-sticking, Outlander-inspired, gluten-free, vegetarian comfort food at its most gratifying.

Serves 4

Ingredients

6 cups Quick Vegetable Stock
    (page 12)

½ ounce (15 grams) dried porcini or
    morel mushrooms

3 tablespoons extra-virgin olive oil, plus
    additional

2 large shallots, diced

½ pound (225 grams) button
    mushrooms (about 8 medium), sliced

1 cup steel-cut oats

1 clove garlic, grated or minced

1 fresh thyme sprig, plus additional
    leaves for garnish

½ cup white wine

2 ounces (60 grams) finely shredded
Parmesan cheese (about 1 cup)

Kosher salt and freshly ground pepper
to taste

Method

In a large pot, over medium-high heat, heat the stock to simmering. In a small bowl, soak the dried mushrooms for 15 minutes in enough hot stock to cover. Scoop out the mushrooms with a fork and chop finely. Strain and pour the soaking liquid back into the hot stock.

In a heavy saucepan or Dutch oven, heat the oil over medium heat. When the oil is shimmering, add the shallots and button mushrooms. Cook until soft and golden, 10 to 12 minutes. Add the oats, garlic, and thyme, stirring, until fragrant, about 1 minute. Add the chopped rehydrated mushrooms and deglaze the pan with the wine. Stir until almost dry.

Add the stock, one or two ladlefuls at a time, stirring constantly. The stock should bubble gently around the oats. When the liquid is almost completely absorbed, add another ladleful or two. Continue cooking, stirring and adding stock, until the oats are tender but still al dente, about 25 minutes. Reduce the heat if necessary to prevent scorching.

Remove the thyme sprig and stir in half of the Parmesan. Season to taste with salt and pepper. Serve immediately, garnishing with the remaining Parmesan and thyme leaves.

Refrigerate leftovers for up to 3 days.

Notes

- *To make this recipe dairy-free and vegan, substitute 1 to 2 tablespoons nutritional yeast for the Parmesan cheese. Garnish with chopped toasted nuts and thyme leaves.*

- *If using store-bought stock, ensure it is low-sodium. Regular packaged stock will result in a VERY SALTY risotto.*

- *Substitute barley or millet for the steel-cut oats for a bit of variety. Note that barley contains gluten.*

- *To include ham as in the excerpt, crisp several slices of pancetta in the hot pan before sautéing the shallots and mushrooms. Drain on a paper towel, crumble the pancetta, and use it to garnish the risotto just before serving.*

STUFFED VEGETABLE MARROW

This proved to be unnecessary, as the sound of the back door opening betokened Dottie's entrance, carrying an apronful of lumpy objects. These proved to be vegetable marrows from the kitchen garden, which cascaded over the floor in a bouncing flood of green and yellow as she let go the apron in order to leap at her father and embrace him.

"Papa!"

For an instant, Hal's face changed entirely, soft with love, and Grey was surprised and disconcerted to feel tears come to his own eyes. He turned away, blinking, and wandered over to the sideboard, meaning to give them a private moment.

—*Written in My Own Heart's Blood,* chapter 93,
"The House on Chestnut Street"

GF | DF | V | VGN

Mrs. Figg may very well have stuffed the marrows in Dottie's apron with a mixture similar to this one of beans, corn, rice, and nuts. This recipe takes some time; make the pilaf up to 2 days ahead to divide the labor, or use leftover Cuban Black Beans and Rice (page 194) as a ready-made filling.

Vegetable marrow is a common term in the UK for any smooth-skinned, tender summer squash, zucchini being the most commonly available in North America.

Serves 6 to 8

Ingredients

½ cup dried kidney beans (see Notes)

1 recipe Rice Pilaf (page 208)

4 vegetable marrows or zucchini, about 1 pound (450 grams) each (see Notes)

¼ cup extra-virgin olive oil

2 teaspoons kosher salt, plus additional

Freshly ground black pepper, to taste

2 fresh thyme sprigs

1 pound (450 grams) onions (about 3 medium), julienned

2 tablespoons sherry vinegar or red wine vinegar

½ cup canned (drained) or cooked corn kernels

½ bunch fresh cilantro or parsley, stems discarded, leaves chopped finely (about ½ cup)

½ teaspoon smoked paprika, or 1 teaspoon sweet paprika

¼ to ½ teaspoon cayenne pepper

Method

In a large bowl, cover the beans generously with water and soak on the counter overnight. Drain and rinse the beans, cover with water by 2 inches in a medium saucepan, and bring to a boil over medium-high heat. Cook them in a slow, rolling boil for 10 minutes, then reduce to medium-low heat, cover, and simmer until tender, about 50 minutes. Drain and combine with the rice pilaf in a large bowl.

Move the rack to the middle rung and heat the oven to 400°F. Line a baking sheet with parchment paper.

Cut the marrows in half lengthwise, and scoop the seeds and flesh out with a sharp-edged spoon, leaving a good ¼ inch of flesh along the inside of the skin. Chop the seeds and flesh roughly and set aside. Place the marrow "boats" on the prepared baking sheet and brush the insides with 1 tablespoon of the olive oil. Sprinkle with salt and black pepper and the leaves from the thyme sprigs. Roast until the tops are light golden and just starting to wrinkle or collapse, 20 to 30 minutes. Set aside to cool.

In a large frying pan, heat the remaining 3 tablespoons oil over medium-high heat until shimmering. Add the onions with 1 teaspoon salt and caramelize, stirring regularly, until they are very soft and deep golden brown, 30 to 35 minutes. Reduce the heat as the onions cook to prevent scorching. Add the chopped marrow seeds and flesh, increase the heat to medium-high, and cook until the marrow releases its water and the pan is dry again, another 25 to 30 minutes. Remove from the heat, stir in the vinegar, and add to the large bowl with the kidney beans and rice.

Stir in the corn, cilantro, paprika, and cayenne to taste. Taste and season with salt and black pepper. Use a large spoon to fill the marrow boats, mounding the stuffing into the squash. Roast until the stuffing is warmed through and the boats are golden, about 20 minutes.

Serve immediately with a plate of Fried Plantains (page 210) and a large green salad.

Notes

- Dried kidney beans must be boiled for 10 minutes to destroy toxins in the raw beans that cause stomach upset and indigestion.
- Use 1½ cups canned kidney beans, drained and rinsed well, in place of the dry.
- This recipe makes use of those often unwanted, homegrown zucchini that everyone with a garden seems desperate to get rid of come late summer.
- If you can only find smaller zucchini, scoop out the seeds with a teaspoon, leaving enough flesh to support the thinner skin once they've been roasted.

CUBAN BLACK BEANS AND RICE

"They call this *moros y cristianos*—that means 'moors and Christians'—the rice being Christians and the black beans Moors, d'you see?"

"Speaking of conception—and Quebec," Grey said, ignoring the food—though it smelled remarkably good, "your son by the Indian woman . . ."

Malcolm did glance at him then. He looked back at his plate, finished chewing, swallowed, and nodded, not looking at Grey.

"Yes. I did make inquiries—once I was mended. They told me the child had died."

—Besieged

GF | DF | V | VGN

It is believed the name *moros y cristianos* came about in the Middle Ages, when southern Spain was occupied by the Moors. It is a popular dish at the Spanish Feast of Saint George, commemorating the Reconquista of 1492, when Christians regained control of the Iberian Peninsula from Muslims.

Serves 6 to 8 as a main dish or 10 to 12 as a side

Ingredients

1 cup dried black beans, rinsed well

1 bay leaf

2 teaspoons kosher salt

2 tablespoons extra-virgin olive oil

1 medium white onion, julienned

1 medium red bell pepper, seeds and
    ribs removed, julienned

2 garlic cloves, minced or grated

1 teaspoon ground cumin

½ cup dry white wine

2 cups long-grain white rice

½ cup chopped fresh cilantro
    or parsley

1 tablespoon minced fresh oregano

Method

In a large saucepan, cover the beans and bay leaf generously with water. Bring to a boil over medium-high heat and reduce to a simmer. Partially cover and simmer gently until tender, 60 to 75 minutes, adding more water if necessary to keep the beans well covered. Remove from the heat, drain, and discard the bay leaf. Season the beans with 1 teaspoon of the salt.

Heat the olive oil in a 6- to 8-quart pot or Dutch oven over medium heat. When the oil is shimmering, add the onion, bell pepper, garlic, cumin, and remaining 1 teaspoon salt. Cook, stirring, until softened, about 10 minutes. Raise the heat to high, add the wine, and reduce by half, about 2 minutes. Add the rice and cook, stirring to coat, for about 1 minute. Add the beans, stir well, and add 4 cups tepid water. Bring to a boil over medium-high heat, cover, and reduce the heat to low. Simmer, undisturbed, until the water is absorbed and the rice and beans are both tender throughout, 20 to 25 minutes.

Season to taste and toss with the cilantro and oregano, gently fluffing the rice.

Serve hot with a large green salad and the Vegetable Stew from OK1. Store in the fridge for up to 3 days.

Chapter 12

❧

Side Dishes

Broccoli Sallet with Radishes and Vinegar

Tobias Quinn's Colcannon

Corn Bread and Salt Pork Stuffing

Salad Greens with Vinegar

Rice Pilaf

Fried Plantains

John Grey's Yorkshire Pudding

Beans Baked with Bacon and Onion

Stewed Pears

Sautéed Turnip Greens

BROCCOLI SALLET
WITH RADISHES AND VINEGAR

Quarry looked him over and shook his head. "Too thin by half! Have to feed you up, I suppose." This assessment was followed by Quarry's ordering—without consulting him—thick soup, game pie, fried trout with grapes, lamb with a quince preserve and roast potatoes, and a broccoli sallet with radishes and vinegar, the whole to be followed by a jelly trifle.

"I can't eat a quarter of that, Harry," Grey protested. "I'll burst."

Quarry ignored this, waving a hand to urge the waiter to ladle more soup into Grey's bowl. "You need sustenance," he said, "from what I hear."

Grey looked askance at him over his half-raised spoon. "What you hear? What do you hear, may I ask?"

Quarry's craggily handsome face adopted the look that he normally wore when intending to be discreet, the fine white scar across his cheek pulling down the eye on that side in a knowing leer.

—*Lord John and the Haunted Soldier*

GF | DF(a) | V | VGN(a)

A fresh-tasting, delicate salad that brings the taste of spring to your lips, even in the depths of winter. Its simplicity belies a flavor made rich with Parmesan cheese and spiked with radish. Serve with Herb-Roasted Salmon (page 169) for an elegant meal without a lot of work.

Serves 6

Ingredients

2 or 3 large broccoli stalks (about 1 pound or 450 grams), florets reserved for another use (see Notes)

2 celery stalks

3 medium radishes, trimmed

¼ cup chopped fresh parsley

1½ ounces (45 grams) Pecorino Romano or Parmesan cheese, shaved into strips with a vegetable peeler (about ½ cup)

2 tablespoons extra-virgin olive oil

1 tablespoon red wine vinegar or
    fresh lemon juice

Kosher salt and freshly ground pepper
    to taste

Method

Use a vegetable peeler to peel the tough outer layer of the broccoli stalks. With a knife, trim the stalks' rough end, about ½ inch. Use a mandoline to slice the remaining stalks paper-thin on the diagonal. Use the peeler to peel the strings from the back of the celery and slice it on the diagonal about ⅛ inch thick using the mandoline. Slice the radishes paper-thin on the mandoline.

In a large bowl, toss together the broccoli, celery, radishes, parsley, and cheese. In a small bowl, whisk together the olive oil and vinegar; toss with the salad. Season to taste with salt and pepper, and toss again before serving.

Notes

- *To make this salad dairy-free and vegan, replace the cheese with toasted, sliced almonds.*
- *If you don't have a mandoline, it is worth buying even a very inexpensive one to make this salad. It is very difficult to slice the vegetables thinly enough by hand.*
- *Use the broccoli florets to make the Broccoli Salad from OK1.*

Tobias Quinn's Colcannon

He'd given his instructions to Tom Byrd on the way back from Glastuig, and the valet had managed accordingly, not packing up all the belongings, as Jamie wished to cause no more stir than there was already, but acquiring what he could for an instant journey.

They found Tom Byrd waiting impatiently by the road with horses, a little way from the ordinary. Tom gave both men a narrow look, glancing from face to face, but said nothing. He had procured a cabbage, and a few potatoes, which he modestly displayed.

"That'll do us fine for a supper," Quinn said, patting Tom approvingly on the shoulder. He looked to the sky. "It's going to rain again," he said in resigned tones. "We'd best find a spot and cook it while we can."

—*The Scottish Prisoner*, chapter 25, "Escape from Athlone"

GF | DF(a) | V | VGN(a)

The word *colcannon* is from the Irish Gaelic *cal ceannann*, meaning "white-headed cabbage." This traditional Irish dish of floury potatoes mashed with cabbage or kale was originally associated with Halloween. Charms were mixed into the colcannon and used to tell the marital future of the diners. A button for a man or a thimble for a woman meant they would remain single for the coming year. A ring foretold marriage, and a coin wealth.

Some women filled their socks with colcannon and hung them from the handle of the front door to attract men, and the first through the door, it was believed, would be her future husband.

Serves 6

Ingredients

3 pounds (1.4 kilograms) russet potatoes (about 6 medium), peeled and quartered

Kosher salt

2 cups shredded cabbage (about ¼ large head) or kale, packed

¾ cup (1½ sticks) butter

1 cup whole milk

4 scallions (white and light green parts),
   thinly sliced

Freshly ground pepper
Chopped fresh parsley, for garnish

Method

Fill a large saucepan with 1 inch of cold water. Add the potatoes and a pinch of salt, cover, and bring to a boil over medium-high heat. Reduce to medium-low and simmer until the potatoes are cooked but not mushy, 15 to 20 minutes.

In a medium saucepan, bring 4 cups water to a boil over high heat. Add the cabbage and keep at a low boil until the cabbage has wilted and is just tender, 3 to 5 minutes, depending on how thinly shredded it is. Do not overcook. Drain, roll in a clean dish towel, and squeeze the excess moisture out, being careful not to burn your hands. Return it to the saucepan and top it with ¼ cup (½ stick) of the butter. Cover to keep warm.

Drain the potatoes and return them to their pan, tossing them briefly to dissipate any excess moisture. Add the milk, ¼ cup (½ stick) of the butter, and the scallions to the saucepan. Warm the milk to steaming, but do not allow it to boil. Use a masher or fork to thoroughly mash the potatoes and combine the mixture. Stir in the cabbage and season with salt and pepper.

To serve, make a well in the center of the colcannon and top it with the remaining ¼ cup (½ stick) butter. Garnish with the chopped parsley. Makes a delicious accompaniment to Roast Beef for a Wedding Feast from OK1.

Store leftovers in the refrigerator for up to 3 days.

Notes

- *To make this recipe dairy-free and vegan, substitute Vegan Cream (page 20) or plant-based milk for the whole milk, and vegan margarine or extra-virgin olive oil for the butter.*

- *Substitute light cream for the milk for richer fare.*

- *Make the leftovers into pancakes by stirring in an egg and enough flour to bind the mixture. Fry in a bit of oil over medium-high heat until crisp on both sides. Makes a delicious, frugal, and hearty breakfast topped with a poached egg.*

CORN BREAD AND SALT PORK STUFFING

The next day, Jamie was called to the commandant's house and didn't come back until after dark.

A man was singing by one of the courtyard fires near St. Clair's quarters, and I was sitting on an empty salt-pork barrel listening, when I saw Jamie pass by on the far side of the fire, heading for our barracks. I rose quickly and caught him up.

"Come away," he said softly, and led me toward the commandant's garden. There was no echo of our last encounter in this garden, though I was terribly aware of his body, of the tension in it and the beating of his heart. Bad news, then.

—An Echo in the Bone, chapter 52, "Conflagration"

GF(a) | DF(a) | V(a) | VGN(a)

Originally created as an Outlander-themed dish for American Thanksgiving, this delicious mix of golden corn bread, crisp bits of pork, and savory vegetables is welcome around any table with a lot of mouths to feed.

The recipe for Corn Bread (page 232) uses the fat rendered from the salt pork in this recipe. If you're short on time or holiday energy, substitute a 1½- to 2-pound loaf of store-bought corn bread to make life easier.

Serves 8

Ingredients

1 pound (450 grams) salt pork, cut into ½-inch cubes

¼ cup (½ stick) butter, plus additional for greasing

¼ cup extra-virgin olive oil

1 large onion, julienned

¾ pound (340 grams) mushrooms, sliced

2 medium carrots or parsnips, grated

3 medium celery stalks, diced

2 garlic cloves, grated or minced

1 tablespoon minced fresh thyme

1 tablespoon minced fresh rosemary

Kosher salt and freshly ground pepper

1 recipe Corn Bread (page 232)

½ cup dried cranberries

2 tablespoons minced fresh sage

¼ cup chopped fresh parsley

2 eggs, lightly beaten

1½ cups Quick Vegetable Stock (page 12) or chicken stock

Method

Place the salt pork in a cold, large cast-iron skillet over medium heat. Cover with a lid and cook until the fat is rendered, stirring very occasionally, 20 to 30 minutes. Remove the lid and cook until the pork is crisp. Scoop the pork onto a plate using a slotted spoon and set aside ¼ cup of the rendered fat for the corn bread, discarding or saving the rest for another purpose. Clean the pan.

In the clean pan, heat the butter and olive oil over medium heat until bubbling. Add the onion, mushrooms, carrots, celery, garlic, thyme, rosemary, 1 teaspoon salt, and ½ teaspoon pepper. Cook, stirring frequently, until the vegetables are soft and golden, 12 to 15 minutes.

Move the rack to the middle rung and heat the oven to 350°F. Grease a 9 x 13-inch baking dish with butter.

Cut the corn bread into bite-size cubes and combine it in a large bowl with the salt pork, vegetables, dried cranberries, sage, and parsley. Taste and adjust the seasonings.

Whisk together the beaten eggs and stock. Pour it over the corn-bread mixture in the bowl and stir to combine. Pour everything into the prepared baking dish, cover with aluminum foil, and bake for 30 minutes. Uncover and cook until golden and crisp on top, about 30 more minutes.

Serve hot with William's Spatchcocked Turkey (page 101) as an alternative to the bread salad. Store leftovers in the fridge for up to 5 days.

Notes

- *To make this recipe gluten-free, use gluten-free corn bread.*
- *To make this recipe dairy-free, eliminate the butter and increase the olive oil to ½ cup.*
- *To make this stuffing vegan, omit the salt pork and the butter as above. Replace the eggs with an egg substitute for baking (see Pantry Notes, page 4).*
- *If the core of a parsnip is particularly large and woody, remove it with a knife and discard before grating.*
- *Prepare this ahead up to mixing the cubed corn bread with the veggies, herbs, and cranberries in a bowl and store in the fridge for up to 2 days. Finish as instructed.*

SALAD GREENS WITH VINEGAR

"What's brought you to London, sir?" Harry asked von Namtzen over the salad. It was plainly meant merely to break the digestive silence caused by the salmagundi, but the Hanoverian's face became shadowed, and he looked down into the plate of greens and vinegar.

"I am purchasing some properties for the captain," Mr. Frobisher put in hurriedly, with a glance at von Namtzen. "Papers to sign, you know . . ." He waved a hand, indicating vast reams of legal requirement.

Grey looked curiously at von Namtzen—who was not only captain of his own regiment but the Graf von Erdberg, as well. He knew perfectly well that the graf had a man of business in England; all wealthy foreigners did, and he had in fact met von Namtzen's property agent once.

Whether von Namtzen had noticed his curiosity or merely felt that more explanation was necessary, he raised his head and expelled an explosive breath.

"My wife died," he said, and paused to swallow. "Last month. I—my sister is in London." Another swallow. "I have brought the . . . my children . . . to her."

"Oh, my dear sir," said Harry, putting a hand on von Namtzen's arm and speaking with the deepest sympathy. "I am so sorry."

—*The Scottish Prisoner,* chapter 9, "Eros Rising"

GF | DF(a) | V(a)

An eighteenth-century Caesar salad made with hard-boiled egg yolks, making it safe for pregnant women and the immune-compromised in the twenty-first century. Serve it with Corn Bread (page 232) and Rosamund's Pulled Pork with Devil's Apple BBQ Sauce from OK1 for an Outlander-inspired picnic.

Serves 6

Ingredients

2 large eggs

3 tinned anchovies, drained and minced

2 teaspoons Dijon mustard

1 garlic clove, grated or minced

½ teaspoon kosher salt,
    plus additional

¼ teaspoon freshly ground pepper,
plus additional
¼ cup extra-virgin olive oil
¼ cup vegetable oil
1 to 2 tablespoons white wine vinegar
or fresh lemon juice

1 large head romaine lettuce
2 ounces Parmesan cheese, grated
(about ½ cup)

Method

Prepare an ice bath by filling a large bowl with cold water and a tray of ice cubes.

In a small pot, cover the eggs with cold water by 1 inch. Bring to a boil over high heat, remove from the heat, cover, and rest for 10 minutes. Pour off the water, roll the eggs around in the pan to crack them slightly (this will make peeling easier), and submerge them in the ice bath to cool.

Peel the cooled eggs, slice them in half lengthwise, and remove the yolks. Slice the whites and set aside. In a medium bowl, mash the egg yolks with 1 teaspoon water until smooth. Whisk in the anchovies, mustard, garlic, salt, and pepper. Combine the two oils and pour a slow, steady stream into the bowl while whisking constantly. When the oil is incorporated, whisk in 1 tablespoon vinegar. Taste and adjust the seasonings and vinegar as needed. Cover and refrigerate.

Tear the lettuce into bite-size pieces and season with a pinch each of salt and pepper. Toss with the cheese and sliced egg whites. Add 2 tablespoons dressing to the salad and toss well. Add more dressing if desired.

Serve with Fish Fried in Batter with Tartar Sauce (page 171) for an indulgent weekend lunch or dinner. Store the leftover dressing for up to 5 days in the refrigerator.

Notes

- *To make this salad dairy-free, replace the Parmesan cheese with toasted nuts.*
- *To make this salad vegetarian, replace the anchovies with 1 tablespoon finely chopped capers.*

Rice Pilaf

Ian lay down with a sack of rice under his head for a pillow. It was hard, but he liked the whisper of the small grains when he turned his head and the faint starched smell of it. Rollo rooted under the plaid with his snout, snorting as he worked his way close against Ian's body, ending with his nose cozily buried in Ian's armpit. Ian scratched the dog's ears gently, then lay back, watching the stars.

—An Echo in the Bone, chapter 13, "Unrest"

GF | DF | V | VGN

A versatile side dish, this recipe is just a starting point for creating pilafs using different spices, dried fruits, and nuts to pair with specific mains, such as a pilaf with crushed fennel seeds, golden raisins, and pine nuts for Coq au Vin (page 98) or cumin, dried apricot, and almond pilaf alongside Lamb Cutlets with Spinach (page 138).

Serves 6

Ingredients

1 tablespoon extra-virgin olive oil

1 large shallot, diced

1 small garlic clove, grated or minced

1 teaspoon brown mustard seeds

1½ cups long-grain rice, rinsed (see Notes)

1 teaspoon kosher salt

¼ cup raisins

2¾ cups Quick Vegetable Stock (page 12) or water

¼ cup lightly toasted chopped nuts, such as hazelnuts, almonds, pine nuts, or cashews

Method

In a small saucepan, heat the olive oil over medium-high heat. Add the shallot and cook until translucent, stirring constantly, 2 to 3 minutes. Add the garlic and mustard seeds, stirring constantly, until the seeds start to pop, about 1 minute. Pour in the rice and salt. Stir until every grain is coated in oil, about another minute. Add the raisins and stock, bring to a boil, reduce the heat to low, stir one last time, cover, and cook until tender, 30 to 35 minutes.

Fluff the rice with a fork, stir in the nuts, re-cover, and rest for 5 minutes. Serve hot or use in Stuffed Vegetable Marrow (page 191). Store leftovers in the refrigerator for up to 3 days.

Notes

- *Basmati is my favorite, but any long-grain rice will do. I often make a mix of 1 cup white basmati and ½ cup brown basmati, which keeps the pilaf light tasting with just a hint of nuttiness. If you decide to mix in brown, increase the cooking time to 45 to 50 minutes.*
- *Millet also makes a delicious pilaf. Substitute the same amount of millet for the rice, and continue with the recipe.*
- *Stock gives your weeknight pilaf special-occasion flavor. Use low-sodium packaged stock if you don't have homemade.*

FRIED PLANTAINS

"You want this?" Accompong waved a hand at Rodrigo. "What for? He's no good to you surely? Unless you want to take him to bed—he won't say no to you!"

Everyone thought that very funny; the clearing rocked with laughter. Grey waited it out. From the corner of his eye, he saw the girl Azeel watching him with something like a fearful hope in her eyes.

"He is under my protection," he repeated. "Yes, I want him." Accompong nodded and took a deep breath, sniffing appreciatively at the mingled scents of cassava porridge, fried plantain, and frying pig meat.

"Sit down, Colonel," he said, "and eat with me."

—A Plague of Zombies

The savory fritters for Manioc and Red Beans with Fried Plantain from OK1 called for green plantains. This recipe uses ripe, yellow plantains to make a sweet, fried snack with caramelized edges and creamy centers; it is equally delicious served beside Ham Steaks with Raisin and Mustard Sauce (page 120) or Cuban Black Beans and Rice (page 194).

Serves 6 as a snack or side dish

Ingredients

4 large ripe, yellow plantains
Vegetable oil, for frying

Kosher salt to taste

Method

With the point of a sharp knife, score the skin of the plantains lengthwise. Peel and discard the skins. Slice the plantains into ½-inch-thick slices on a sharp diagonal.

Fill a heavy skillet or saucepan with ½ inch of vegetable oil. Heat over medium-high heat until shimmering but not smoking. Fry the plantains, in batches to avoid overcrowding the pan, to a deep golden brown, 3 to 4 minutes per side, reducing the heat to medium, if necessary, to prevent them from burning.

Transfer to paper towels to drain, and season with salt. Repeat with the remaining plantains.

Serve hot.

John Grey's Yorkshire Pudding

And in the late summer dusk of the first day, Manoke had wiped his fingers after eating, stood up, casually untied his breechclout, and let it fall. Then waited, grinning, while Grey fought his way out of shirt and breeches.

They'd swum in the river to refresh themselves before eating; the Indian was clean, his skin no longer greasy. And yet he seemed to taste of wild game, the rich, uneasy tang of venison. Grey had wondered whether it was the man's race that was responsible or only his diet?

"What do I taste like?" he'd asked, out of curiosity. Manoke, absorbed in his business, had said something that might have been "cock" but might equally have been some expression of mild disgust, so Grey thought better of pursuing this line of inquiry. Besides, if he did taste of beef and biscuit or Yorkshire pudding, would the Indian recognize that? For that matter, did he really want to know, if he did? He did not, he decided, and they enjoyed the rest of the evening without benefit of conversation.

—The Custom of the Army

DF | V

Dripping puddings were originally cooked under the roast, to catch the fat dripping before they smoked on the hot coals below. The simple dough of flour, eggs, and water was later renamed Yorkshire pudding by Hannah Glasse in *The Art of Cookery Made Plain and Easy,* published in London, 1747.

Makes 12 individual puddings or 1 large

Ingredients

1¾ cups all-purpose flour

1 teaspoon kosher salt

4 large eggs, lightly beaten

½ cup whole milk

3 tablespoons beef dripping or
    vegetable oil

Method

Move the rack to the upper-middle rung and heat the oven to 450°F.

In a medium bowl, whisk together the flour and the salt. Make a well in the flour

and add the beaten eggs and milk. Whisk until smooth, add ⅔ cup water, and whisk again to make a batter the consistency of whipping cream. Cover and set aside at room temperature for 30 minutes.

Divide the beef dripping among a 12-hole muffin tin (¾ teaspoon per cup) or pour into a 13 x 9-inch baking pan. Put it in the oven and heat the dripping until almost smoking, about 10 minutes.

Remove the tin from the oven and, working quickly, pour in the batter. If the dripping doesn't sizzle when you add the first spoonful, put the tin back into the oven for another few minutes.

Cook the puddings in the oven until well risen and golden, 18 to 25 minutes (or up to 30 minutes for a large single pudding). DO NOT OPEN THE DOOR until you're sure they're ready—otherwise they will sink.

Serve immediately, cutting a large, single pudding into slices.

Notes

- *To make these dairy-free, substitute almond, soy, or rice milk for the whole milk.*
- *To make the British childhood favorite toad-in-the-hole, add browned sausages to the batter in the hot dripping and bake as directed.*
- *Stuff any leftovers with the filling from Benedicta's Steak and Mushroom Pie (page 93) and enjoy this Grey-themed snack hot or cold any time of day.*

Beans Baked with Bacon and Onion

Harry gave the window a look of deep suspicion and shook his head. "Not a chance. Steward!"

Mr. Bodley was already tottering toward them under the weight of a tea tray laden with seedcake, sponge cake, strawberry jam, marmalade, hot buttered crumpets in a basket wrapped in white linen, scones, clotted cream, almond biscuits, sardines on toast, a pot of beans baked with bacon and onion, a plate of sliced ham with gherkins, a bottle of brandy with two glasses, and—perhaps as an afterthought—a steaming teapot with two china cups and saucers alongside.

"Ah!" said Harry, looking happier. "I see you expected me."

Grey smiled. If not on campaign or called away by duty, Harry Quarry invariably entered the Beefsteak at four-thirty on a Wednesday.

—*An Echo in the Bone,* chapter 32, "A Flurry of Suspicion"

GF | DF | V(a) | VGN(a)

Pilgrims at Plymouth learned to make baked beans from Native Americans. As recipes developed, molasses was added to local baked bean recipes in New England, creating what we now know as Boston baked beans. Baked beans were traditionally cooked on Saturday and left in the oven overnight. The beans were still hot the next day, allowing people to indulge in a hot meal while still observing Sunday as the Sabbath.

I suspect Lord John would have run into these sweet, syrupy beans during his travels to the colonies, and assume he made a special request of the Beefsteak kitchen.

Serves 6 as a side

Ingredients

1 pound (450 grams) dried white beans, such as navy or Great Northern

¼ cup molasses (not blackstrap) or black treacle

¼ cup dark brown sugar, lightly packed

1 tablespoon mustard powder

¼ teaspoon freshly ground pepper, plus additional

6 ounces (170 grams) bacon or salt pork, chopped roughly

1 small onion, chopped

Kosher salt to taste

Method

Pour the beans into a large bowl and cover generously with water. Soak overnight on the counter.

Drain the beans and add them to a Dutch oven or large, ovenproof pot. Cover with water by 1 inch and bring to a boil. Reduce to a simmer, cover, and cook until just tender, 60 to 75 minutes.

Move the rack to the lower rung and heat the oven to 250°F. In a small bowl, combine the molasses, brown sugar, mustard powder, pepper, and ½ cup hot water.

Drain the beans and put them back in the pot. Add the bacon and onion to the pot, burying them under the beans. Pour the molasses mixture over the beans and stir to combine. Pour in just enough water to cover the beans, put on the lid, and bake in the oven until soft and tender, about 6 hours, checking occasionally and adding a little extra water to keep the beans just covered if necessary.

Increase the heat to 350°F, uncover the pot, and cook for another 30 minutes to thicken the sauce. Remove from the oven and season to taste with salt and pepper.

Serve hot with the Heart of Palm Frittata (page 28) for a hearty meal with lots of leftovers. Store the leftover beans in the fridge for up to 5 days.

Notes

* *To make the beans vegan, omit the bacon and mix 2 tablespoons extra-virgin olive oil into the molasses mixture before pouring it over the beans.*

* *Quick-soak method for the beans: Cover the dried beans with water by 2 inches and bring to a boil over high heat. Boil for 2 minutes, remove from the heat, and cover for 1 hour. Drain and proceed with the recipe.*

* *To cook this in a slow cooker, combine the cooked beans with the bacon and onion. Stir in the molasses mixture, pour in just enough water to cover, and cook on low for 8 hours or on high for 4 to 5 hours.*

STEWED PEARS

"I'll go and order some breakfast for William, shall I?" he said. "Take him into the parlor, why don't you, my dear, and give him a dish of tea."

"Tea," Willie breathed, his face assuming the beatific air of one beholding—or being told about—some prodigious miracle. "I haven't had tea in weeks. Months!"

Grey went out to the cookhouse, this standing at a little distance behind the house proper so that the latter should not be destroyed when—not if—something caught fire and burned the cookhouse to the ground. Appetizing smells of fried meat and stewed fruit and fresh bread floated out of this ramshackle structure.

—An Echo in the Bone, chapter 73,
"One Ewe Lamb Returns to the Fold"

GF | DF | V | VGN

Popular since antiquity, the only varieties of pears available prior to the sixteenth century were those that required cooking. This recipe for stewed pears is inspired by a Dutch recipe for *stoofperen,* traditionally served as a side dish for game, such as The Old Fox's Roast Haunch of Venison (page 155).

The specific variety of stewing pear used by the Dutch is not available outside Europe, so this recipe has been tweaked to work with widely available varieties, such as Bosc and Concorde, that remain firm when ripe.

Serves 6

Ingredients

2 pounds (900 grams) firm pears, such as Bosc or Concorde (about 4 medium)

1 cup red wine

1 cinnamon stick

2 tablespoons sugar or honey

1 teaspoon vanilla extract

Method

Peel the pears. Cut them in quarters lengthwise and remove the cores.

In a large pot, combine the pears, wine, cinnamon, and sugar. Cover with cold water and cook over low heat until very tender but not falling apart, 1½ to 2 hours, stirring occasionally.

With a slotted spoon transfer the pears to a medium bowl. Bring the syrup to a boil over high heat and boil until reduced by half, about 10 minutes. Remove from the heat, stir in the vanilla, and cool for 15 minutes before pouring the syrup over the pears in the bowl.

Serve warm as a side dish for meat and game or chilled as a dessert with whipped cream or sweetened Vegan Cream (page 20). Store in the fridge for up to a week.

Sautéed Turnip Greens

Siverly had made it into the ornamental wood; Grey couldn't see the man, but he heard the snap and crunch of a body forcing its way through undergrowth in a hurry. Follow, or go round?

He hesitated for no more than an instant, then ran to the left. The man must be heading for the stables; he could cut him off.

He vaguely saw servants in the distance, pointing at him and shouting, but paid them no mind. He'd lost his hat, but that didn't matter, either. He galloped through the kitchen garden, leaping a basket of turnip greens set dead in the middle of the walk, and dodging the openmouthed cook who'd set it there.

—The Scottish Prisoner, chapter 23, "Plan B"

GF | DF | V | VGN

First mentioned in print in 1699's *A Discourse on Salads* by John Evelyn, one of Britain's first advocates for a meatless diet, turnip greens have long been celebrated for their fresh taste and medicinal benefits. In her *Cook and Housekeeper's Complete and Universal Dictionary* from 1823, Mary Eaton says of the green shoots that pop up from last year's turnips, "They make very nice sweet greens, and are esteemed great purifiers of the blood and juices."

Serves 6

Ingredients

2 tablespoons extra-virgin olive oil or bacon grease

2 large shallots, minced

2 garlic cloves, grated or minced

3 or 4 large bunches turnip greens (about 2 pounds or 900 grams), stems removed and discarded, leaves chopped

1 teaspoon kosher salt, plus additional

½ teaspoon crushed red pepper flakes

1 cup Quick Vegetable Stock (page 12) or chicken stock

1 tablespoon red wine vinegar

Method

In a large pan, heat the oil over medium heat. When the oil is shimmering, add the shallots and garlic. Cook, stirring occasionally, until the aromatics are softened and starting to brown, about a minute. Add the greens, salt, and red pepper flakes, and sauté, stirring constantly, until wilted and bright green, about 2 minutes. Stir in the stock, increase the heat to medium-high, and cook until the greens are tender, 10 to 15 minutes. Stir in the vinegar and season with salt to taste.

Serve immediately with Chicken and Cornmeal Stew (page 113) for a Southern-inspired feast.

Note

- *Mustard, beet, and other vegetable greens can be cooked in the same way. Adjust the timing based on the green, cooking them just until they are tender.*

Chapter 13

❧

Breads and Baking

German Brötchen

Cuban Flauta

Dottie's Millet Loaf

Corn Bread

Cassava Bread

Scones with Preserved Lemon

Rumm's Tea Cakes

Seed Cake

German Brötchen

He was aware that some of the English junior officers considered this garment mildly contemptible, but then, they hadn't been shot at yet. Grey had, repeatedly. It wouldn't save him from close fire, but the fact was that most of the French muskets had a very short range, and thus a good many musket balls were near spent by the time they reached a target. You could see them, sometimes, sailing almost lazily through the air, like bumblebees.

Coats, epaulets, gorget, laced hat . . . roll. Tom, always prepared, had thrust a crusty German roll into his hand, thickly buttered, Grey crammed the last of it into his mouth, shook crumbs from his lapels, and washed it down with coffee—one of the other orderlies had brewed some over a spirit lamp, the smell of it bracing.

—Lord John and the Brotherhood of the Blade,
chapter 29, "Dawn of Battle"

DF | V | VGN(a)

Ubiquitous across Germany, these crusty rolls have a light, airy interior that makes them popular for breakfast.

Makes 12 rolls

Ingredients

3¾ cups bread flour or all-purpose flour, plus additional for dusting

2½ teaspoons instant yeast

1½ teaspoons kosher salt

1½ teaspoons sugar

2 large egg whites

½ teaspoon vegetable oil, for the bowl

Method

In the bowl of a stand mixer, combine the flour, yeast, salt, and sugar. Mix thoroughly, using the paddle attachment on low speed. Add 1 of the egg whites to a measuring cup and top up with enough tepid water to make 1½ cups liquid in total. Whisk lightly with a fork, then add to the dry ingredients and increase the mixer speed to medium-low. When the mixture has come together in a rough ball, change to the dough hook attachment and knead on medium-low until the dough is soft, slightly tacky, and elastic, about 6 minutes.

Alternatively, mix the dough by hand in a large bowl and knead on a lightly floured counter for 8 to 10 minutes.

Rest the dough on the counter, covered, for 15 minutes. Use your fingertips to press and pull the dough into a rough 8 x 10-inch rectangle. Using a bench scraper if the dough sticks, fold the long end in thirds, like a letter. Rotate the dough one quarter turn, and fold the short ends in thirds as well, making a rough square. Place the dough seam side down, cover, and rest for 15 minutes. Repeat the pressing out, folding, and resting sequence two more times. Place the dough in a lightly oiled bowl, cover, and let rise in a warm, draft-free place until doubled in size, about 60 minutes.

Divide the dough into twelve equal pieces and cover with plastic wrap or a clean dishcloth. On a lightly floured counter, working with one piece of dough at a time, draw the edges of the dough into the center, making a ball. Turn the ball over and roll it under your palm in a tight circle on the counter five or six times, to tighten the surface tension of the dough and ensure an even rise. Rock the dough under your palm one last time to give it an oblong shape. Repeat with the remaining pieces of dough. Arrange on a parchment-lined baking sheet, cover with plastic, and let rise on the counter until nearly doubled, 45 to 60 minutes.

Move the racks to the lower and middle rungs and heat the oven to 450°F. Place an old metal baking pan on the bottom shelf to serve as a steam pan. In a small bowl whisk the remaining egg white with 1 teaspoon water.

Brush the proofed buns gently, but thoroughly, with the egg wash. Use a sharp knife to slash each bun vertically down the middle about ¼ inch deep. Pour 1 cup hot water into the steam pan before closing the oven door and bake the buns until dark golden, 22 to 25 minutes. Turn the oven off, remove the steam pan, prop open the door slightly, and leave the buns to cool for 10 minutes before removing them to a cooling rack.

Best eaten the same day. Keep in a paper bag for up to 2 days after baking and warm gently in the oven before serving.

Note

- *To make these rolls vegan, eliminate the egg whites. Use 1½ cups tepid water in the dough, and brush the proofed buns with water before baking.*

Cuban Flauta

"No!" he said aloud, clenching his fists. "No, that's bloody not going to happen."

"What's not going to happen?" Tom inquired, backing into the room with a small wheeled table festooned with edibles. "There's a lot of beer, me lord. You could bathe in it, should the fancy take you."

"Don't tempt me." He closed his eyes briefly and took several deep breaths. "Thank you, Tom."

Plainly, he couldn't do anything tonight, and no matter what he did in the morning, he'd do it better if he had food and rest.

Hungry as he'd been half an hour before, his appetite seemed now to have deserted him. He sat down, though, and forced himself to eat. There were small patties of some kind of blood sausage, made with onions and rice, a hard cheese, the light, thin-crusted Cuban bread—he thought he'd heard someone call it a *flauta,* could that be right? Pickled vegetables of some kind. Beer. More beer.

—Besieged

DF(a) | V | VGN(a)

The first American bakery to produce Cuban bread was most likely La Joven Francesca Bakery, established in a thriving Cuban-Spanish-Italian community in Tampa in 1896. Known as *pan cubano,* it is the only choice for an authentic Cuban sandwich.

A traditional loaf of Cuban bread is rectangular in shape, rather than rounded like French or Italian loaves, and about 3 feet long. This recipe makes two shorter loaves instead, so it is easier getting them in and out of our home ovens.

Makes 2 small loaves

Ingredients

2 cups bread flour

2 cups all-purpose flour, plus more
 for dusting

1 tablespoon instant yeast

2 teaspoons sugar

1 teaspoon kosher salt

1 tablespoon lard or butter (see Notes)

½ teaspoon vegetable oil, for the bowl

Method

In the bowl of a stand mixer fitted with the paddle attachment, combine the flours, yeast, sugar, and salt on low speed. With the machine running, break up the lard into smaller pieces with your hands and add to the bowl. Add 1⅔ cups warm water and increase the mixer speed to medium-low. When the mixture has come together into a rough ball, change to the dough hook attachment and knead on medium-low until the dough is soft and very tacky, 7 to 8 minutes.

Alternatively, mix the dough by hand in a large bowl and knead on a lightly floured counter for 10 minutes.

Place the dough in a lightly oiled bowl, cover, and set aside to rise in a warm, draft-free place until doubled in size, about 60 minutes.

Divide the dough into two equal pieces. On a piece of baking-sheet-size parchment and using lightly floured fingertips, press the first piece out into a rectangle roughly 6 x 8 inches. Fold the long edge in thirds, like a letter. Pinch the seam and ends closed and turn the dough over so the seam is on the bottom. Rock the loaf under both palms to settle and shape it into an oblong about 3 inches wide. Repeat with the second piece of dough. Move the dough and the parchment to a baking sheet, cover with plastic, and let rise on the counter until nearly doubled, 45 to 60 minutes.

Move the rack to the middle rung and heat the oven to 450°F.

Use a sharp knife to slash each loaf about ¼ inch deep lengthwise down the middle. Brush the loaves with water and bake until light golden, 18 to 22 minutes. Cool at least 15 minutes before slicing.

Notes

- *Lard is the traditional fat used in flauta. To make this bread dairy-free and vegan, use refined coconut oil or vegan margarine instead.*

- *Wet or well-hydrated doughs like this result in an open and tender crumb, and the steam keeps the dough soft while it expands at the beginning of the bake. As baking continues, it dissolves and caramelizes the dough's sugar, resulting in a crisp crust out of the oven.*

Dottie's Millet Loaf

"It's that moment when you can convincingly imagine the delightful prospect of eating everything the establishment has to offer," he told Dottie. "Momentarily untroubled by the knowledge that one's stomach has a limited capacity and thus one must, alas, choose in the end."

Dottie looked a little dubious, but, thus urged, she took a deep sniff of the atmosphere, to which the scent of fresh-baked bread had just been added as the serving maid came in with a great loaf and a dish of butter with a four-leafed clover—this being the name of the establishment—stamped into its oleaginous surface.

"Oh, that smells wonderful!" she said, her face lighting. "Might I have some, please? And a glass of cider?" He was pleased to see her nibble hungrily at the bread and take a deep breath of the cider—which was aromatic enough to challenge even the squid, his own reluctantly final choice, though this was accompanied by a dozen fresh-shucked oysters to fill whatever crevices might remain. Dottie had chosen the baked hake, though she had only picked at it so far.

—Written in My Own Heart's Blood, chapter 125,
"Squid of the Evening, Beautiful Squid"

DF | V | VGN

A vegan, 40% whole-wheat loaf that's big on flavor and can settle a queasy stomach straight out of the oven. *Outlander Kitchen* recipe testers proclaimed it to be their new favorite bread. Serve it with a bowl of Annie MacDonald's Chicken Noodle Soup (page 44) for a hearty and flavorful lunch.

Makes 1 large round or 2 sandwich-style loaves

Ingredients

1¼ cups boiling water

½ cup millet

3 cups all-purpose flour, plus
    additional for dusting

2 cups whole-wheat flour

½ cup sunflower seeds

1 tablespoon instant yeast

2 teaspoons kosher salt

1 cup plant-based milk

2 tablespoons vegetable oil, plus more
   for greasing

1 tablespoon molasses

Method

In a small bowl, pour the boiling water over the millet and set aside for 20 minutes.

In the bowl of a stand mixer fixed with the paddle attachment, combine the all-purpose flour, whole-wheat flour, sunflower seeds, yeast, and salt; mix thoroughly on low. Add the softened millet and water, milk, oil, and molasses. Increase the mixer speed to medium-low and, when it has come together in a rough ball, change to the dough hook attachment and knead on medium-low for 12 to 15 minutes. The dough will transition from very sticky to soft and slightly tacky.

Alternatively, mix the dough by hand in a large bowl and knead the sticky dough on a lightly floured counter for 20 minutes.

Form the dough into a ball and set in a large, clean bowl to rise in a warm, draft-free place until at least doubled, about 90 minutes.

Move the rack to the middle rung and heat the oven to 400°F.

If making sandwich loaves, grease two 5 x 9-inch bread pans with oil. Divide the dough in half. On a lightly floured counter, press each piece into a rectangle about 5 x 8 inches. Starting on the shorter end, roll the dough into a log. Pinch the final seam closed with your fingers, then gently rock the loaf on the counter, seam side down, to even it out. Do not taper the ends. Transfer to the prepared pans, ensuring the loaves touch both ends of the pan for an even rise. Cover loosely with plastic wrap or a clean dish towel and proof on the counter until the dough has doubled in size and is cresting the top of the pans, 30 to 45 minutes (see Notes).

For a single large round loaf, draw the edges of the dough into the center, gently stretching the dough to create surface tension while forming a ball. Pinch the creases on the bottom together tightly and twist them slightly to further tighten the surface tension, ensuring an even rise. Transfer the dough, seam side up, to a well-floured 10-inch banneton or medium bowl lined with a clean, natural-fiber cloth (see Notes). Enclose the dough in a plastic bag, seal, and proof on the counter until the dough has doubled in size, 45 to 60 minutes.

Bake the sandwich loaves for 15 minutes. Reduce the heat to 325°F and bake until dark golden and the loaves feel light and sound hollow when you tap on the bottom, another 25 to 30 minutes. Remove the loaves from the tins immediately after removing from the oven. Cool at least 1 hour before slicing.

For the large round loaf, turn the banneton upside down and transfer the loaf gently but quickly from your palm to a 10- to 12-inch cast-iron pan. Bake for 15 minutes, reduce the heat to 325°F, and bake until dark golden and the loaf feels light and sounds hollow when you tap on the bottom, another 40 to 50 minutes. Cool at least 1 hour before slicing.

Store the bread in a paper bag on the counter for up to 3 days or freeze for up to 3 weeks.

Notes

- *The loaves are proofed and ready for the oven when a finger poked into the loaf results in an indentation that fills slowly and incompletely.*

- *A banneton is a basket made especially for baking round loaves, or* boules. *It provides shape and structure to dough during the proofing stage. To replicate a banneton, lightly spray or brush a medium bowl no larger than 10 inches in diameter with oil. Line the bowl with a clean muslin, burlap, or linen cloth, and spray or brush the cloth with more oil. Dust the cloth with flour to coat.*

CORN BREAD

Rodney was not a chatterbox, but we kept up an amiable conversation as we walked. He said that he and his *opa* had walked up to the head of the pass every day for the last week, to be sure of meeting us.

"Mam and Missus Higgins have a ham saved for ye, for supper," he told me, and licked his lips in anticipation. "And there's honey to have with our corn bread! Daddy found a bee tree last Tuesday sennight and I helped him smoke 'em. And . . ."

I replied, but absentmindedly, and after a bit we both lapsed into a companionable silence. I was bracing myself for the sight of the clearing where the Big House had once stood—and a brief, deep qualm swept through me, remembering fire.

—*Written in My Own Heart's Blood,* chapter 137,
"In the Wilderness a Lodging Place"

V

This traditional recipe for corn bread comes straight from North Carolina and belongs to one of the *Outlander Kitchen* recipe testers, Anna. It was passed down to her from her mother, a first-generation Italian American, who most likely learned it from her mother-in-law, who was from an Irish-immigrant family and born in Tennessee. A story reminiscent of Jamie's involved dissertations on the origins of his family, don't you agree?

Use in Corn Bread and Salt Pork Stuffing (page 203), or alongside Ham Steaks with Raisin and Mustard Sauce (page 120).

Serves 8 to 10

Ingredients

¼ cup salt pork fat, bacon fat, or vegetable oil

1 cup yellow cornmeal

1 cup all-purpose flour

2 tablespoons sugar (optional)

1 tablespoon baking powder

½ teaspoon kosher salt

1 cup buttermilk

1 egg, lightly beaten

Method

Move the rack to the middle rung and heat the oven to 425°F. Heat the fat in an 8- or 9-inch cast-iron pan over medium heat.

In a large heatproof bowl, combine the cornmeal, flour, sugar (if using), baking powder, and salt. Pour the buttermilk and beaten egg into the dry ingredients and mix until just combined. When the fat is shimmering in the pan, pour in the batter in an even layer. Bake until a toothpick stuck in the middle comes out clean, 20 to 25 minutes. Cool in the pan for 15 minutes before removing to a metal rack to cool further.

Serve warm as a side.

Best eaten shortly after baking, but leftovers smothered with butter and heated under the broiler are also delicious the next day.

Note

- *If you are making this to use in the recipe for Corn Bread and Salt Pork Stuffing (page 203), render the salt pork first and use that fat for this recipe.*

CASSAVA BREAD

He saw her at once; her back was turned to him, hair hanging casually down her back in a long, thick plait, and she was talking, waving her hands, to a coal-black woman who was squatting, barefooted, on the tiles of the courtyard, patting out some sort of dough onto a hot greased stone.

"That smells good," he said, walking up beside her. "What is it?"

"Cassava bread," she said, turning to him and raising an eyebrow. "And *platanos* and *ropa vieja*. That means 'old clothes,' and while the name is quite descriptive, it's actually very good. Are you hungry? Why do I bother asking?" she added before he could answer. "Naturally you are."

"Naturally," he said, and was, the last vestiges of seasickness vanishing in the scents of garlic and spice. "I didn't know you could speak Spanish, Mother."

—*Besieged*

GF | DF | V | VGN

Cassava bread, or *casabe,* is gluten-free, fiber rich, and low in cholesterol, with no sodium and a moderate carbohydrate content. Traditionally made with yuca that has been peeled, ground, compressed, and sifted, this recipe uses commercially prepared cassava flour, which is available in specialty markets and online.

Makes 4 tortilla-like round flatbreads

Ingredients

1 cup cassava flour

Method

In a large bowl, mix the cassava flour with ½ cup room-temperature water until all of the flour is moistened. The dough will be very lumpy and grainy.

Use your fingers or the back of a spoon to break up all of the lumps until the dough is the texture of wet sand, about 10 minutes.

Heat a large, heavy pan over medium heat. Place the ring from a 7- to 8-inch springform pan in the center of the pan. Sprinkle a slightly heaping ½ cup of the

dough into the ring and spread it evenly. Flatten it down firmly all over, especially at the edges, with a potato masher or the bottom of a glass.

Cook until the bread separates from the ring, 3 to 4 minutes. Remove the ring, flip the bread with a spatula, and cook the other side until golden, 3 to 4 minutes. Cool on a rack and repeat with the remaining dough.

These stay soft for a few hours after cooking but are best used the day they are cooked. For longer storage, air-dry the bread on a rack for 2 days until completely dry. Wrap and store for up to 2 weeks.

Note

- *Lee Ann's Tester Tip: "For cassava crepes, make a thin batter and pour a thin layer into the pan, tilting the pan to spread the batter evenly. Cook until light brown on both sides."*

SCONES WITH PRESERVED LEMON

Quarry nodded and refilled Grey's glass. "You're not eating," he observed.

"I lunched late." Quite late. In fact, he hadn't had luncheon yet. He took a scone and spread it desultorily with jam.

"And Denys Wossname?" Quarry asked, flicking the letter with a pickle fork. "Shall I inquire about him, too?"

"By all means. Though I may make better progress with him on the American end of the matter. That's at least where he was last seen." He took a bite of scone, observing that it had achieved that delicate balance between crumbliness and half-set mortar that is the ideal of every scone, and felt some stirrings of appetite return. He wondered whether he should put Harry onto the worthy Jew with the warehouse in Brest, but decided not. The question of French connections was more than delicate, and while Harry was thorough, he was not subtle.

—*An Echo in the Bone,* chapter 32, "A Flurry of Suspicion"

V

A luscious, decadent scone made with cream and an egg, resulting in a tender crumb and slightly longer shelf life. The addition of Preserved Lemons (page 10) takes the taste from traditional to distinctively new world.

Makes 8

Ingredients

¼ cup granulated sugar

1½ Preserved Lemons (page 10), rinsed, flesh and pith discarded, peel minced (about ¼ cup)

3 cups all-purpose flour, plus additional for dusting

2 teaspoons baking powder

½ teaspoon baking soda

½ teaspoon kosher salt

½ cup (1 stick) butter, chilled or frozen

1 large egg, lightly beaten

1¼ cups whipping cream, plus additional for brushing

Coarse demerara sugar, for sprinkling

Method

In a large bowl, toss together the granulated sugar and preserved lemons. Stir in the flour, baking powder, baking soda, and salt. Grate in the butter; toss to coat. Make a well in the center and add the beaten egg and cream. Mix with a fork, incorporating the dry ingredients a little at a time, until a shaggy, slightly dry dough forms.

Turn out onto a lightly floured surface and knead gently into a ball. Press or roll out to a 6 x 12-inch rectangle and fold the long edge in thirds, like a business letter. Rotate the dough one quarter turn and roll it out again into another 6 x 12-inch rectangle. Cut into eight square scones, or use a round cutter if you prefer. Brush the dough with cream and sprinkle with the demerara sugar. Transfer to a baking sheet lined with parchment paper or a silicone sheet and refrigerate for 15 minutes.

Move the rack to the middle rung and heat the oven to 375°F.

Bake the scones until they are golden brown, 25 to 30 minutes. Cool on a rack.

Serve with butter and jam. Keep leftovers in an airtight container for up to 3 days.

Notes

- *Store-bought preserved lemons are generally small. You may need up to 3 or 4.*

- *For triangular scones, roll the dough into a 1-inch-thick round and cut it into eight even wedges.*

RUMM'S TEA CAKES

It took less than five minutes over the cake plate at Rumm's for Minnie to realize the depths of her father's treachery.

"Your style is very good, my dear," said Lady Buford. The chaperone was a thin, gray-haired lady with an aristocratically long nose and sharp gray eyes under heavy lids that had probably been languorously appealing in her youth. She gave a small, approving nod at the delicate white daisies embroidered on Minnie's pink linen jacket.

"I had thought, with your portion, that we might set our sights on a London merchant, but with your personal attractions, it might be possible to aim a little higher."

—*A Fugitive Green,* chapter 5, "Strategy and Tactics"

DF(a) | V | VGN(a)

Tea cakes originated in England and, in most regions of the country, refer to light, sweet, yeast-leavened buns containing dried fruits that are typically split, toasted, buttered, and served with afternoon tea.

Makes 8 tea cakes

Ingredients

3½ cups all-purpose flour, plus
   additional for dusting
¼ cup granulated sugar
1 tablespoon instant yeast
1½ teaspoons kosher salt
Zest and juice of 1 orange
1 teaspoon ground cinnamon

¾ teaspoon ground cardamom
¼ cup (½ stick) cold butter, cut into
   small pieces
½ teaspoon vegetable oil
½ cup chopped dried apricots
½ cup dried cranberries
½ cup confectioners' sugar

Method

In a large bowl, combine the flour, granulated sugar, yeast, salt, orange zest, cinnamon, and ½ teaspoon of the cardamom. Mix in the butter with your hands, breaking it up into pea-size lumps, and make a well in the center. Pour in 1 cup of room-temperature water and bring the dough together with your hands, adding more water a tablespoon at a time, if necessary, to make a rough dough.

On a lightly floured counter, knead the dough through its initial stickiness until it forms a soft, tacky dough with a smooth skin, 5 to 10 minutes. Rub the oil over the surface of the dough and transfer it to a large bowl. Cover with a clean dish towel and let rise on the counter until the dough ball has doubled in size, 60 to 90 minutes.

Add the apricots and cranberries to the bowl, and begin to work them into the dough. Tip the dough onto the counter and knead until the dried fruit is evenly incorporated.

Divide the dough into eight equal pieces and gently roll each piece under your palm in small circles on the counter to form a ball. Use a rolling pin to flatten the ball into disks about ¾ inch thick.

Move the rack to the middle rung and heat the oven to 375°F. Line a baking sheet with parchment paper.

Arrange the tea cakes on the baking sheet. Cover them loosely with plastic wrap and proof until doubled in size, about an hour. Bake until golden, 12 to 15 minutes.

In a small bowl, mix the confectioners' sugar with 1 tablespoon of the orange juice and the remaining ¼ teaspoon ground cardamom to make a glaze.

Transfer the tea cakes to a cooling rack and lay the parchment paper under the rack to catch the glaze as you brush it over the hot cakes.

Serve warm, with butter, or as Minnie had them, with clotted cream and tea. Tea cakes are possibly even more delicious the next day, served toasted with lots of butter.

Notes

- *To make this recipe dairy-free and vegan, substitute refined coconut oil or vegan margarine for the butter.*
- *Switch up the spices and the dried fruit to create your own house special tea cakes.*
- *These buns proof very well on the stovetop while the oven is heating. If your stove vents through one of your stovetop elements, avoid placing the pan over that vent.*
- *Helen's Tester Tip: "Really liked these. They are easy to make and have a nice shelf life. I shared some with friends the other afternoon at mah-jongg—they loved them, too. They get better the next day and the next."*

SEED CAKE

"Will you take something, sir? A little wine, perhaps?" Tom had appeared, manfully lugging an enormous tray equipped with a rattling array of bottles, decanters, glasses, and an immense seed cake. Where had he got that? Grey wondered.

"Oh! No, I thank you, my lord. I d-do not take spirits. We are Methodist, you understand."

"Of course," Grey said. "We'll have tea, Tom, if you please."

Tom gave Mr. Lister a disapproving look, but decanted the cake onto the table, hoisted the tray, and rattled off into the recesses of the apartment.

—Lord John and the Haunted Soldier

V

This traditional British cake flavored with caraway was very popular from the late Middle Ages through the Victorian era. It makes a delicious afternoon snack with a cup of tea.

Makes 1 loaf

Ingredients

1 cup (2 sticks) butter, softened, plus additional for the pan

1½ cups all-purpose flour, plus additional for the pan

¾ cup sugar

2 tablespoons finely ground almonds

2½ teaspoons caraway seeds

1½ teaspoons baking powder

½ teaspoon kosher salt

3 large eggs

½ cup brandy

Zest of 1 orange

Method

Move the rack to the middle rung and heat the oven to 350°F. Butter and flour a 5 x 8-inch loaf pan.

In a large bowl, cream together the butter and sugar with a hand mixer on medium speed until light and fluffy, about 2 minutes. In a small bowl, stir together the flour, ground almonds, caraway seeds, baking powder, and salt. Add the dry ingredients to the butter and sugar. Mix on low speed until well combined. Add the eggs, brandy, and orange zest, and mix on medium speed until smooth, about 2 minutes.

Scrape the batter into the prepared loaf pan and smooth the top. Bake until golden, well risen, and a toothpick inserted into the middle of the cake comes out clean, about 90 to 105 minutes.

Cool in the pan for 30 minutes, remove, and cool completely on a rack.

Serve with tea. The cake will keep on the counter, well wrapped, for up to 3 days.

Chapter 14

❧

Sweets and Desserts

Dried Apricot Tart

Cranachan with Brian and Jenny

Argus House Chocolate Cake

Mistress Abernathy's Apple Pandowdy

Tarte Tatin

Almond Biscuits

Currant Biscuits

Lemon, Lime, and Orange Ice

Oliebollen

DRIED APRICOT TART

Once more he was late for dinner. This time, though, a tray was brought for him, and he sat in the drawing room, taking his supper while the rest of the company chatted.

The princess saw to his needs, and sat with him for a time, flatteringly attentive. He was worn out from a day of riding, though, and his answers to her questions brief. Soon enough, she drifted away and left him to a peaceful engagement with some cold venison and a tart of dried apricots.

He had nearly finished, when he felt a large, warm hand on his shoulder.

—*Lord John and the Succubus*, chapter 5, "Dark Dreams"

GF(a) | DF(a) | V

Choose the plumpest, largest apricots you can find for this delicate, slightly sweet dessert. The Turkish apricots in Lord John's tart would have been much larger than the ones we see in this century.

Makes one 10-inch tart

Ingredients

½ cup dry white wine

½ cup honey

Zest and juice of 1 medium orange

1-inch piece of fresh ginger, halved, or ½ teaspoon ground ginger

7 ounces (200 grams) dried apricots (about 1 cup)

3 tablespoons all-purpose flour, plus additional for dusting

½ recipe Vegan Short Crust Pastry (page 13)

½ cup (1 stick) butter, softened

½ cup sugar, plus 1 tablespoon for sprinkling

2 large eggs

1 teaspoon vanilla extract

½ teaspoon baking powder

Method

Move the rack to the center rung and heat the oven to 375°F.

In a medium saucepan, combine the wine, honey, orange juice, and ginger with ½ cup water. Bring to a simmer over medium-high heat and add the apricots. Cover, reduce to low, and poach the apricots until plump, about 30 minutes. Drain (see Notes).

On a lightly floured board, roll the short crust into a 12-inch circle about ⅛ inch thick. Transfer to a 10-inch tart pan, pressing the dough into the corners and trimming the excess, leaving an extra ½ inch beyond the pan's edge. Fold the excess to the outside, so the edges are a double thickness, and press into the sides of the pan.

Using a fork, poke holes all over the bottom of the crust. Cover the dough with parchment paper or aluminum foil, and fill the crust with pie weights or dried beans. Bake 15 minutes, remove the weights and parchment, and return to the oven until the pastry looks dry, about 10 more minutes.

In a large bowl, cream together the butter and ½ cup sugar until pale and fluffy; beat in the eggs and vanilla. In a small bowl, combine the flour, baking powder, and orange zest. Gently fold into the wet mixture until well combined.

Spoon the custard into the short crust, then arrange the apricots on top. Sprinkle with the remaining 1 tablespoon sugar and bake until golden, 25 to 30 minutes. Cool on a rack.

Serve with Ulysses's Syllabub from OK1. Cover and refrigerate leftovers for up to 3 days.

Notes

- *To make this recipe gluten-free, substitute the Press-In Crust (page 17) for the Vegan Short Crust and use brown rice flour in place of the all-purpose flour.*
- *To make it dairy-free, substitute nondairy margarine for the butter.*
- *Reserve the apricot poaching liquid to mix with club soda and spirits for creative cocktails—especially those made with gin.*

CRANACHAN WITH BRIAN AND JENNY

"But where is Bombay?" asked the younger of the housemaids, wrinkling her brow and looking from one face to another.

"India," said Jenny promptly, and pushed back her chair. "Senga, fetch the cranachan, aye? I'll show ye where India is."

She vanished through the swinging door, and the bustle of removing dishes left Roger with a few moments' breathing space. He was beginning to feel a little easier, getting his bearings, though still agonized with worry for Jem. He did spare a moment's thought for William Buccleigh and how Buck might take the news of the date of their arrival.

Seventeen thirty-something . . . Jesus, Buck himself hadn't even been born yet! But, after all, what difference did that make? he asked himself. He hadn't been born yet, either, and had lived quite happily in a time prior to his birth before. . . . Could their proximity to the beginning of Buck's life have something to do with it, though?

—*Written in My Own Heart's Blood,* chapter 52,
"Return to Lallybroch"

GF | DF(a) | V | VGN(a)

A traditional Scottish dessert of raspberries, whisky, and cream, originally cranachan was made with crowdie cheese and called a crowdie cream. This twenty-first-century version, popular on OutlanderKitchen.com for years, uses whipped cream. Substitute a batch of homemade Crowdie Cheese from OK1, or blend a bit of crowdie and whipped cream together, and enjoy the best of both worlds.

Serves 4

Ingredients

¼ cup quick-cooking oats or coarsely
    ground whole oats

1 cup whipping cream

2 tablespoons honey

2 tablespoons whisky

1½ cups fresh raspberries

Method

In a small pan, toast the oats gently over medium heat, stirring occasionally, until just aromatic and lightly golden, 4 to 5 minutes. Remove from the heat and cool.

In a medium bowl, whip the cream to soft peaks. Add the honey and whisky and beat until combined.

Stir half the oats into the cream. Add half the raspberries and use a fork to break them. Reserve a few berries for garnish, then gently fold the remainder into the cream, keeping them whole.

Gently spoon the mixture into parfait glasses or bowls. Garnish with the reserved raspberries and a sprinkle of the remaining toasted oats.

Serve chilled. Cranachan can be made up to 3 hours ahead of time and kept covered in the refrigerator. Spoon into serving bowls when ready to serve.

Note

- *To make this dessert dairy-free and vegan, replace the whipping cream and honey with two batches of sweetened Vegan Cream (page 20), thinned and blended to the texture of whipped cream. (A blender will produce the light texture of whipped cream much better than a food processor.)*

ARGUS HOUSE CHOCOLATE CAKE

He'd known her as Mina Rennie; God knew what her real name was. She'd been the seventeen-year-old daughter of a bookseller in Paris who dealt in information and more than once had carried messages between her father and Jamie, during his days of intrigue there before the Rising. Paris seemed as distant as the planet Jupiter. The distance between a young spy and a duchess seemed even greater.

"For the sake of the cause we once shared." Had they? He'd been under no illusions about old Rennie; his only loyalty had been to gold. Had his daughter really considered herself a Jacobite? He ate a slice of cake, absently enjoying the crunch of walnuts and the richly exotic taste of cocoa. He hadn't tasted chocolate since Paris.

—*The Scottish Prisoner,* chapter 8, "Debts of Honor"

DF(a) | V

A steamed sponge rich with chocolate, moist in texture, and light as air, this dessert is worthy of the cook and kitchens in the Greys' residence, located on the southern edge of London's affluent Hyde Park.

Makes one 9-inch cake

Ingredients

6 tablespoons butter, melted and cooled slightly, plus additional for greasing

1 cup all-purpose flour

⅓ cup natural cocoa powder (see Notes)

1 teaspoon baking soda

1 teaspoon cinnamon

½ teaspoon kosher salt

1 cup light brown sugar, packed

2 large eggs

½ cup whole milk

2 teaspoons white vinegar

2 teaspoons vanilla extract

1½ cups walnut pieces

Confectioners' sugar, for dusting (optional)

Method

Lightly scrunch a 20-inch piece of aluminum foil into a snake about 1 inch thick. Form into a circle and set on the bottom of a large Dutch oven. Fill the pot with enough water to reach three-quarters up the foil circle. Grease the bottom and sides of a 9-inch round cake pan with butter. Line the bottom with parchment paper and place the prepared pan on top of the coil.

Sift the flour, cocoa, baking soda, and cinnamon together into a medium bowl. Stir in the salt. In a large bowl, whisk together the brown sugar and eggs until lightened, about 30 seconds. Whisk in the milk, butter, vinegar, and vanilla. Add the flour mixture and whisk until just combined. Gently fold in the walnuts.

Pour the batter into the prepared pan and smooth the top. Cover the Dutch oven with a clean dish towel held taut, then the lid. (The dish towel will absorb any drips caused by condensation.) Heat on high heat until the water boils. Reduce the heat to low and steam, covered, until a toothpick inserted in the center comes out clean, 20 to 25 minutes. Use caution when opening the lid to check for doneness; steam burns.

Turn off the heat and remove the lid and dish towel. Remove the cake pan from the Dutch oven when the pan is cool enough to handle. Transfer the pan to a cooling rack. Let the cake cool completely before running a small knife around the inside edge of the pan. Invert the cake onto a plate, remove the parchment, and invert it back onto another plate.

Dust with confectioners' sugar before serving, if desired.

Cover and store leftovers for up to 3 days.

Notes

- *To make this recipe dairy-free, substitute plant-based milk for the whole milk.*
- *Because Dutch-process cocoa is made from beans that have been washed in an alkali solution, it does not work in recipes that use baking soda as the leavening agent. Use only natural cocoa in this recipe.*
- *Use a spatula in one hand and an oven glove on the other to maneuver the cake pan out of the Dutch oven after it has cooled slightly.*

MISTRESS ABERNATHY'S APPLE PANDOWDY

"Decayed flesh," she said. "Ye'd ken what that smells like, would ye?"

It must have been her accent that brought back the battlefield at Culloden and the stench of burning corpses. He shuddered, unable to stop himself.

"Yes," he said abruptly. "Why?"

She pursed her lips in thought. "There are different ways to go about it, aye? One way is to give the *afile* powder to the person, wait until they drop, and then bury them atop a recent corpse. Ye just spread the earth lightly over them," she explained, catching his look. "And make sure to put leaves and sticks over the face afore sprinkling the earth, so as the person can still breathe. When the poison dissipates enough for them to move again and sense things, they see they're buried, they smell the reek, and so they ken they must be dead." She spoke matter-of-factly, as though she had been telling him her private recipe for apple pandowdy or treacle cake. Weirdly enough, that steadied him, and he was able to speak calmly past his revulsion.

—A Plague of Zombies

GF(a) | DF | V | VGN

This colonial-era skillet pie, or pandowdy, from the Old English *doude* for "unkempt" or "inelegant," was a favorite of Abigail Adams. Although much juicier in, and just out, of the oven than an apple pie, as it cools the liquid is absorbed into the crust, making it more like a pudding than a pie.

Makes one 9-inch deep-dish pie

Ingredients

Refined coconut oil, for greasing

3 pounds (1.4 kilograms) tart, crisp apples (7 or 8 medium), peeled, cored, and sliced ¼ inch thick

3 tablespoons dark brown sugar

1½ teaspoons cinnamon

1 teaspoon kosher salt

1 teaspoon ground ginger

¼ teaspoon freshly grated nutmeg

⅓ cup maple syrup

½ recipe Vegan Short Crust Pastry (page 13)

2 tablespoons plant-based milk, for brushing	1 teaspoon demerara sugar, for sprinkling

Method

Move the rack to the middle rung and heat the oven to 400°F. Generously grease a 9-inch skillet or pie pan with sides at least 2 inches high.

In a large bowl, combine the apples, brown sugar, cinnamon, salt, ginger, and nutmeg; toss well. Pour into the prepared pan. Combine the maple syrup with ½ cup water and toss with the apples.

Roll the short crust into a rectangle about ¼ inch thick. Use a sharp knife to cut the pastry into roughly 3-inch squares and arrange these randomly over the apples, overlapping the pastry in places, tucking it over the apples in others, and leaving a few spaces for steam vents. Brush the crust with milk and sprinkle with the demerara sugar.

Bake until the crust is set and beginning to brown, about 40 minutes. Remove from the oven and, with the back of a spoon, gently press about half of the squares down into the apples and their juices. Return to the oven until the juices are bubbling and the crust is golden, 10 to 15 more minutes.

Cool for at least 30 minutes. Serve warm or at room temperature with Ulysses's Syllabub from OK1 or vanilla ice cream. Leftovers will keep, covered on the counter, for up to 2 days.

Notes

- *To make this recipe gluten-free, substitute a sheet of gluten-free pastry for the short crust.*
- *Abigail Adams most likely used Newtown Pippins in her recipe, a late winter, heritage apple prized for baking. Honeycrisp, Pink Lady, or Braeburns are good easy-to-find options.*

Tarte Tatin

They ate heartily, and separately, in their rooms. Jamie was beginning to feel that the second helping of tarte tatin with clotted cream had been a mistake, when Rebekah came into the men's room, followed by her maid carrying a small tray with a jug on it, wisping aromatic steam. Jamie sat up straight, restraining a small cry as pain flashed through his head. Rebekah frowned at him, gull-winged brows lowering in concern.

"Your head hurts very much, Diego?"

"No, it's fine. No but a wee bang on the heid." He was sweating and his wame was wobbly, but he pressed his hands flat on the table and was sure he looked steady. She appeared not to agree and came close, bending down to gaze searchingly into his eyes.

—Virgins

GF(a) | DF(a) | V | VGN(a)

This classic French dessert is named after the Hotel Tatin, where it was accidentally created by one of two sisters who ran the hotel in the late nineteenth century. Overworked and flustered, as the story goes, she started to make a traditional apple pie but overcooked the filling on the stove. In an attempt to save the disaster, she quickly covered it with pastry and put it into the oven to finish. Guests were delighted with the upside-down dessert, and the rest is culinary history.

Makes one 9- or 10-inch tart

Ingredients

All-purpose flour, for dusting

1 sheet puff pastry (10 to 12 ounces or 285 to 340 grams)

2 pounds (900 grams) sweet-tart baking apples, such as Granny Smith or Gala (about 4 medium or 6 small)

½ cup sugar

6 tablespoons butter, chilled and diced

Method

Move the rack to the middle rung and heat the oven to 350°F.

On a lightly floured surface, roll out the pastry to a ⅛-inch thickness and cut a circle to fit the top of a 9- or 10-inch cast-iron or other heavy ovenproof pan. Lay it on a parchment-lined baking sheet and cover with plastic; freeze while preparing the apples.

Peel, core, and quarter the apples. Sprinkle the sugar in an even layer in the cast-iron pan set over medium-high heat. Cook the sugar to a dark amber syrup that's just starting to smoke, swirling the pan occasionally once the sugar has mostly melted. DO NOT STIR WITH A SPOON. Remove from the heat and carefully stir in ¼ cup of the diced butter, watching for any splatters.

Pack the apple quarters very tightly in a circle around the edge of the pan, rounded sides down, then repeat to fill in the middle. Melt the remaining 2 tablespoons butter and brush it over the apples.

Bake for 30 minutes, then remove and place the disk of frozen puff pastry on top. It will quickly soften; tuck the edges inside the pan and, with a sharp knife, prick four or five holes in the pastry to allow steam to escape. Return to the oven and bake until the pastry is golden brown and crisp, 40 to 45 minutes.

Allow to cool for an hour before running a knife around the edge of the pan and inverting it onto a large serving plate.

Serve with Clotted Cream from OK1, crème fraîche, or vanilla ice cream. Store leftovers on the counter, covered, for up to 2 days.

Notes

- To make this recipe gluten-free, ensure your puff pastry is gluten-free.
- To make it dairy-free and vegan, substitute refined coconut oil or vegan margarine for the butter.
- Any fruit that holds its shape during baking makes a good tarte tatin—pears, peaches, even tomatoes.

ALMOND BISCUITS

Before he could answer, the door opened and Germain came in, a bundle of broadsheets under one arm and a scowl on his face. The latter disappeared like the morning dew as he spotted us, though, and he came to hug me.

"*Grand-mère!* What are you doing in here? *Maman* said you went to buy fish."

"Oh," I said, suddenly guilty at thought of the laundry. "Yes. I am—er, I mean, I was just on my way. . . . Would you like a bite, Germain?" I offered him the plate of almond biscuits, and his eyes lighted up.

"One," said Fergus firmly. Germain rolled his eyes at me but took a single biscuit, lifting it with two fingers in exaggerated delicacy.

—*Written in My Own Heart's Blood,* chapter 112,
"Daylight Haunting"

GF(a) | V

Slightly sweet and crunchy, this icebox shortbread flavored with almonds makes an ideal pairing with an afternoon cup of tea.

Makes about 30

Ingredients

1 cup (2 sticks) butter, softened

¾ cup confectioners' sugar

¾ cup almond meal

½ teaspoon kosher salt

½ teaspoon almond extract

1¾ cups all-purpose flour, plus
    additional for dusting

Method

In a large bowl, combine the butter, confectioners' sugar, almond meal, salt, and almond extract. Blend, using a hand mixer on medium-low speed, gradually increasing to medium-high and beating until smooth and fluffy, about 2 minutes.

Reduce the speed to low and gradually add the flour, mixing to form a uniform dough. Roll the dough into a log about 2 inches in diameter, lightly flouring your counter and hands if necessary. Wrap the log tightly in plastic wrap. Refrigerate until firm, at least 1 hour and up to 3 days (see Notes).

Move a rack to the upper-middle rung and heat the oven to 350°F. Line a baking sheet with parchment paper.

Unwrap the dough and use a sharp knife to cut ¼-inch-thick slices. Arrange the slices 1 inch apart on the prepared baking sheet. Bake until just golden at the edges, 12 to 15 minutes.

Cool 5 minutes on the baking sheet, then transfer to a wire rack and cool completely. Store in a sealed container for up to a week.

Notes

- *To make this recipe gluten-free, replace the all-purpose flour with your favorite commercially prepared gluten-free all-purpose flour mix.*

- *Dough logs can also be frozen for up to 1 month. Defrost on the counter for 15 minutes before slicing.*

CURRANT BISCUITS

Harry made a low noise in his throat indicating complete understanding and sympathy—he'd been by Hal's side through his father's suicide and all the bloody mess that came afterward. Hal smiled at his friend and half-lifted his glass in silent acknowledgment.

"As to what he said, he greeted me very affably, asked me to sit, and offered me a currant biscuit."

Harry whistled.

"My God, you are honored. I hear he only gives biscuits to the king and the first minister. Though I imagine he'd give one to the queen, too, should she choose to visit his lair."

—A Fugitive Green, chapter 17, "Red Wax and Everything"

DF(a) | V | VGN(a)

Currants are small, dried Corinthian seedless grapes that first came to Britain in the late Middle Ages. Originally known as raisins of Corinth, their name eventually evolved into currants.

Called Garibaldi biscuits after the great Italian general Giuseppe Garibaldi, who unified Italy and achieved near cult status during his celebrated visit to Britain in 1864, these subtly sweet biscuits are made from currants baked between two thin layers of dough, and were first produced commercially by Peek Freans in the late nineteenth century.

Makes 28 biscuits

Ingredients

1½ cups all-purpose flour, plus additional for dusting

2 tablespoons confectioners' sugar

1 teaspoon baking powder

½ teaspoon kosher salt

6 tablespoons butter, chilled

3 to 4 tablespoons whole milk, chilled

1 large egg

1⅓ cups currants

3 tablespoons demerara sugar, for sprinkling (optional)

Method

In a medium bowl, whisk together the flour, confectioners' sugar, baking powder, and salt. Break the butter into small pieces, scatter over the dry ingredients, and work them in with your fingertips until the butter is reduced to pea-size lumps and the flour is the color of cornmeal. Make a well in the center of the bowl.

Pour 3 tablespoons of the milk into the well and use your fingertips to bring the dough into a slightly crumbly ball that just holds together. Add more milk 1 teaspoon at a time, if needed, but avoid making a sticky dough.

Divide the dough in half, and shape each half into two 1-inch-thick rectangles. Wrap separately in plastic wrap and refrigerate each piece for 30 minutes.

Move the rack to the upper-middle rung and heat the oven to 350°F. Line a baking sheet with parchment paper. Lightly beat the egg with 1 teaspoon water to make an egg wash.

Roll one piece of dough out on a lightly floured counter into a rough 9 x 15-inch rectangle about ⅛ inch thick. Brush the surface of the dough lightly with some of the egg wash, then spread one long half of the dough with half the currants, pressing them in gently. Fold the other half of the dough over the currants, and roll it into a rectangle about 7 x 16 inches. Some of the currants may pop through; that's okay.

Brush the top of the dough lightly with the remaining egg wash and sprinkle with half the demerara sugar, if using.

Use a baker's scraper or a pizza wheel to trim away the ragged edges so you have a 6 x 15-inch rectangle. Cut the dough into two 3-inch-wide strips, then cut each strip into seven pieces, for a total of fourteen cookies.

Transfer the cookies, as well as the scraps, to the prepared baking sheet. Space them close together, as they need very little room for expansion. Repeat the entire process with the remaining piece of dough, fitting all of the cookies and the scraps onto a single baking sheet.

Bake the cookies to a light golden brown, 12 to 14 minutes. Remove them from the oven and transfer to a rack to cool. Store, covered, for up to 3 days.

Notes

- *To make these dairy-free and vegan, replace the butter with refined coconut oil, the whole milk with plant-based milk, and brush the tops of the cookies with more of the plant-based milk instead of the egg wash before baking.*

- *Original Garibaldi biscuits are not sprinkled with coarse sugar, but I think it gives the cookies a nicer finish and, of course, a slightly sweeter taste.*

- *I prefer these biscuits when they're made with finely chopped golden raisins, which are sweeter and juicier than their small cousins.*

LEMON, LIME, AND ORANGE ICE

"Mother Claire!" I had been feeling pleasantly invisible and, startled out of this delusion, now glanced across the room to see Willie, his disheveled head sticking out from the red-crossed tabard of a Knight Templar, waving enthusiastically.

"I do wish you could think of something else to call me," I said, reaching his side. "I feel as though I ought to be swishing round in a habit with a rosary at my waist."

He laughed at that, introduced the young lady making goo-goo eyes at him as Miss Chew, and offered to get us both an ice. The temperature in the ballroom was rising eighty, at least, and sweat darkened not a few of the bright silks.

—*An Echo in the Bone,* chapter 98, "Mischianza"

GF | DF | V | VGN

A frozen descendant of the Arabic *sharbat* described in the headnote to Rosewater Sherbet (page 279), this simple combination of citrus results in a surprisingly flavorful and refreshing treat. Serve as a palate cleanser between courses or as a light ending after a heavy meal, such as Pork Tenderloin with Cider Sauce and German Fried Potatoes (page 122).

6 small servings

Ingredients

⅓ cup sugar

6 tablespoons fresh orange juice

2 tablespoons fresh lemon juice

2 tablespoons fresh lime juice

6 fresh mint sprigs, for garnish

Method

In a medium saucepan over medium-high heat, combine the sugar with the citrus juices and 1½ cups water. Bring to a low boil. Reduce the heat to medium and stir until the sugar is dissolved, about 2 minutes. Cool slightly.

Pour into a 13 x 9-inch dish; cover and freeze for 45 minutes, or until the edges begin to firm. Stir, re-cover, and return to the freezer. Repeat every 30 minutes until slushy, about 90 minutes total. Transfer to a glass or ceramic bowl, cover, and freeze until ready to serve, up to a day.

Serve in small chilled glasses or dishes, garnished with mint sprigs.

OLIEBOLLEN

Minnie carefully brushed powdered sugar off the ledger. The early queasiness of pregnancy had mostly passed, replaced by the appetite of a ravening owl, according to her father.

"An *owl*?" she'd said, and he nodded, smiling. His shock had passed along with her queasiness, and his face took on a rapt look sometimes when she caught him watching her.

"You look at food, *ma chère,* and turn your head to and then fro, as though you expect it to bolt, and then you swoop on it and—*gulp!*—it's gone."

"Bah," she said now, and looked to see if there were more *oliebollen* in the pottery jar, but, no, she'd finished them. Mortimer's antics had abated and he'd fallen into a stupor, as he usually did when she ate, but she was still hungry.

—*A Fugitive Green,* chapter 7, "Annunciation"

DF(a) | V

Dutch for "oil balls," *oliebollen* are traditionally made using yeast. This updated recipe uses baking powder as leaven, so that you spend less time in the kitchen and more time enjoying delicious, light-tasting apple and raisin doughnuts with your family and friends.

Makes 3 to 4 dozen small doughnuts

Ingredients

Vegetable oil, for frying

2¾ cups all-purpose flour

2½ teaspoons baking powder

1½ teaspoons kosher salt

2 tablespoons sugar

2 tablespoons butter, softened

1 large egg

2 cups whole milk

1 bottle (10 ounces or 295 milliliters) dark ale, such as stout or porter (see Notes)

1 medium apple, cored and grated

¼ cup raisins

Confectioners' sugar, for dusting (optional)

Method

Into a large, heavy pot, such as a Dutch oven, pour 4 inches of vegetable oil and heat over medium-high heat. Keep an eye on the oil while you mix up the batter.

In a medium bowl, stir together the flour, baking powder, and salt. In a large bowl, cream the sugar and butter. Beat in the egg until well combined, then mix in the milk and ale. Stir in the flour mixture to make a thick batter; add the grated apple and raisins.

Increase the heat under the oil to high. When the oil reaches 360°F on an instant-read thermometer, fry tablespoonfuls of batter until golden on all sides, 3 to 4 minutes total. Allow the temperature of the oil to come back up in between batches. Transfer to a plate lined with paper towels to drain.

Cool slightly and dust with confectioners' sugar, if desired.

Store in an airtight container for up to 3 days.

Notes

- *To make the oliebollen dairy-free, use plant-based milk instead of the whole milk and non-dairy margarine for the butter.*

- *Choose a beer low in hops, such as Innis & Gunn ales or Guinness, as hops get bitter when cooked.*

- *Mix it up with cranberries instead of raisins.*

Chapter 15

Drinks and Cocktails

GIN AND ORANGE FLOWER COCKTAIL

"Are you all right, madam?" one of the men asked, leaning forward. His voice cracked sharply on "madam," and she actually looked at him properly for the first time. Sure enough, he was a beardless boy. Taller than his companion, and pretty well grown, but a lad nonetheless—and his guileless face showed nothing but concern.

"Yes," she said, and, swallowing, pulled a small fan from her sleeve and snapped it open. "Just . . . a little warm."

The older man—in his forties, slender and dark, with a cocked hat balanced on his knee—at once reached into his pocket and produced a flask: a lovely object made in chased silver, adorned with a sizable chrysoberyl, she saw with surprise.

"Try this," he said in a pleasant voice. "It is orange-flower water, with sugar, herbs, the juice of blood oranges, and just a touch of gin, for refreshment."

"Thank you." She repressed the "drugged and raped" murmuring in her brain and accepted the flask. She passed it unobtrusively under her nose, but there was no telltale scent of laudanum. In fact, it smelled divine and tasted even better.

—*A Fugitive Green,* chapter 6, "Unexpected Introductions"

GF | DF | V | VGN

A multisensory cocktail created by photographer Rebecca Wellman: "I see cocktail engineering as a bit of a science. The way that the layers dance sequentially on your tongue from light to dark: citrus, sweet, and bitter. Part of the cocktail experience includes your nose, making the orange wheel and the rosemary garnish an important part of the equation. If you are feeling adventurous, light the rosemary garnish on fire, then blow it out immediately to add a smoky scent."

Serves 2

Ingredients

1 batch hot Simple Syrup (page 15)

7 fresh thyme sprigs

7 fresh rosemary sprigs

¼ teaspoon vanilla extract

4 ounces fresh blood orange juice

2 ounces London dry gin

1 ounce fresh lemon juice

¼ teaspoon orange blossom water

Orange wheels, for garnish

Fresh rosemary sprigs, for garnish

Club soda (optional)

Method

Immediately after removing the simple syrup from the heat, stir in 5 sprigs each of the thyme and rosemary, as well as the vanilla. Infuse on the counter until completely cool, preferably overnight. Strain.

Add the remaining 2 sprigs each of thyme and rosemary to a cocktail shaker and muddle lightly. Add the blood orange juice, gin, lemon juice, 1 ounce of the infused simple syrup, and orange blossom water to the shaker and cover. Shake to blend. Add 4 large ice cubes and shake vigorously.

Strain into 2 rocks glasses filled with ice and garnish with orange wheels and rosemary. Top with a splash of club soda, if desired.

Store leftover simple syrup in the fridge, covered, for up to 1 week.

Note

* *Oranges and lemons can vary greatly in sweetness, so adjust the cocktail to your taste with more simple syrup or lemon juice.*

ICED NEGUS

"To be desirable, it is necessary to be talked about, my dear," Lady Buford told her over a glass of iced negus at Largier's tea shop (Madame Largier was French and thought tea itself a distinctly second-class beverage). "But you must be talked about in the right way. You must not suggest any hint of scandal, and—just as important—you must not cause jealousy. Be sweet and unassuming, always admire your companions' frocks and dismiss your own, and do not bat your eyes at their sons or brothers, should such be present."

"I've never batted my eyes at anyone in my life!" Minnie said indignantly.

"It isn't a difficult technique to master," Lady Buford said dryly. "But I trust you take my point."

—*A Fugitive Green,* chapter 10, "Down to Business"

GF | DF | V | VGN(a)

An early-eighteenth-century port punch flavored with lemon, sugar, and aromatics that refreshes and restores.

Serves 4

Ingredients

2 cups ruby port
½ cup fresh lemon juice
½ teaspoon vanilla extract
½ cup sugar

1-inch strip of lemon zest
1-inch strip of orange zest
Orange or lemon twists, for garnish
Cinnamon sticks, for garnish

Method

In a large, heatproof pitcher or bowl, stir together the port, lemon juice, and vanilla.

In a medium saucepan, combine the sugar, lemon zest, and orange zest with 2 cups water. Bring to a boil over high heat, stirring to dissolve the sugar. Boil for 1 minute, then pour over the port mixture, stir, and cool completely on the counter to give the flavors time to meld. Cover and refrigerate until chilled.

Serve over ice, garnished with a citrus twist and cinnamon sticks.

Notes

- *Not all port is vegan. See Beer, Wine, and Spirits in Pantry Notes (page 3) for more information.*

- *Unless you already have a favorite, choose a mid-priced ruby port.*

- *It is much easier to zest the lemon before you juice it.*

- *To serve hot, add the port mixture to the saucepan after the sugar syrup has boiled, and heat gently.*

WHISKY AND COCONUT MILK

"India, I heard," Lady Mumford went on, frowning slightly as she fingered the cloth of his uniform sleeve. "Now, you'll have your new uniform ready ordered, I hope? A nice tropical weight of superfine for your coat and weskit, and linen breeches. You don't want to be spending a summer under the Indian sun, swaddled to the neck in English wool! Take it from me, my dear; I went with Mumford when he was posted there, in '35. Both of us nearly died, between the heat, the flies, and the food. Spent a whole summer in me shift, having the servants pour water over me; poor old Wally wasn't so fortunate, sweating about in full uniform, never could get the stains out. Drank nothing but whisky and coconut milk—bear that in mind, dear, when the time comes. Nourishing and stimulating, you know, and so much more wholesome to the stomach than brandywine."

—*Lord John and the Private Matter*

GF | DF | V | VGN

This exotic and creamy whisky punch offers a unique way to cool down from the summer heat.

Serves 4

Ingredients

1 batch hot Simple Syrup (page 15)

2 chai tea bags, or 2 teaspoons loose chai in a tea ball

1 cup coconut milk

8 ounces (240 milliliters) whisky (see Notes)

Crushed ice (optional)

Lime twists, for garnish

Method

Immediately after removing the simple syrup from the heat, add the tea to the pan. Steep until completely cool. Discard the tea, and cover and chill the syrup in the refrigerator.

In a small bowl, blend the coconut milk and the chai syrup with an immersion blender or whisk until smooth. Slowly add the whisky, stirring continuously until combined. Pour it into a pitcher, cover, and chill in the refrigerator for at least an hour before serving.

Stir to recombine and pour into glasses over crushed ice, if desired. Garnish with a twist of lime.

Notes

- *Choose a non-peaty single malt whisky for this recipe, such as Glenmorangie and The Macallan, or a blended whisky, such as Chivas Regal and Johnnie Walker.*
- *Becky's Tester Tip: "For the best taste, chill for several hours before serving. At first the whisky overpowered the other flavors, but it balanced out with time. I used 6 ounces of Tomatin, a Highland single malt—not at all peaty."*

ROSEWATER SHERBET

The crowd was funneling in to a large central hall, where Princess Augusta—or so Minnie assumed the pretty, bejeweled woman with the big blue eyes and the incipient double chin to be—was greeting her guests, supported by several other gorgeously dressed ladies. Minnie casually faded into the crowd and bypassed the receiving line; no need to call attention to herself.

There were enormous refreshment tables at the back of the house, and she graciously accepted a glass of sherbet and an iced cake offered her by a servant; she nibbled as she wandered out into the gardens, with an eye to its design and the locations of various landmarks. She was to meet Mr. Bloomer at three o'clock, in the "first of the glasshouses." Wearing green.

Green she was, from head to toe: a pale-green muslin gown, with a jacket and overskirt in a printed French calico. And, of course, the parasol, which she erected again once outside the house.

—*A Fugitive Green,* chapter 11, "Garden Party"

GF | DF | V | VGN

The word *sherbet* comes from the Arabic *sharbat,* which means "a drink." This family of sweet, nonalcoholic drinks made from fruit, cane juice, herbs, and spices was introduced to India in the sixteenth century by the conquering Mughals, who regularly sent to the Himalayas for large loads of ice. By the seventeenth century, sherbet powders, made from dried fruit and flowers mixed with sugar, had made their way to England.

This recipe is a version of *gulab sharbat,* a cordial usually mixed with water or milk that is popular across the Middle East and the Indian subcontinent.

Makes about 1 quart (1 liter)

Ingredients

1 cup fresh organic, culinary-grade
    rose petals, or ¾ cup dried
2 to 3 cups boiling water

½ teaspoon cardamom seeds
1½ cups fresh lemon juice
1 cup sugar

½ cup fresh pomegranate juice

Kosher salt

Crushed ice, for serving

Club soda or milk, for serving

Method

In a large glass or ceramic bowl, crush the rose petals with a pestle or the back of a spoon. Add 2 cups boiling water to fresh petals, or 3 cups to dried. Stir in the cardamom seeds, cover, and leave on the counter overnight.

Strain the mixture and discard the solids. Pour the rosewater into a pitcher and stir in the lemon juice, sugar, pomegranate juice, and a pinch of salt, mixing until the sugar dissolves. Strain and cool completely.

Serve in a glass with crushed ice and top up with club soda or milk. Store the undiluted cordial in the refrigerator for up to 2 weeks.

Notes

- Rosa damascena, *commonly known as the damask rose, is prized for its fine scent and is the best choice for use in the kitchen.*

- *Dilute with two parts cold water and freeze as per the directions for Lemon, Lime, and Orange Ice (page 265) for a sweet, botanical, and frozen treat.*

LEMON BARLEY WATER

"Indeed there are," Grey said. "Who do you propose to help?"

Fraser narrowed his eyes a bit but had plainly been thinking about it.

"Well, there's my sister and her husband. They've the six bairns—and there are my tenants—" He caught himself, lips compressed for a moment. "Families who *were* my tenants," he corrected.

"How many?" Grey asked, curious.

"Maybe forty families—maybe not so many now. But still . . ."

Hal must have come well up to scratch on the reward, Grey thought.

Grey didn't wish to dwell on the matter. He coughed and rang the bell for a footman to bring him a drink. His chances of getting anything stronger than barley water in his bedroom were slim, and he wasn't fond of sherry.

—*The Scottish Prisoner,* chapter 8, "Debts of Honor"

DF | V | VGN

Used for centuries as a restorative for the sick and dehydrated, barley water was adopted into the kitchens of Auguste Escoffier, a French chef and restaurateur in the late nineteenth and early twentieth centuries. A stickler for order and discipline, among the many changes he made to his kitchen brigades was to ban the drinking of alcohol. Instead, each Escoffier hotel kitchen was home to a barrel of lemon barley water that kept his staff hydrated and alert in a hot and stressful environment.

Makes about 1 quart (1 liter)

Ingredients

½ cup pot or pearl barley

Zest of 2 lemons, cut into 1-inch strips
(see Notes)

¼ cup lemon juice

¼ cup honey or sugar

Method

In a large saucepan, bring 2 quarts (2 liters) water to a boil.

Rinse the barley in cold water. In a small pot, cover the barley with 2 cups of cold water and bring to a boil. Boil for 5 minutes, drain, and add to the large pot of boiling water. Reduce the heat to medium and simmer briskly, uncovered, until the water is reduced by half, about 30 minutes. Strain and cool for 15 minutes.

Add the lemon zest, lemon juice, and honey to a pitcher. Strain the barley water into the pitcher and stir well. Stir, refrigerate, and serve chilled.

Store in the refrigerator for up to 5 days.

Notes

- *It is easier to zest the lemons before you juice them.*
- *The remaining barley can be used in soups, like Scotch Broth at Cranesmuir (page 52), stews, or baking.*

COCOA WITH THE MacKENZIES

He and Brianna had been sitting below that very window at the time, but he glanced reflexively at the window beside him, which reflected only the domestic scene of which he was a part. The man in the glass looked wary, shoulders hunched in readiness to lunge at something. He got up and drew the curtains.

"Here," he said abruptly, sitting down and reaching for Mandy. She came into his arms with the slow amiability of a tree sloth, sticking her wet thumb in his ear in the process.

Bree went to fetch them cups of cocoa, returning with a rattle of crockery, the scent of hot milk and chocolate, and the look of someone who's been thinking what to say about a difficult matter.

—*An Echo in the Bone,* chapter 21, "The Minister's Cat"

GF | DF(a) | V | VGN(a)

Made from cocoa, milk, and sugar, this cocoa is lighter and sweeter than the fuller-bodied Hot Chocolate with La Dame Blanche from OK1. Serve it with a plate of Almond Biscuits (page 260) to drive away nightmares of the scariest Nuckelavee on the darkest winter night.

Serves 4

Ingredients

⅓ cup natural cocoa powder

⅓ to ½ cup sugar (see Notes)

¼ teaspoon kosher salt

4 cups whole milk

Vanilla or peppermint extract
  to taste (optional)

Method

In a medium saucepan, whisk together the cocoa, sugar, and salt. Stir in ¼ cup of the milk and blend to a smooth paste before stirring in the rest of the milk. Heat over medium heat until very hot, stirring constantly to prevent the bottom from scorching. Do not allow the milk to boil. Remove from the heat and add vanilla or peppermint, if using.

Divide the cocoa between 4 mugs and serve.

Notes

* *To make this recipe dairy-free and vegan, replace the milk with your favorite plant-based milk.*

* *Natural cocoa is simply ground, roasted cocoa beans, while Dutch-process cocoa is made from beans that have been washed in an alkali solution to remove some of their bitterness. It is darker, with a more complex flavor than natural cocoa. While they cannot always be used interchangeably in baking, an equal amount of Dutch-process cocoa can be substituted in this recipe.*

* *Start with the lesser amount of sugar and, once the milk starts to heat up, taste and add additional sugar, or not, to suit your taste.*

MULLED CIDER

"I've resigned my commission," he said, a little stiffly. "Under the circumstances, there seemed little point to my remaining in the army. And I have business that requires somewhat more independence of movement than I should have as one of Sir Henry's aides."

"Will you come and have something hot to drink with me? You can tell me about your business." I'd rushed out without my cloak, and a chilly breeze was fingering me with more intimacy than I liked.

"I—" He caught himself, frowning, then looked at me thoughtfully and rubbed a finger down the long, straight bridge of his nose, just as Jamie did when making up his mind. And just as Jamie did, he dropped his hand and nodded briefly as though to himself. "All right," he said, rather gruffly. "In fact, my business may be of some . . . importance to you."

Another five minutes saw us in an ordinary off Ellis Square, drinking hot cider, rich with cinnamon and nutmeg. Savannah wasn't—thank God— Philadelphia, in terms of nasty winter weather, but the day was cold and windy, and the pewter cup was delightfully warm in my hands.

—*Written in My Own Heart's Blood*, chapter 127, "Plumbing"

GF | DF | V | VGN

Hot mulled cider most likely finds its roots in the pagan new year's tradition of wassailing. From the Anglo-Saxon toast *waes hael*, meaning "good health," the wassail was a drink made of mulled ale or wine, curdled cream, roasted apples, an egg or two, spices, and sugar. Merrymakers carried it in huge bowls from house to house, spreading good cheer and singing songs, a tradition that has evolved into Christmas caroling.

Serves 12

Ingredients

1 gallon (3.75 liters) apple cider

1 tablespoon whole allspice berries

3 cinnamon sticks

1 vanilla bean, split lengthwise

6 whole cloves

½ teaspoon freshly grated nutmeg

½ to 1 cup Calvados (apple brandy) (optional)

Method

In a large pot, combine the cider, allspice berries, cinnamon sticks, split vanilla bean, cloves, and nutmeg. Bring just to a simmer over medium heat, reduce to medium-low, and cook just below a simmer for about an hour.

Strain the cider through a sieve into another pot or heatproof punch bowl; discard the solids. Add Calvados to taste, if desired. Ladle into cups and serve.

Hot Rum Punch
with Preserved Lemon

"Do you love the young woman, William?" he asked, very quietly. The tavern wasn't busy, but there were enough men drinking there that no one was noticing them.

William shook his head, helpless.

"I—tried to protect her. To save her from Harkness. I—I bought her for the night. I didn't stop to think that he'd come back—but of course he would," he finished bitterly. "I likely made things worse for her."

"There wouldn't have been a way of making them better, save marrying the girl or killing Harkness yourself," Lord John said dryly. "And I don't recommend murder as a way of settling difficult situations. It tends to lead to complications—but not nearly as many as marriage." He got up and went to the bar, returning with two steaming cups of hot rum punch.

"Drink that," he said, pushing one in front of William. "You look chilled through."

He was; he'd taken a table in a far corner, nowhere near the fire, and a fine, uncontrollable shiver was running through him, enough to ripple the surface of the punch when he wrapped his hand round the pewter cup. The punch was good, though made with preserved lemon peel, sweet, strong, and hot and made with good brandy as well as rum. He hadn't eaten anything in hours, and it warmed his stomach immediately.

—*Written in My Own Heart's Blood*, chapter 132, "Will-o'-the-Wisp"

GF | DF | V | VGN

Strong, dark rum combines with brandy, sugar, amber rum, and preserved lemons to make a warm and bracing libation for a crowd. This recipe is inspired by a favorite punch recipe of Charles Dickens, an enthusiastic host renowned for his Christmas and Twelfth Night parties, and modified with the substitution of preserved lemon for his fresh peel.

Serves 12

Ingredients

4 Preserved Lemons (page 10), rinsed, flesh and pith removed and discarded

Zest and juice of 1 small orange

¾ cup demerara sugar

Juice of 4 or 5 fresh lemons

1¼ cups amber or aged rum

1¼ cups overproof rum

1 cup brandy, preferably Cognac

1 quart (1 liter) boiling water

Freshly grated nutmeg

Method

Cut the preserved lemon peel into ½-inch strips. Using a vegetable peeler, remove the zest from the orange in strips, being careful not to include any of the white pith; juice the orange and reserve it. In a heatproof, nonreactive punch bowl or pitcher, combine the preserved lemon and orange peels with the sugar, and muddle it together using a muddler, pestle, or the back of a wooden spoon. Cover and set the mixture on the counter overnight to infuse.

Combine the orange and lemon juices to make ¾ cup juice in total.

When ready to serve, pour both the rums and the brandy into the bowl with the sugar and peels. Add the reserved citrus juice and boiling water; stir well. Grate nutmeg over the top of the punch and ladle into punch glasses.

Notes

- *Brandy in general means any kind of distilled spirit made from fermented fruit juice. Only a grape brandy produced in the Cognac region of France can be called Cognac. So you see, all Cognac is brandy, but not all brandy is Cognac. Choose according to your budget and enjoy!*

- *Quality amber rum gets its color from charred oak barrels. Overproof rum is more than 50% alcohol.*

- *Demerara sugar was originally manufactured and shipped from the port of Demerara in British Guyana. Its flavor is lighter than that of conventional brown sugar. Substitute light brown sugar (unpacked) if demerara is unavailable.*

Chapter 16

❧❧

Condiments and Preserves

Minnie's Sauerkraut

Rachel Murray's Dill Pickles

Mrs. Bug's Piccalilli

Brandied Peaches

Seville Orange Marmalade

Jerked Beef

Mushroom Catsup

Prepared Horseradish

Minnie's Sauerkraut

Minnie lay in bed, the remains of breakfast on a tray beside her, and contemplated the shape of her first day in London. She'd arrived late the night before and had barely taken notice of the rooms her father had engaged for her—she had a suite in a townhouse on Great Ryder Street, "convenient to everything," as he'd assured her, complete with a housemaid and meals provided from the kitchen in the basement.

She had been filled with an intoxicating sense of freedom from the moment she'd taken an affectionate leave of her father on the dock at Calais. She could still feel the pleasure of it, bubbling in the slow, pleasant fashion of a crock of fermenting cabbage under her stays, but her innate caution kept a lid on it.

—*A Fugitive Green,* chapter 3, "Irish Rovers"

GF | DF | V | VGN

Pickling as a food preservation technique originated four thousand years ago in the Tigris valley of Mesopotamia, where cucumbers from India were lacto-fermented in saltwater brine until they were no longer considered raw and vulnerable to spoilage.

Here, the cabbage is immersed in a salt bath to encourage the development of lactic acid, which in turn produces an acidic environment that inhibits the growth of spoiling bacteria.

Makes about 1 quart (1 liter)

Ingredients

2 pounds (900 grams) white cabbage
4 teaspoons kosher salt, plus additional

½ cup filtered or distilled water
   (see Notes)

Method

Wash a 1-quart (1-liter) mason jar and its lid in hot, soapy water. Rinse thoroughly and set on the dish rack to air-dry. Wash your hands in hot, soapy water and shake dry.

Remove the outside dirty or wilted leaves from the cabbage and discard; cut the cabbage into quarters. Using a mandoline or food processor fitted with the slicing blade, shred the cabbage between ⅛ inch and ⅜ inch thick. In a large bowl or bucket, toss the cabbage with the salt. Set aside for 15 minutes.

Add the water to the cabbage and mix and squeeze with your hands for a few minutes to release the juices. Use your hands to pack the cabbage tightly into the clean jar, pushing down with a spoon to compact it further. Fill the jar, leaving ¾ inch of headspace at the top. Pour in the remainder of the brine to cover, leaving ½ inch of headspace. Cover with the lid and set aside in a warm (65 to 72°F) spot for at least 7 days.

After 24 hours, open the lid gently to release the accumulating gases and to check that the cabbage is submerged. Top up with the filtered or distilled water and a pinch of salt. Burp the lid again at 36 hours and at 48 hours, also checking to ensure the cabbage is still covered by liquid.

After 7 days, taste. If fermented to your liking, refrigerate the sauerkraut and start to consume; it will still be crunchy and fresh tasting. For more sour and softer kraut, ferment longer, up to 21 days.

Use in Gail Abernathy's Brats and Sauerkraut (page 128), a Reuben sandwich, or as the pickle with a plate of meat and cheese. Store in the refrigerator for up to 1 month.

Notes

- *Chlorine and fluoride, found in much of the tap water around the planet, can inhibit the fermentation process. Use filtered or distilled water for best results.*

- *Fermenting crocks or lids are widely available. Many have a burp bubble to release extra gases without having to open the lid.*

- *To double or triple the batch, make sure to maintain the desired ratio of 2 to 2.5% salt to cabbage by weight. Every 2 pounds (900 grams) of cabbage uses 0.6 to 0.8 ounce (18 to 23 grams) of salt.*

- *Flavor it with coriander, bay leaves, mustard seeds, or garlic. Add color with grated carrot or a pinch of turmeric.*

RACHEL MURRAY'S DILL PICKLES

"D'ye no mean to eat that?" he inquired, coming up beside her stirrup.

"I do," she said calmly, "but all in good time." She licked the substantial length of the warty green thing with a long, slow swipe of her tongue and then—holding his eyes—sucked deliberately on the end of it. He walked straight into a springy pine branch, which swiped him across the face with its needles.

He swore, rubbing at his watering eyes. She was laughing!

"Ye did that on purpose, Rachel Murray!"

—*Written in My Own Heart's Blood*, chapter 140, "Woman Will Thou Lie with Me?"

GF | DF | V | VGN

Traditional recipes for dill pickles involve fermenting cucumbers in barrels full of saltwater brine for several weeks. In contrast, this recipe is for fresh-pack pickles, meaning that the fresh cucumbers are expeditiously acidified with vinegar in jars before immediately being processed in boiling water, a home-canning technique made possible in 1858 by the invention of mason jars by John Mason of New York, and one that reduced the time required for pickles from 3 weeks to a single afternoon.

Makes six 1-quart (1-liter) jars

Ingredients

2 quarts (2 liters) apple cider vinegar or distilled vinegar (5% acetic acid)

8 pounds (3.6 kilograms) 4- to 6-inch pickling cucumbers

12 fresh dill heads

6 garlic cloves, minced

6 tablespoons pickling or coarse salt

6 teaspoons pickling spice

Method

Place six clean 1-quart (1-liter) mason jars, six rings, and six lids into a boiling-water canner and fill the pot with water to cover. Heat over high until just boiling and boil for 10 minutes. Turn off the heat and keep the pot covered to stay hot. In a large nonreactive (see Notes) pot, combine the vinegar with 2 quarts (2 liters) water and bring to a boil over high heat.

Scrub the cucumbers clean. Slice off and discard ⅛ inch from the blossom ends. Cut the cucumbers into spears, if large.

Remove one of the jars from the boiling-water canner, emptying the water back into the pot. In the bottom of the hot jar, place 1 dill head, 1 clove minced garlic, 1 tablespoon pickling salt, and 1 teaspoon pickling spice. Pack the jar with cucumbers, leaving ¾ inch of headspace at the top. Top with 1 dill head and ladle the boiling pickling liquid into the jar to cover the cucumbers, leaving ½ inch of headspace. Slide a rubber or silicone spatula between the glass and the food to remove any air bubbles. Wipe the jar rim with a CLEAN damp cloth to remove any stickiness and cover with a hot lid. Screw the ring on until just finger-tight. Return the jar to the canner and repeat with the remaining jars and cucumbers.

Ensure the jars in the canner are covered by at least 2 inches of water. Place the lid on the canner and return the water to a gentle boil for 15 minutes. Remove the jars and cool overnight. Check to ensure the seals are airtight.

Wipe, label, and store the jars in a cool, dark place for up to 2 years. Refrigerate after opening.

Notes

- *Nonreactive materials include stainless steel, glass, and enamel.*
- *The blossom ends of cucumbers contain an enzyme that softens the pickles over time, and so they are removed.*
- *The timing and temperatures in this recipe will work at altitudes of up to 1,000 feet. Those at higher altitudes should consult the National Center for Home Food Preservation (nchfp .uga.edu), an excellent resource for all things preserved.*
- *Reprocess any unsealed jars, or refrigerate those jars and consume them first.*

Mrs. Bug's Piccalilli

Jamie reached into his cloak and drew out his flask. Uncorking this, he leaned forward and carefully poured a few drops of whisky on the head of each of the dead women, then lifted the flask in silent toast to Grannie MacLeod, then to Mrs. Bug.

"Murdina, wife of Archibald, ye were a great cook," he said simply. "I'll recall your biscuits all my life, and think of ye wi' my morning parritch."

"Amen," I said, my voice trembling between laughter and tears. I accepted the flask and took a sip; the whisky burned through the thickness in my throat, and I coughed. "I know her receipt for piccalilli. That shouldn't be lost; I'll write it down."

—*An Echo in the Bone*, chapter 4, "Not Yet Awhile"

GF(a) | DF | V | VGN

Pungent, sweet, festively golden, and slightly addictive, piccalilli makes a pretty hostess gift when tied with a tartan ribbon. It's also a tasty addition to a potluck or picnic table at any time of year, especially alongside some ham, a wedge of strong cheese, and a bottle of ale.

Makes about four 1-pint (500-milliliter) or eight 1-cup (250-milliliter) jars

Ingredients

4 cups small cauliflower florets

1½ cups deseeded and diced
  English cucumber

1½ cups julienned yellow onion

1 cup trimmed and diced
  green beans

½ cup shredded carrot

5 teaspoons kosher salt

½ cup mustard powder

½ cup all-purpose flour

1 tablespoon ground turmeric

½ teaspoon white pepper

½ teaspoon freshly grated nutmeg

¼ cup apple cider vinegar

1 tablespoon coriander seeds

¼ cup light brown sugar,
  lightly packed

1½ cups malt vinegar

Method

In a large bowl, combine the cauliflower, cucumber, onion, green beans, carrot, and salt. Mix well, cover, and refrigerate overnight.

Place four 1-pint (500-milliliter) or eight 1-cup (250-milliliter) mason jars into a boiling-water canner with their matching lids and rings. Add water to cover, heat over high until just boiling, and boil for 10 minutes. Turn off the heat and keep the pot covered to stay hot.

Drain the vegetables. In a large saucepan, whisk together the mustard powder, flour, turmeric, white pepper, and nutmeg. Add the cider vinegar and 2 cups water. Whisk until smooth and add the vegetables, coriander seeds, brown sugar, and malt vinegar.

Bring to a simmer over medium heat, stirring occasionally to prevent scorching on the bottom. Simmer 10 to 15 minutes, until the sauce thickens enough to coat the back of a spoon. Add more water if the sauce becomes too thick. Remove from the heat.

Remove one of the jars from the boiling-water canner, emptying the water back into the pot. Ladle the piccalilli into it, leaving ½ inch of headspace. Slide a rubber or silicone spatula between the glass and the food to remove any air bubbles. Wipe the jar rim with a CLEAN damp cloth to remove any stickiness and cover with a hot lid. Screw the ring on until just finger-tight. Return the jar to the canner and repeat with the remaining jars and piccalilli.

Ensure the jars in the canner are covered by at least 2 inches of water. Place the lid on the canner and return the water to a gentle boil for 10 minutes. Remove the jars and cool overnight. Check to ensure the seals are airtight.

Wipe, label, and store the jars in a cool, dark place for up to 2 years. Refrigerate after opening.

Notes

- *To make this recipe gluten-free, substitute additional cider vinegar for the malt vinegar, and brown rice flour for the all-purpose flour.*

- *The timing and temperatures in this recipe will work at altitudes of up to 2,000 feet. Those at higher altitudes should consult the National Center for Home Food Preservation (nchfp .uga.edu), an excellent resource for all things preserved.*

- *A canning funnel, while not absolutely necessary, makes ladling anything into jars much easier and helps to keep your jars and work space clean.*

Brandied Peaches

The snow was falling thickly over the Channel, and now swept nearly horizontal as the howling wind changed direction and the ship gave a sickening lurch. The other man shook himself and went below, leaving Grey to eat brandied peaches with his fingers from a jar in his pocket and stare bleakly at the oncoming coast of France, visible only in glimpses through low-lying clouds.

—*An Echo in the Bone*, chapter 24, "Joyeux Noël"

GF | DF | V | VGN

Originally domesticated in China, *Prunus persica*, commonly known as the peach tree, is a member of the rose family and closely related to cherry, plum, almond, and apricot trees. It's species name, *persica*, refers to its widespread cultivation in Persia, from where it eventually made its way to Europe and the New World.

I'm not sure if it's still socially acceptable to eat brandied peaches from a jar in your pocket, but it certainly sounds like a delectably better-than-average way to pass the time at sea in a storm.

Makes five 1-pint (500-milliliter) jars

Ingredients

5 pounds (2.25 kilograms) ripe but firm, blemish-free peaches

3 cups sugar

1½ cups brandy, preferably Cognac

Method

Place five 1-pint (500-milliliter) mason jars, five rings, and five lids into a boiling-water canner and fill the pot with water to cover. Heat over high heat until just boiling and boil for 10 minutes. Turn off the heat and keep the pot covered to stay hot.

Prepare an ice bath by filling a large bowl with cold water and a tray of ice cubes.

Bring a large pot of water to a boil. Using a small sharp knife, make a shallow X in the bottom of each peach. Blanch the peaches in batches in the boiling water for 1 minute, then plunge into the ice bath. Peel the peaches and quarter the flesh, discarding the pits.

In a medium pot, combine the sugar with 3 cups water and bring to a boil. Boil until it thickens slightly, 3 to 5 minutes. Remove from the heat.

Pour ¼ cup of the brandy into each jar. Gently pack the peaches into the jars and spoon or funnel the syrup over the fruit, leaving ½ inch of headspace at the top. Run a rubber spatula around the inside of the jars to release any air bubbles. Wipe each jar rim with a CLEAN damp cloth to remove any stickiness and cover with a hot lid. Screw on each ring until just finger-tight. Return the jars to the canner.

Ensure the jars in the canner are covered by at least 2 inches of water. Place the lid on the canner and return the water to a gentle boil. Process for 20 minutes. Turn off the heat, remove the cover, and allow the jars to sit for 5 minutes before removing them from the water. Allow them to cool, untouched, for 4 to 6 hours.

Check the seals and store in a cool, dark place for up to a year. Refrigerate after opening.

Note

- *The timing and temperatures in this recipe will work at altitudes of up to 1,000 feet. Those at higher altitudes should consult the National Center for Home Food Preservation (nchfp .uga.edu), an excellent resource for all things preserved.*

SEVILLE ORANGE MARMALADE

"Geneva Dunsany is dead." Benedicta, Dowager Countess of Melton, set down the black-bordered letter very gently by her plate, her face pale. The footman froze in the act of presenting more toast.

For an instant, the words had no meaning. The hot tea in Grey's cup warmed his fingers through the china, fragrant steam in his nostrils mingling with the scents of fried kippers, hot bread, and marmalade. Then he heard what his mother had said, and set down his cup.

"God rest her soul," he said. His lips felt numb, in spite of the tea. "How?"

—Lord John and the Brotherhood of the Blade,
chapter 3, "Pet Criminal"

GF | DF | V | VGN

Hercules, as one of his twelve labors, was tasked to steal three golden apples of immortality from a tree at the center of Hera's garden. After days of battle with its guardian dragon, he slayed the beast, collected the fruit, and set off to return them to his king. Along the way, he sat down to rest, exhausted, and a single fruit dropped from his bag. That fruit grew into a beautiful tree around which rose the city of Seville.

Sevillanos today believe that Hercules's golden apples were actually the bitter oranges that now adorn their city in the thousands. Sour beyond palatable, filled with seeds, and dry of flesh, modern tales say we have a thrifty Dundee housewife to thank for marmalade, after she boiled the rough, dimpled, and terrible-tasting citrus her husband, a grocer, bought at a steep discount from a Spanish ship sheltering in the harbor.

Makes three 1-pint (500-milliliter) jars

Ingredients

2¼ pounds (1 kilogram) Seville
    oranges (6 to 8)
2 lemons

5 cups sugar
¼ cup scotch whisky (optional)

Method

Scrub the oranges and lemons under warm water with a soft brush; cut the fruit into quarters.

In a large stockpot, cover the oranges and lemons with 2 quarts (2 liters) water and bring to a boil over high heat. Reduce to a simmer and cook until the peel is very soft and almost translucent, 1½ to 2 hours. Strain the fruit over a large bowl, pressing down on the fruit with a spoon or spatula to extract as much liquid as possible.

Wash the stockpot. Place three 1-pint (500-milliliter) mason jars and their rings and lids into another large pot and fill with water to cover. Heat over high until just boiling and boil for 10 minutes. Turn off the heat and keep the pot covered.

Slice the peel and fruit into narrow ⅛- to ¼-inch strips, depending on your preference, discarding the seeds and any large pieces of membrane. Return the sliced peel, flesh, and reserved juice to the cleaned stockpot. Stir the sugar into the mixture and heat over medium heat, stirring constantly, until the sugar has dissolved, 2 to 3 minutes. Return it to a full boil over high heat, then reduce the heat to maintain a gentle boil. Stir occasionally while cooking to prevent scorching. Continue cooking until it has reached the gel point, about 218°F on an instant-read thermometer, anywhere from 15 to 60 minutes.

Immediately remove from the heat and stir in the whisky, if using. Remove one of the jars from the boiling-water canner, emptying the water back into the pot. Ladle in the marmalade, leaving ½ inch of headspace. Slide a rubber or silicone spatula between the glass and the food to remove any air bubbles. Wipe the jar rim with a CLEAN damp cloth to remove any stickiness and cover with a hot lid. Screw the ring on until just finger-tight. Repeat with the remaining marmalade and jars. Allow them to cool, untouched, for 8 hours.

Check the seals and store in a cool, dark place for up to a year. Refrigerate once opened and use within 1 month.

Notes

- *To test the marmalade without a candy thermometer, REMOVE THE PAN FROM THE HEAT and put a small amount of marmalade on a plate that has been chilled in the freezer and briefly return it to the freezer. After 2 or 3 minutes, it should be slightly jelled and will wrinkle just a bit when you slide your finger through it. If not, continue to cook until it is.*

- *For more information about canning and preserving check out the National Center for Home Food Preservation's comprehensive website (nchfp.uga.edu).*

JERKED BEEF

Jamie snorted but smiled nonetheless as he stood to shake Dan's hand. Then he turned back to the litter on the table, stowing the papers and purse—and a stray quill that Dan had abandoned, overlooked—into the bag. He was grateful for the food; the scent of jerked meat and journeycake floated out of the canvas depths, and he could feel the hard shape of apples at the bottom. He'd left the printshop without breakfast, too.

—Written in My Own Heart's Blood, chapter 10,
"The Descent of the Holy Ghost upon a Reluctant Disciple"

GF | DF

Preserving meat under the sun or over the smoke of a fire has kept people fed and nourished for thousands of years. The simple flavor of beef in a salt-and-pepper brine blooms with the addition of a little smoke.

The addition of vinegar and coriander comes from South African biltong, which may seem out of place in an Outlander cookbook, but is a centuries-old method that has been a personal favorite for decades. You may live where the sun is hot enough to dry it outside, but if not, dry it in your oven.

Makes about 1½ pounds (680 grams) beef jerky

Ingredients

3 pounds (1.4 kilograms) outside or bottom round of beef

Kosher salt and freshly ground pepper

½ cup coriander seeds, toasted and ground, for biltong

1 cup apple cider vinegar, for biltong

Method

Freeze the beef until firm, but not solid, 2½ to 3 hours. With a sharp knife, remove all the exterior fat from the beef. Cut it parallel to the grain into ⅛- to ¼-inch-thick slices. In a small bowl, mix the salt and pepper together.

JERKED BEEF: Generously sprinkle salt and pepper into the bottom of a container with a tight-fitting lid. Lay the beef down in a single layer and sprinkle generously with salt and pepper. Repeat until all the meat is layered with seasoning. Cover and refrigerate for 8 hours. Flip the container over and refrigerate for another 8 hours.

BILTONG: Generously sprinkle salt, pepper, and coriander into the bottom of a container with a tight-fitting lid. In a large bowl, toss the beef with the vinegar until every piece is coated. Shaking off the excess vinegar, lay the beef down in a single layer and sprinkle generously with salt, pepper, and coriander. Repeat until all the meat is layered with seasoning. Cover and refrigerate for 8 hours. Flip the container over and refrigerate for another 8 hours.

IN THE OVEN: Move the rack to the middle rung and heat the oven to 150°F, or as low as your oven will go. Use the convection setting if you have it; the fan increases air circulation and decreases drying time.

Arrange the beef in single layers on metal cooling racks set inside rimmed baking sheets. Dehydrate the beef, rotating the racks two or three times, until the outside of the beef is dry and leathery, 8 to 10 hours, depending on the thickness of the meat. If your oven does not go as low as 150°F, prop the door open with a wooden spoon to allow the excess heat to dissipate.

IN THE SMOKER: Arrange the beef in single layers on your smoker's racks. Smoke at 150°F for 3 to 4 hours. Continue to dehydrate without smoke at 150°F, either in your smoker or oven, until the outside of the beef is dry and leathery, 4 to 6 more hours, depending on the thickness of the meat.

Dried jerky/biltong should not be crumbly, but instead it should be firm, flexible, and easily bend back on itself without snapping. Finish drying the meat on racks at room temperature for another 12 to 24 hours. Store in airtight containers in a dark, cool spot for up to 1 month. Refrigerate or freeze for longer life.

Notes

- *Slicing the meat across the grain will result in much more fragile jerky, that, while easier to chew, reduces to crumbles with any amount of handling. Beef sliced with the grain travels much better.*

- *To use a food dehydrator, follow the manufacturer's instructions.*

- *Biltong is traditionally made with large cuts of beef or game that are hung in the sun, then sliced or shredded to serve. Here, I've combined North American jerky slices with the taste of South African biltong.*

MUSHROOM CATSUP

An hour later, Grey and Wainwright bade farewell to Signor *Berculi and the* salle des armes, *and turned toward Neal's Yard, where one of Grey's favorite chophouses did a bloody steak with roast potatoes and the proprietor's special mushroom catsup—an appealing prospect to ravenous appetites.*

—Lord John and the Brotherhood of the Blade, chapter 10,
"Salle des Armes"

GF | DF | V | VGN

Brought home by eighteenth-century English explorers to the Malay Peninsula, *kecap* was originally a thin sauce for fish made from walnuts, oysters, or mushrooms. Mushroom catsup quickly caught on in London, and secret recipes dominated restaurants and gentlemen's clubs for decades, until the rise of tomato catsup in the mid-nineteenth century.

Serve it on steak, or stir it into soups and stews. It's a vegan, umami-rich, hundreds-years-old secret sauce that makes a delicious, plant-based alternative to Worcestershire.

Makes about 2 cups

Ingredients

2 pounds (900 grams) brown
    mushrooms, cleaned and sliced

2 tablespoons kosher salt

2 bay leaves

Zest of 1 lemon, grated

1-inch piece of fresh ginger,
    quartered lengthwise

1 teaspoon whole peppercorns

6 whole allspice berries

3 whole cloves

1 medium onion, julienned

¼ cup apple cider vinegar

1 tablespoon sugar

2 teaspoons hot or sweet paprika

Method

In a large nonreactive bowl (see Notes), layer the mushrooms, sprinkling salt between each layer and finishing with salt. Press down on the mushrooms firmly with the back of a large spoon, cover with a plate, and leave the bowl in a cool, dark place for 24 hours, pressing down on the mushrooms twice as they macerate.

Enclose the bay leaves, lemon zest, ginger, peppercorns, allspice berries, and cloves in a tea ball or tie them in a square of muslin to make a bouquet garni.

Pour the sliced mushrooms and any liquid from the bowl into a large saucepan or stockpot. Add the onion, bouquet garni, vinegar, sugar, and paprika. Bring to a boil over medium-high heat, lower the heat to medium-low, and simmer, stirring occasionally, for 20 minutes.

Wash a 1-quart (1-liter) mason jar and its lid in hot, soapy water. Rinse thoroughly and set on the dish rack to air-dry.

Discard the bouquet garni. Pour the mushroom mixture into a strainer lined with three layers of cheesecloth or a clean muslin or linen dish towel. Allow to drain until cool enough to handle, then twist and squeeze all the liquid from the mushrooms. Cool completely and pour the liquid into the sterilized jar.

Refrigerate for up to 1 month. Use in An Echo in the Bone Broth (page 46), Vegan Sausage Rolls (page 75), or in any dish that needs a punch of vegan umami.

Notes

- *Nonreactive materials include stainless steel, ceramic, and glass.*
- *Change up the flavor and use horseradish root instead of the ginger or lime zest for the lemon. Keep them guessing!*

Prepared Horseradish

"Malingering bugger," Harry said, reaching for the brandy. "How is he?"
"Quite his usual self, to judge from his correspondence." Grey handed Quarry the unfolded letter, which the latter read with a burgeoning grin.

"Aye, Minnie will have him sorted like a hand of whist." He put down the letter, nodding at it as he raised his glass. "Who's Richardson and why do you want to know about him?"

"Ezekiel Richardson, Captain. Lancers, but detached for intelligence work."

"Oh, intelligence laddie, eh? One of your Black Chamber lot?" Quarry wrinkled his nose, though it was not clear whether this was a response to the notion of intelligence laddies or the presence of a dish of grated horseradish accompanying the sardines.

—*An Echo in the Bone,* chapter 32, "A Flurry of Suspicion"

GF | DF | V | VGN

The word *horseradish* originated in the late sixteenth century and combines *horse,* formerly used to mean "strong" or "coarse," with the word *radish,* for "root." It is the classic accompaniment for Roast Beef for a Wedding Feast from OK1.

Makes about 1½ cups

Ingredients

8- to 10-inch-long fresh horseradish
    root, peeled
½ teaspoon kosher salt

1 tablespoon white or apple cider
    vinegar

Method

Chop the horseradish root into ½-inch pieces. Add the pieces to a food processor with the salt and 2 tablespoons water. Pulse until finely ground but not mushy.

Transfer to a bowl and taste for pungency. When it is to your taste, stir in the vinegar. The horseradish will continue to get hotter until the vinegar is added to stabilize it, so do not wait too long.

Store in a closed jar in the refrigerator for up to 1 month.

Notes

- *Caution: Ground or grated horseradish is much more potent than freshly chopped onions. Work in a well-ventilated room, and keep the horseradish at arm's length.*
- *Apple cider vinegar will result in a slightly darker finished product. If you want white horseradish, use white vinegar.*

The Diet and Cookery of Eighteenth-Century Highlanders

"The food was either terribly bad or terribly good," Claire had said, describing her adventures in the past. "That's because there's no way of keeping things; anything you eat has either been salted or preserved in lard, if it isn't half rancid—or else it's fresh off the hoof or out of the garden, in which case it can be bloody marvelous."

—*Drums of Autumn*

Prior to the Clearances that forced tens of thousands from the land and left it as one of the least densely populated areas in all of Europe, the Scottish Highlands were home to a much larger population, mostly tenant farmers living in small collective groups of crofts called townships. These townships typically housed a hundred people, often extended family, who grew, raised, foraged, and, if near the water, fished to survive among the north's unforgiving landscape with its short growing season, harsh climate, and poor soil.

The typical diet of a Highland Scot through the first half of the eighteenth century varied widely, according to their place in the economic and social structure. The tables of the great halls in castles such as Leoch and the dining rooms of manor houses like Lallybroch were laden with venison and wild boar, beef and lamb, fowl and songbirds.

They had imported delicacies in their storerooms: dried fruit, citrus peel, expensive spices like pepper, cloves, and cinnamon. Sugar, still a very expensive commodity in the early eighteenth century, was used to make sumptuous desserts and puddings.

They drank beer brewed on their estates, as well as whisky—*uisge beatha*, or the water of life, malted and distilled onsite—and enjoyed fine wines from Europe's best grape-producing regions.

The cook in a wealthy kitchen turned a bountiful combination of locally grown produce and ingredients from afar into a tasty and nourishing assortment of dishes distinct from those in the rest of the British Isles. Scotland's near-four-hundred-year Auld Alliance with France against the English left a lasting influence on Scottish culture, including her cuisine. Terms such as the French *escalope* became the Scot's *collop*, for a slice of meat, and a boiling fowl, *Hetoudeau*, became *Howtowdie*, a dish of boiled chicken with spinach and poached eggs.

The diet of the poorer classes, including the crofter, was a much leaner, plain, and monotonous one. Bannocks, oatcakes, porridge, and vegetable pottages, very occasionally enriched with a small piece of meat or a bone, made up the bulk of a farmer's diet. Meat was expensive and eaten rarely. Farmers grew crops of oats, barley, and pease (peas) at a subsistence level and raised animals, especially cattle, primarily for their by-products, such as milk, butter, and cheese. Wheat for leavened bread wouldn't grow on the poor, unimproved soil, and there was no oven in a farmer's croft in which to bake it.

Kitchen gardens, or kailyards, supplemented farmers' families' diets with year-round crops of kale, leeks, and other vegetables hardy enough to survive the ruthless winters. Kale's historical popularity as a mainstay of Scottish cooking owes much to the simple fact that it can survive a Highland winter. So ubiquitous was kale that its name became metonymically associated with everything food, from the family vegetable plot to the dinner bell:

> But hark! The kail-bell rings, and I Maun gae link aff the pot;
> Come see, ye hash, how sair I sweat To stegh your guts, ye sot.
> (Watty and Madge, *David Herd's Collection of Scottish Songs, Volume ii*, p. 199)

Mustard, spinach, carrots, and cabbage from the garden provided welcome variety in a crofter's diet from summer through early winter. The hardest time of year was undoubtedly after the failing of the previous winter's kale crop in early spring, through until the first harvests in early summer, when food stores were near bare and the last of the kale had gone to seed. Foraged wild vegetables such as nettles, sorrel, and garlic filled in the food gap and provided much-needed nourishment to fuel the plowing and planting activities of spring. Wild berries in summer were a rare sweet treat.

The first recorded example of potatoes being grown in Scotland is 1701, but it wasn't until the last quarter of the century that they found their way into the average family's vegetable plot. Turnips were introduced at about the same time, adding diversity and substance to the Highland diet. Both vegetables also stored well, improving food security.

Near the shores, most men split their time between the fields and the sea. These fishermen–farmers had the most varied, nutrient-rich diet of the Highlands' working poor, thanks to plentiful fish and seafood. They used seaweed to fertilize their gardens and made salt to season and preserve their food, as well as to barter with it with the inland population.

Across the Highlands, food for the workingman was required to be easily transportable and resistant to spoilage. Men would commonly carry a small bag of oatmeal in their sporrans, which could quickly be made into a basic porridge or oatcake while in the fields or away from home. This type of food-to-go is thought to account for the origins of haggis, but it's important to note that the first printed reference to that eminently Scottish dish is in an English cookbook, although it most likely extends back much further, to the Viking occupation of Britain.

Crofts were sturdy, small, windowless homes built to shelter their inhabitants from the ruthless conditions in the Highlands. Just inside the single door used by both humans and animals was a sunken room with a cobbled floor, where the animals, mostly cattle and chickens, were kept, along with the farmer's *cas-chrom*, or foot plow, and his wife's milk churn.

Up a step from the byre was the croft's center section, which served as the family's living room, dining room, kitchen, and bedroom. The floor was packed dirt, and the walls were made of thickly cut turf or clay and wattle. The roof was thatched in whatever was available—heather, broom, bracken, straw, or rushes.

The peat fire in the center of the living area burned day and night to provide light and warmth. The family sat around the fire on low wooden stools, where the smoke was not as thick, and if there was fish, they were hung above the fire to smoke. An opening in the roof was offset from the fire to allow smoke to escape, but the walls and roof were covered with black ash from the fire. The walls were scraped of ash, which was collected along with the blackened thatching to use as fertilizer in the fields; this may explain why their oat crops grew so well in the substandard soil.

Cooking equipment and utensils were very basic, and cooking was a necessary chore that held none of the creative appeal seen in today's ergonomic and sanitary kitchens. The woman of the house prepared and cooked her family's meals from her perch on the edge of her stool, with only the dim fire to light her efforts, unless the family could afford an oil-burning rush lamp for additional lighting.

The cast-iron girdle (griddle) was nestled into the ashes of the fire and used to bake bannocks and oatcakes. The kettle for cooking the family's porridge and pottage was either balanced on top of the fire or hung just above it, from a chain attached to the ceiling. The pot was perpetually filled morning to night with the family's next meal, bubbling away unobserved while the woman of the house completed the rest of her exhaustive list of chores, including the backbreaking work of fetching water for cooking and cleaning, as well as hauling back and stacking the peat cut by the men in the fields to ensure a constant supply of fuel for the fire.

In stark contrast to the dim picture painted of the crofter's living space and cooking area were the large—sometimes vast—kitchens in clan castles and large homes, which were generally housed on the building's lowest level and equipped with at least one major hearth and chimney. The inventory of large equipment would have included a brick oven beside the hearth for baking, as well as a stew hole in the wealthiest and most up-to-date of kitchens.

The stew hole was a raised freestanding structure that allowed the cook to stand instead of sitting or crouching at the hearth and was a precursor to the cast-iron stove. A fire was built in the base, and pots were set on grates over the fire to cook or warm, depending on their distance from the heat.

In addition to iron kettles and girdles, the list of small equipment would likely have included spits to turn the meat and fowl, copper and clay pots, a variety of knives, tongs, ladles, mallets, sifters, and molds, all designed to make the preparation of modern, more refined foods faster and easier.

Meal times were also dependent on class and status. While breakfast in a croft was an almost nonexistent pre-dawn sup of milk and a bowl of hastily consumed porridge or brose, praise was sung from as far as London regarding the wide variety of fish and meat available at the laird or clan chief's morning feast, taken later in the morning. Supper was a light evening meal for all classes, with the exception of celebratory feasts, and was usually leftovers from that day's most substantial meal, dinner, which was eaten at or around midday.

Defeat at Culloden saw the systematic destruction of the clan system and a need for cash to satisfy the demands of the court in London. These changes were at least partially responsible for the switch in the Highlands from a barter economy to a cash-based one. Tenant farmers who had paid their rent with labor and goods in kind for generations now found themselves unable to come up with the coin their landlords demanded.

Over subsequent decades, the majority of the land was enclosed for grazing and, often, entire townships evicted to make room for more-profitable sheep. The more fortunate evictees were relocated to the cities of Edinburgh and Glasgow, while the less fortunate were transported to faraway colonies such as Australia and North America, most never to see their homeland again. Many of the poor who arrived on America's Atlantic shores moved into the backcountry, including wilderness areas of North Carolina like the fictional Fraser's Ridge.

To begin, their diet remained based primarily on boiled grains and vegetable stews, although they quickly adapted to incorporate a number of locally grown ingredients such as corn (maize), beans, squash, and collards, a close cousin to kale. Potatoes, which were still new to the first emigrants forced from the Highlands, became an important staple. The lush natural larder of their new home also regularly provided animal protein, in the form of small game and birds, resulting in a much more varied and nutritionally complete diet for all.

Because they were released into the woods as young shoats to run wild until they matured, hogs were relatively simple and low-cost to raise. Eventually, much of the North Carolina and surrounding colonies' diets were based on pork and corn, with the average person consuming five pounds of pork for every pound of beef. This "hog and hominy" diet, as it came to be called, stretched across all levels of society, with the wealthiest consuming the choicest cuts of the animal and leaving their workers and slaves with what remained. All parts of the animal were consumed or repurposed, and the diet was supplemented with a bevy of collard greens or cabbage.

As they had been at home in the Highlands, smoking and salting were the primary means used to preserve meats and fish. Potted meat, the process of sealing cooked meat in fat, was another common technique. Salted meat was perpetually on the menu in most homes and taverns. Hogs were never slaughtered in summer, and their meat was seldom eaten fresh, except after a large slaughter, when giant smoking pits would be dug and people were invited for miles around to join the feast. The great tradition of Southern barbecue originates from these early gatherings.

In their new home, fruits and vegetables were dried and pickled, then packed in fresh straw to sit alongside cheese and barrels of salted meat, as well as cider and beer, in the cool air of small underground house cellars. In cold seasons, fresh meat was also stored for short periods of time. Those without such spaces stored food for a short time in springs or wells, in containers set into the cold water. Only the very wealthy, as well as large dairies, possessed separate icehouses.

In the homes of plantation owners, large farmers, and wealthy merchants, traditional foods were being transformed at the hands of their African cooks. Spices were used heavily to enhance flavors as well as to disguise spoiled meat in the warm climate. Vitamin-rich "pot likker," the previously discarded cooking water in which vegetables had been slow-cooked, was now kept and savored. Slave cooks produced fried chicken and fritters, adding the African method of deep-fat frying to the growing list of new cooking techniques.

Access to cheap sugar, for centuries so costly as to be out of the reach of all but the very rich, meant that everyone could now afford to make puddings, custards, and other sweet treats regularly. The imposition of heavy taxes on staple foodstuffs also resulted in dietary changes. Examples include the replacement of the popular molasses-based rum with liquor made from locally grown corn and the rise in popularity of coffee as the supply of tea dried up leading up to the American Revolution.

The settlers' wooden backcountry cabins were small; however, they included a fireplace with hearth and chimney, an important improvement over a croft's centrally located fire on the floor. As it had been back home, cooking of any meal was a major undertaking and equipment was basic. Activity was centered on the fireplace, with the cast-iron pot hanging from a chain or rod over the wood fire and the baking kettle and/or girdle nestled into the ashes of the fire.

In larger households, the kitchen was often separated from the house to keep the heat, smells, and staff far from living quarters and guests. These kitchens contained the same basic equipment and tools as found in backcountry cabins but better made and from higher-quality materials. In addition, more-expensive inventory, such as mechanized spit jacks and stew holes, made the cook's job faster and easier, while allowing more control over the final taste and appearance of the dish.

The other large feature of wealthier kitchens—including those of the burgeoning middle class, such as merchants and tradesmen—was the presence of a bread oven, either beside the hearth or outside the house. Baking was an all-day affair undertaken once per week and involved the baker rising early to prepare her dough and light the fire within the oven. Once the fire had reduced to ashes, the oven floor was swept clean and the loaves and pies placed inside, with the help of a long wooden or cast-iron peel. The oven door was then closed and the contents left to bake. It was often well after dark when a day's baking was finally done, and meals on these days were generally leftovers or simple stews that could be left to cook unattended.

Much like it had been in the Highlands, breakfast was taken early if you were poor and later for those of greater means. For most, it began with home-brewed cider or beer and a bowl of porridge cooked overnight in the embers of the fire. It was among the Southern planters that breakfast became a leisurely and delightful meal, more like our modern brunch, featuring large spreads of breads, cold meats, and cheeses.

Dinner was the main meal of the day, served in early afternoon. A typical wealthier family in the late 1700s served two courses for dinner. The first included soups, meats, savory pies, pancakes and fritters, and a variety of sauces, pickles, and catsups. Desserts appeared with the second course, which included an assortment of fresh, cooked, or dried fruits, custards, tarts, and sweetmeats. "Sallats," or salads, were more popular for supper, a light meal served just before bed, but were sometimes served at dinner to provide decoration for the center of the table.

The life of an eighteenth-century Highland crofter was one of constant toil and strife. The workday was long, food scarce. And while their relocation to the Americas resulted in death for some and a cruel loss of country and family for thousands more, eventually those who survived in the New World adopted a life of continuing hard work but greater food and nutritional reward. The increase in protein and variety of diet undoubtedly fueled many Highlanders' rise from crushing poverty and their contribution to the fight for their new nation's independence.

ACKNOWLEDGMENTS

As always, my first thank-you goes to Diana Gabaldon, for her epic stories full of food, love, loss, and laughter. Your years of support for *Outlander Kitchen* are a gift and guiding force.

To my husband, and My Englishman, Howard. You put your own dreams on hold to support our little family, and encouraged me every step of the way along the journey to fulfilling my dream. I look forward to fulfilling more of our dreams together.

My agent, Susan. Your ability to listen, problem solve, and gently encourage makes you more valuable than precious jewels.

Anne, my editor, and everyone I have the pleasure of working with at Random House. I cherish our smooth working relationship. You let me do my thing but are always there when I have a question.

Outlander Kitchen photographer, Rebecca Wellman, who cooked, styled, and shot the majority of the photos in OK1 and OK2, including both covers. I am grateful to work with such a talented artist.

Cookbook authors from across the centuries, especially the women, including Mrs. McLintock, who published the first Scottish cookbook, *Mrs. McLintock's Receipts for Cookery and Pastry-Work*, in 1736. Also Mrs. Hannah Glasse's *The Art of Cookery Made Plain and Easy*, first published in London in 1747, and F. Marian McNeill's *The Scots Kitchen*, first published in 1929. All were a source of tradition, lore, and inspiration.

A huge round of applause, bows, and gratitude to the group of eleven *Outlander Kitchen* recipe testers, who all returned from testing OK1 to diligently test at least twenty recipes in six weeks each for this cookbook. It's a lot of work, and expense, and I'm sure a source of grief for some of them, when their families face another unfamiliar and "experimental" dish for dinner, although they've never complained. For their hard work and culinary courage, I give thanks to Janet Lee Anderson,

Rhiannon McVean, Darcy Gagne, Jennifer Broughton, Anna Lapping, Jason and Jen Davis, Brianne Begley, Becky Inbody, Helen Bullard, and Lee Ann Monat, as well as all of their friends and family.

Long-distance hugs and kisses to my Coven. After our Outlander obsession brought us together from across the globe almost ten years ago, we're still going strong. I'm proud and grateful for our extraordinary friendship.

The eateries of Pender, including Port Browning Pub, Jo's Place, Woods on Pender, Vanilla Leaf Bakery, and Slow Coast Coffee. Thank you for keeping me fed, caffeinated, and for pouring an ice-cold beer when the moment, or a gap in creativity, demanded it. Mine can be a very solitary occupation, so I appreciate your warm greetings and camaraderie.

Pender Island is an incredibly beautiful and peaceful place to live. Thank you to all of my island friends and neighbors, especially Susan and Dan Charman for the cucumbers that made Rachel Murray's Dill Pickles, Anna and Darren Law for the roast from a local deer that became The Old Fox's Roast Haunch of Venison, Kathy Cronk for the emergency bottle of golden syrup, and Kim Pollard for her friendship.

Finally, my deepest love to all of *Outlander Kitchen*'s fans. Your enthusiasm, emails, and photos keep my tank full. Thank you for the greatest decade a cook and food writer could hope for.

RECIPE INDEX

A food lover and bookworm from birth, THERESA CARLE-SANDERS grew up exploring the multicultural restaurant mecca that was, and still is, Vancouver, British Columbia, with her parents and two brothers. After years of travel as an early adult, she settled down and married the Englishman of her dreams, only to find herself, a few years later, blindly pursuing an unwanted corporate dream.

She and her husband, Howard, gave up the city life in 2003 and moved to the rain forests of Pender Island, BC, for a quieter, gentler life at a less hurried pace. In 2008, Theresa returned to Vancouver temporarily to follow her lifelong dream of culinary school, graduating at the top of her class in 2009.

Back on Pender, between cooking for local restaurants and catering private functions, she began writing, cooking, and photographing her own recipes for her first blog, *Island Vittles*. In 2011, she began her second blog, *Outlander Kitchen*, a collection of writing and recipes based on her favorite Outlander series, by Diana Gabaldon.

Today, Theresa and Howard are happily ensconced in their little cabin in the woods on Pender, accompanied by their seventeen-year-old Shiba Inu, Koda.

A visual artist from an early age, Rebecca Wellman has surveyed the world through a camera lens for most of her life. She also has a strong love for beautiful food and all things culinary. Eventually, the two passions collided into a joyful career.

Rebecca has worked as a professional photographer, specializing in food and lifestyle for more than fifteen years. She has worked on set with Food Network Canada, is the editor at large for *EAT* magazine, and recently released her own book, *First, We Brunch: Recipes and Stories from Victoria's Best-Loved Breakfast Joints.*

Rebecca lives in beautiful Victoria, on the west coast of British Columbia, Canada.

You can find her at RebeccaWellman.ca.